Tempest at Ox Hill
The Battle of Chantilly

★————————————★

"Have I not heard great ordnance in the field,
And heaven's artillery thunder in the skies?"

— William Shakespeare

Tempest at Ox Hill
The Battle of Chantilly

★————————————————★

David A. Welker

DA CAPO PRESS

Copyright © 2002 David A. Welker

Cataloging-in-Publication Data is available from the Library of Congress.

First Da Capo Press edition 2002
ISBN 0-306-81118-9

Published by Da Capo Press
A Member of the Perseus Books Group
http://www.dacapopress.com

Da Capo Press books are available at special discounts for bulk purchases in the U.S. by corporations, institutions, and other organizations. For more information, please contact the Special Markets Department at the Perseus Books Group, 11 Cambridge Center, Cambridge, MA 02142, or call (800) 255-1514 or (617) 252-5298, or email j.mccrary@perseusbooks.com.

1   2   3   4   5   6   7   8   9—05   04   03   02   01

To Margaret

Whose love, support, and inspiration made this
work, and makes all things, possible.

CONTENTS

Acknowledgments   8

Preface   9

Chapter 1   ★ The Long Road to Chantilly   15
May to August 30, 1862

Chapter 2   ★ The Confluence of Two Lives   41

Chapter 3   ★ Movement and Machinations   81
Sunday, August 31, 1862; Dawn to Midday

Chapter 4   ★ Stuart's Salutation   95
Sunday, August 31, 1862; Midday to Nightfall

Chapter 5   ★ The Gathering Storm   109
Monday, September 1, 1862; Midnight to Noon

Chapter 6   ★ Duel at Jermantown   123
Monday, September 1, 1862; 11:00 A.M. to 5:00 P.M.

Chapter 7   ★ Stevens's Battle   137
Monday, September 1, 1862; 3:00 to 5:00 P.M.

Chapter 8   ★ Kearny Takes Command   169
Monday, September 1, 1862;
Late Afternoon to Early Evening

Chapter 9   ★ The Aftermath   195
Monday, September 1, 1862; Nightfall to Midnight

Chapter 10   ★ The Honor of Two Lives   209

Chapter 11   ★ A Retreat On All Fronts   215
             Tuesday, September 2 to Wednesday,
             September 3, 1862

Chapter 12   ★ An Afterword   229
               Who Won the Battle of Chantilly?

             Photo Section   after page 193

             Order of Battle   248

             Chapter Notes   255

             Bibliography   267

             Index   273

ACKNOWLEDGMENTS

★————————————★

There are so many people who helped make this book possible that it is difficult to name them all. Indeed, many of those who offered crucial aid to my work did so at the end of an internet and email link, never knowing the results of their efforts. To all of you—at numerous university libraries, historical societies, and museums—thank you so very much. There are some individuals, however, who deserve special mention and thanks: my wife, Margaret, who endured too many evenings alone while I researched or wrote this book. My children Rebecca and Thomas, who endured regular side trips to the remaining field of Chantilly during nearly every visit to the toy store now standing at the center of what had been Jackson's rear area. My brother-in-law Jeffery Fortais, who is a fellow historian and kindred Civil War enthusiast. Jeff's excellent maps provide a graphic dimension that magnify my words a thousand fold. Bob Pierce, Jeff's student assistant whose computer skill so aided Jeff's cartographic task. Harry Pfanz, whose review of my first draft offered untold guidance, both in revealing the mystery that is a Civil War battle and in the craft of writing Civil War history. John Hennessy, who selflessly offered me the fruits of his own research by pointing out the locations of important documents that may otherwise never have crossed my path. My comrades-in arms in the 28th Massachusetts Infantry, Company B, and all the various Civil War reenactors with whom I've crossed paths over the years who helped me gain a glimpse of 19th-century soldiering life. Ed Wenzel, whose care of Chantilly Battlefield in the face of adversity is a model for us all. Mario Espinola, whose dedication to preserving the archeological record of Chantilly is a gift to future generations of Americans. The entire staff of the U.S. Army History Institute at Carlisle Barracks, without whose assistance untold precious hours would have been wasted; their research and historical expertise is staggering. The staff of the Fairfax County Public Library's Virginia Room, whose love of helping people find information shows through in the care they take to help each patron, whatever their subject or purpose.

PREFACE

★————————————————————————————★

I had driven past it dozens of times without ever knowing it was there at all—a small patch of a county park that, save for an inconspicuous sign, resembled an empty lot overgrown by trees. Lots like these, after all, are scattered throughout northern Virginia, spots on which for one reason or another developers couldn't fit a building. Only years later, when I started researching my adopted hometown of Centreville's history, did I become aware that this apparently empty plot of ground was the scene of one of the Civil War's more notable small struggles, the battle of Chantilly.

The Confederates called the battle Ox Hill, I would soon discover. But I could learn little more than that the battle was fought in a torrential downpour, when the brilliant bolts of lightning and the pounding of thunder competed with the cannon's roar and flash, and that it claimed the lives of two Union generals. Joining in the "Third Battle of Manassas" in 1989, I heard repeatedly from preservationists that they were fighting the developers to prevent at Manassas what had already happened at Chantilly and more than once I heard or read that Chantilly was a "lost" battlefield. But still, the prospect that a Civil War battle took place so near my home intrigued me. Turning to a county road map I finally found the Ox Hill Battlefield Park and eagerly hopped in my car, filled with excitement and anticipation.

Driving out the route taken by the Union army in its retreat to Washington that 1st of September, 1862, I wondered what the field would look like and began to construct mental pictures of it in my mind. Stopping at the last traffic light near my destination I turned my head in search of some sign of the field. It was then that I realized just where I was, by the little park I had passed so often on the way to shop at the mall. Surely this wasn't it? Venturing from my car I beheld nothing that looked like the battlefields I was familiar with; no interpretive signs, no markers, no guide paths, just an empty lot framed by tall stands of oak and maple trees. Wandering deeper into the lot I soon found an old house, long since abandoned. Next to the old house stood a wire mesh fence that struggled vainly to separate the park from a tightly packed collection of apartments and townhouses. Wandering back through the woods I could still find no evidence of a battle, only evidence of human carelessness in the form of litter and trash. Only as I was about to leave the park did I see it, the small reminder that once men had fought and died here.

Perched on the edge of the lot, separated from the sidewalk only by a thin screen of young maples and poison ivy, sat two large gray stones protected by a rusting black iron pipe fence. Carved on these two stones were the names "Stevens" and "Kearny." Were these possibly the gravestones of these Union generals, I wondered, and searched vainly for some explanation. Nearby, however, I found more evidence that this was special ground—a low granite rock carved into the shape of a stump engraved with the legend "Kearny stump" and topped by a cross. The spot was careworn but it certainly held its share of mystery. Walking back to my car I noticed one more sign that I had bypassed earlier, "Relic Hunting Prohibited" it warned.

My visit to this largely neglected field only piqued my interest in the battle. Visits to the local library and my own collection of Civil War histories yielded little; no books on the battle were available and the information contained in the wider histories of the war offered little. Though there were a few articles dating from the Civil War centennial that gave good overall accounts of the facts of the battle of Chantilly. As my personal research progressed I found that it altered forever how I viewed common places and landmarks of my everyday existence. I discovered that the toy store I regularly take my kids to is built at the center of where Jackson's Confederate line stood during the battle; that the Fairfax County trash dump where I leave my trash each week is where the Millan House—in which Union surgeons struggled to save the lives of the battle's wounded—once stood; that my doctor's office is perched nearly on top of Ox Hill, where Stuart's artillery guns once stood; that the parking lot of the Sears store at Fair Oaks Mall is the site on which the 51st New York faced the Stonewall Brigade; and near the mall's movie theaters was where the 21st Massachusetts stumbled into a slaughter in a dark and rainy woods. Suddenly, all these innocuous places of everyday living were no longer so common.

Concurrent with this interest in the battle of Chantilly, I began to explore writing Civil War history. My professional work entailed writing and it seemed natural to use my talents in this way, for pleasure if not profit. My early forays into writing included a series of newspaper articles for the *Washington Times'* Civil War page and, after publishing several of these four or five pages articles, I determined to use my research on Chantilly to write an article and pass on the story of the battle to local readers who might not be aware of the history in their very backyard. After writing the article I felt confident that it was a solid, if basic, effort. But at the suggestion of a friend I passed the article to the local head of a citizen's group dedicated to preserving Chantilly battlefield for review and comments. His response, I soon discovered to my great sadness, would be less than enthusiastic.

He broke the news of his concerns about the piece in a polite manner and told me not to despair, for other writers had tried the same thing and come up short, too. But when I protested that I had used all the information I could find in published accounts of the battle, he again responded that I shouldn't feel too bad because there were no good modern accounts of the battle and many of the firsthand accounts were stilted, making it hard to sort out truth from fiction. He pointed out some of the more glaring errors in my article, demonstrating an impressive knowledge of the battle in the process. When I suggested that he should consider writing the article he demurred that he was no writer. Perhaps, he mused, someday someone will try to write the story of Chantilly and sort through all the conflicting information. I hung up the phone quite depressed that my effort had come up short and set the project aside.

Later, after my first book had been accepted for publication, I began to search around for a new project to tackle and quite unexpectedly came across my thick folder of notes on the battle of Chantilly. In the meantime I found that a few other authors had done what I had failed to do—produce a magazine article on the battle that was historically accurate. Finding copies of these articles at my library provided some enjoyable and informative reading. I finally had a basic understanding of the battle. But although they were informative, it seemed to me that there was more of a story contained in the fight than could be conveyed in any magazine article. The thought of the untold stories that had evaded the magazines sent me back to my folder of research, the Manassas National Battlefield Park Library, the Library of Congress, and to any other place I could find regimental histories, personal memoirs, biographies, and accounts written by those who were at Chantilly on September 1, 1862. The accounts of suffering, heroism, cowardice, and endurance I found in all these places convinced me that the story of this battle needed to be told. It was then that I began the long process that led to the creation of this book.

As I searched for firsthand accounts of the battle I discovered at least one reason that may explain why no one had previously published a volume on Chantilly. There simply is a dearth of firsthand sources from men who observed what happened there. In some cases the lack of an account or official report is understandable. Generals Stevens and Kearny lost their lives at Chantilly and naturally could leave no account of their actions or thinking that day. Other key actors in the drama that was the battle of Chantilly perished in battle shortly thereafter and apparently didn't have time to prepare an official report. Colonel Strong—commanding Hays's Brigade—was killed at Antietam and never filed an official report of his actions. Because his brigade was one of those that bore the brunt of Stevens's attack, the absence of his report is a major hurdle for historians to overcome. Several other senior commanders at Chantilly filed short official reports but were unable to elaborate because they, too, were killed in battle. These include Generals Jackson and Reno, both of whom filed little more than sketchy outlines of their actions. General McGowen—who commanded Gregg's Brigade but was wounded and thus absent on September 1—failed to permit the acting commander that day to submit a detailed report in his place. McGowen's report simply notes his absence and that the brigade fought there, but offers no other details of their actions at Chantilly. Even the common soldiers failed to provide the wealth of letter and diary accounts, as is the case with so many other battles. Why this is remains undetermined. But whatever the cause, we are left to draw on very few accounts to determine the experience of the common soldier at Chantilly. Added to this are the accounts of veterans who claim things that they could not possibly know, but perhaps fabricated in their golden years. Chief among these are the many "firsthand" accounts of Confederate veterans who claimed they personally killed Philip Kearny. Anyone who has ever observed a reenactment or fired a reproduction Springfield or Enfield musket knows that such a claim, even in broad daylight, is nearly impossible to substantiate. Similar challenges face nearly all Civil War historians but they provide an even greater hindrance to the historian who would unravel the fight at Chantilly.

Despite this considerable challenge, carefully piecing together the available official reports and firsthand accounts provided a glimpse into what really happened on September 1, 1862, at Chantilly. The movement of key Confederate brigades and most Union forces engaged there was clearly outlined in these sources. And important individual vignettes— both those of individual soldiers, and their companies and regiments— emerged from personal collections, libraries, archives, and history societies around the country, putting a human face on the events at Chantilly. Bit by bit, account by account, the story of the battle of Chantilly slowly emerged in my mind. The process of transforming my research into a written history, though, revealed gaps in the historical record that could not be left unfilled if the story of the Ox Hill fight was to be told. In an effort to fill these gaps I have taken a historian's "best guess" of what may have happened in these few cases and indicated that effort in appropriate endnotes. After years of obscurity, the tales of human suffering, sacrifice, courage, and endurance that unfolded at Chantilly on that late summer's day in 1862 are accessible to modern Americans.

I cannot in good conscience close this introduction without passing on my thoughts on the state of Chantilly Battlefield today, for the lack of respect accorded this field has cost modern America a priceless treasure. The story of what happened to Chantilly Battlefield in the 1980s must be remembered if we are to learn anything from its loss and to move beyond partisan anger to begin honoring the veterans who fell at Chantilly.

For decades after the conclusion of the war the field on which Chantilly was fought sat vacant or was used as farmland, but looked very much like it had on September 1, 1862. By 1915, what had been the Reid farm and much of the land of the Millan farm had been purchased by a former Confederate soldier named John Ballard. It was Ballard who donated a 50 feet by 100 feet section of his land on which the first New Jersey Brigade Society erected two stone markers as a memorial to Isaac Stevens and Philip Kearny. Part of the agreement between Ballard, the Society, and the State of Virginia was that there would be a Confederate memorial erected sometime in the future and that signs would eventually be erected to explain the battle to visitors. Although the stone memorials to Stevens and Kearny remain today, no such memorial was ever erected to the Confederate dead at Chantilly, and it was not until 1998 that a marker was finally erected explaining the battle.

In the late 1970s and early 1980s the rapid growth of building in the area around Chantilly battlefield caught Civil War historians and other citizens almost completely by surprise. Fledgling preservationists finally raised objections to building plans in the field's vicinity, and the chairman of the Fairfax County Board of Supervisors, Jack Herrity, asked the United States Department of the Interior if it was interested in buying a 200 to 300 acre tract surrounding the battlefield. Secretary of the Interior Cecil Andrus replied that the department had no interest in buying the land and the die was cast for Chantilly Battlefield.

As the 21st century opens, building continues on ground that properly should be a historic park. Most of the land on which the Reid farm's orchard, cornfield, and grassy field once stood—on which men fought and died—now is literally riddled with townhouses and parking spaces. The flat plain south of the Reid house site now is the location of a set of monstrous apartment buildings. The last remnants of a fence that once bordered the Reid farmhouse yard lies hidden nearby the apartments in a thick overgrowth, rotting and forgotten. The only bow the developers have made to the notion that the land they are building on is at all special is a postage-stamp-sized park and some street names calling to mind the fight at Chantilly.

Today the encroachment on what remains of the key portion of the Chantilly Battlefield has been stopped, thanks to the efforts of the small but dedicated group of citizens who comprise the Chantilly Battlefield Association. These men and women struggled to save the remains of this historic spot even when the odds seemed to move against them. Thanks to this tenacity, a few of the key portions of the field have been preserved for posterity. The spot where General Isaac Stevens was killed holding the colors of the 79th New York, the woodline where the 79th New York and the 28th Massachusetts clashed with A. P. Hill's Division, and some portion of the grass and cornfields remain undeveloped. And the markers to Stevens and Kearny remain where the Chantilly veterans themselves placed them. The latest good news for the Chantilly battlefield has arrived in its placement on a Virginia Civil War Trails list and the erection of a historic maker to explain the significance of the battle to visitors.

My hope is that this book will enliven interest in the story of Chantilly; its personal tales of sacrifice, suffering, and glory, its importance in determining the course of the Civil War, and its call to modern America. For too long the tale of Chantilly has been ignored, buried, and forgotten, and it is in part that fact that has allowed the land on which this conflict raged to be squandered. As on September 1, 1862, when the sight of Confederates on this ground called Isaac Stevens to action, it calls to us today. Will our response be worthy of their sacrifice?

1

THE LONG ROAD TO CHANTILLY

MAY TO AUGUST 30, 1862

Few of the many observers of the course of the American Civil War in early 1862 would have guessed that the two competing armies would soon come as near to the Union's capital as the tiny hamlet of Chantilly, Virginia. The year had opened with nearly all the key political and military stars aligning in the Union's favor. Kentucky, Missouri, and western Virginia were all in Union hands and regiments from those regions already were forming to bolster the Federal war effort. New Orleans was under Union control and Federal expeditions were well-established on the Atlantic coast in both North and South Carolina. Union forces were also operating in Tennessee with every expectation of making headway at freeing the state—particularly Unionist eastern Tennessee—from Confederate control. At the same time, George McClellan's Army of the Potomac was making steady, if slow, progress in its drive up Virginia's peninsula toward the Confederate capital at Richmond. Things were going so well that Union Secretary of War Edwin Stanton even closed the army recruiting stations, anticipating no more need for volunteers to fill the ranks. But just when it looked like the Union might wrap up the war in less than a year, a former professor from the Virginia Military Institute began to stir up trouble in the Shenandoah Valley.

Thomas J. "Stonewall" Jackson, an eccentric if misunderstood teacher and soldier, would almost single-handedly reverse the war's course and breath renewed life into the Confederacy's military prospects. In what would come to be known as the Valley Campaign, Jackson unleashed a series of defeats on Union troops that were startling in both their military skill and their speed. First, Stonewall defeated Union troops under the command of Major General John C. Fremont, west of the Shenandoah Valley. Next, he turned and struck Union forces at Front Royal and, then two days later, crushed Major General Nathaniel P. Banks's command at Winchester. Union leaders in Washington became convinced that Jackson's next target would naturally be the Federal capital itself and every spare unit available in the Union seat of government was mobilized in preparation to meet an attack. But, much to the eventual relief of the citizens of Washington and their defenders, it was not to be.

Jackson, in fact, had no intention of striking Washington. He had already achieved Richmond's goals in the Valley—freeing the Confederacy's "breadbasket" from Union control and drawing Union reinforcements away from assisting McClellan in his drive up the Virginia peninsula. Confederate leaders now had other plans for Jackson's victorious army. After forestalling a planned Union pincer attack by defeating its two parts in turn—beating Fremont's men again in the battle of Cross Keys and Irvin McDowell's vanguard division at Port Republic— Jackson's men boarded trains heading for the peninsula to join Robert E. Lee's forces in stopping McClellan's advance on the Confederate capital. By mid-June of 1862, the Union's war effort was once again in tatters.

Clearly, Washington had to do something before the tide of war in the east turned irrevocably against the Union cause. General McClellan's answer was to give his drive on Richmond a much-needed shot in the arm by adding 30,000 fresh troops; any fewer reinforcements than this, he argued, would leave him too weak to confront Lee's allegedly larger force guarding Richmond. One easy way to assemble the needed troops, McClellan argued, was to combine Fremont's, McDowell's, and Banks's forces under his command. President Lincoln and Secretary of War Stanton greeted the general's proposal with skepticism, for while both agreed that McClellan's peninsula campaign should continue, they genuinely feared for the safety of the capital if all of Washington's defensive forces were moved south. The president and secretary of war similarly saw through this blatant power grab by McClellan, of whom Lincoln was growing personally and professionally tired. General McClellan had repeatedly demonstrated his scorn for the president's authority and, in any case, Lincoln must have doubted the general would really drive on Richmond with even twice as many men. McClellan's proposal was rejected; he would have to press on toward Richmond with his existing force. But McClellan was right about one thing—Fremont's, McDowell's, and Banks's forces would have to be united to be of any military value. Consequently, Lincoln and Stanton agreed to join these troops in a new army-sized formation—the Army of Virginia.[1]

To command this new, united force President Lincoln selected John Pope, a successful young senior officer from the West, who he hoped would bring a promise of similar victory east with him. President Lincoln's choice certainly appeared justified, for at 40 years of age Major

General John Pope had amassed an admirable military record indeed. An 1842 West Point graduate—in the top third of his class—and veteran of the Mexican War, Pope had served with distinction in the Western theater, claiming victories in Missouri and in command of the attacks on New Madrid, Island No. 10, and Corinth. General Pope also had impeccable personal credentials. A descendant of George Washington and the Pope family of Virginia, which had originally settled in southwestern Fairfax County only miles from the Manassas battlefield, John had been born in Kentucky in 1822 and soon after moved with his family to Illinois. Related by marriage to Mary Todd Lincoln's family, his uncle was a United States Senator from Kentucky and his father was a Federal judge. On top of all that, John Pope was already personally acquainted with the president, for then-Captain John Pope had been one of two military officers who had escorted President-elect Lincoln on his train ride to Washington in 1860.[2]

On the same day that John Pope received his new assignment, George McClellan and the Army of the Potomac were thrown into the first of several fights that would come to be known as the Seven Days' Campaign. These actions—comprising the battles of Mechanicsville, Gaines' Mill, Savage's Station, Frayser's Farm, and Malvern Hill—were an effort by Robert E. Lee to drive the Federal threat from Richmond's gates before his defense of the city ran out of men and steam. Despite the fact that Lee nearly lost the tactical fight and that the much-touted hero of the Shenandoah Valley—Stonewall Jackson—had performed dismally, the Seven Days' Campaign was a turning point in McClellan's drive on Richmond and a major blow to the Union's war plans. When the last action of the Seven Days' fight was over, the Army of the Potomac was retreating in demoralized confusion down the peninsula, having clearly failed in its effort to take the Confederate capital. McClellan put the best spin possible on the loss, arguing in his dispatches to Washington that it was not a defeat at all but rather an intentional shift of grand strategy. He was, he claimed, merely moving his base of operations from the Pamunkey River to the James River, and that once this move was completed and the army fully reinforced, he would renew the drive on Richmond. But no one, from the president to the men in the Army of the Potomac's ranks to the northern public, was fooled by the "change of base" story; McClellan and his army had been beaten—though just barely—and to try this strategy once again would be sheer folly.

While his own army was forming, John Pope served as the president's temporary military advisor. Pope relished this role and was in his element hobnobbing with the nation's leaders and steering the direction of the war.

Regardless of the opinion various people had about General Pope, all would agree that he knew well how to promote himself and how to cultivate friendships with influential people. During his brief tenure as military advisor to the president, the Army of Virginia's new commander managed to ingratiate himself with anyone who might help his personal fortunes. Pope's Republican politics and long-held antislavery views also were a plus during his informal chats with the powerful and well-connected at evening parties, and the general always seemed to know the right thing to say to the right person.

At the same time, John Pope spent much of his time in Washington doing all he could to undermine McClellan's political standing. Pope argued to anyone who cared to listen that McClellan and his army should be withdrawn from the peninsula and sent north to reinforce his own forthcoming drive against Richmond's line of communications. With this number of troops under his command, he argued, he could quickly achieve his objectives and then turn to attack the Confederate capital. He even went so far as to argue to Secretary of the Treasury Salmon P. Chase—a personal friend—that McClellan should be relieved of command due to his "incompetency and indisposition to active movements," and the Army of the Potomac's forces merged with the Army of Virginia.[3]

George McClellan had taken the news of the appointments of Pope and General Henry W. Halleck—Lincoln's recently appointed chief of the Union army—with all the grace he could muster; no mean feat for the ambitious young general who believed Pope was getting the troops that might permit him to successfully seize Richmond. But when he heard of the appointment of Halleck to replace him as the commander of Union armies—a move that now officially "demoted" him to a single army command and made him Pope's "equal"—he could not restrain his anger. Adding insult to injury, McClellan learned of this blow through the newspapers rather than via an official channel. "I see it reported in this evening's papers that Halleck is to be the new Genl in Chief. Now let them take the next step & relieve me & I will once more be a free man," he wrote his wife Mary Ellen, to whom McClellan could express his true feelings. But McClellan understood politics as well as any general in the Union army, and resigned himself to this change as well. "I shall have to remove the three stars from my shoulder & put up with two—Eh bien—it is all for the best I doubt not."[4]

Despite General McClellan's initial acceptance of these professional and personal slights, their implications soon began to chafe in his mind. Pouring out his frustrations in a letter to Mary Ellen on July 22, he wrote,

"I see that the Pope bubble is likely to be suddenly collapsed—Stonewall Jackson is after him, & the paltry young gentleman who wanted to teach me the art of war will in less than a week either be in full retreat or badly whipped." Turning to his other rival, Henry Halleck, McClellan continued, "I see that the fickle press (& I presume the people) are beginning to turn and worship Halleck as the rising star—as soon as Stanton & the Presdt feel they can safely do so they will either supersede me or do something to put me out of the service. I do not like the political turn that affairs are taking . . ." As the days of late July and early August 1862 passed, George McClellan became increasingly convinced that somehow his political decline with Washington was due not to any action—or inaction—on his part, but rather to the appearance of Pope and Halleck on the scene. His letters to Mary Ellen and other personal friends reflect this belief and his growing, brooding mood of anger and resentment. When asked by his personal correspondents what he might do in response to these slights, McClellan replied time and again that what had happened was clearly God's will and that, while he would not act to hurt the fortunes of either Halleck or Pope, he nonetheless did not have to actively help them succeed in their endeavors.[5]

Then, on August 3, General Halleck ordered McClellan to withdraw his army from the Virginia peninsula to join General Pope's force in northern Virginia, a move that predictably left George McClellan seething. "I have received my orders from Halleck," McClellan complained to Mary Ellen by mail, "I cannot tell you what they are, but if you will bear in mind what I have already written to you, you can readily guess them when I say that they are as bad as they can be & that I regard them as almost fatal to our cause." Halleck's professional slap in the face was more than George McClellan could bear and his patience with Halleck and Pope was now worn out. In the same letter of August 4, McClellan hinted to Mary Ellen his planned course of action; he would now almost openly resist Halleck and Pope's efforts. "I will issue tomorrow an order giving my comments on Mr. Jno Pope—I will strike square in the teeth of all his infamous orders & give directly the reverse instructions to my army . . ." Such talk of hindering Pope's efforts, though bordering on disloyal, would soon seem tame. For as the temperate days of August wore on, McClellan's frustration with his own fading standing in Washington grew and with it his hatred of John Pope. By August 10, General McClellan wrote his wife, "I have a strong idea that Pope will be thrashed during the coming week— & very badly whipped he will be & ought to be—such a villain as he is ought to bring defeat on any cause that employs him." That George

McClellan would write such words of treason was perhaps forgivable in light of his tremendous ego and its recent battering by Washington. But in the coming days McClellan's loyalty to the Union would be put to the test and he would be given the opportunity to reinforce these disloyal thoughts with commensurate action.[6]

Throughout the time that the conflict between Pope and McClellan continued to brew, Pope's army was forming—albeit slowly—over a vast region covering most of northern Virginia. The Army of Virginia's I Corps, newly under the command of Major General Franz Sigel, consisted of about 11,500 men posted in the Shenandoah Valley near Middletown. The II Corps, comprised of 8,800 men formed into only two small divisions, remained under the command of Major General Nathaniel P. Banks and also was deployed in the Shenandoah Valley near Sigel's I Corps. The III Corps, the army's largest element consisting of 18,500 men organized into two large divisions, remained under the command of Major General Irvin McDowell. But the III Corps itself was as dispersed as the entire army, with one of its divisions posted on the old Manassas battlefield and the other sitting outside Fredericksburg, nearly a two-day march apart. The Army of Virginia's Reserve Corps, under the command of Brigadier General Samuel D. Sturgis was still forming in Alexandria, as was its cavalry division, consisting of 5,000 or so troopers. All told, the new Army of Virginia would be 43,800 men strong when it finally merged and took to the field. And once it was underway, it would indeed give General Lee and his fellow Confederate military leaders something new to worry about.[7]

The Army of Virginia now rapidly evolved into a fighting force that controlled northern Virginia from the Shenandoah Valley to Fredericksburg and it soon would be ready for offensive operations. McClellan's Army of the Potomac remained on the peninsula, poised to resume attacks on Richmond at any time. But what worried Robert E. Lee most was the prospect of these two armies attacking in unison from their current locations. He knew the Confederate Army of Northern Virginia could handle either Union force alone but if McClellan and Pope launched a coordinated attack on Richmond from the east and north, Lee's forces would be spread too thin to stage a successful defense of the capital. Lee's only hope in the face of this threat was to follow the strategy that already had served him so well—he would seize the initiative and strike first, before his Union counterparts could attack.

In early July, Lee developed a plan to trap Pope's army in a V-shaped area where the Rappahannock and Rapidan rivers meet, striking before

Pope could be reinforced by McClellan's army. On July 13 Lee ordered Jackson's Command to Gordonsville to launch this effort. But Lee's entire army moved too slowly into position and the general soon received intelligence that McClellan's men were beginning to leave the peninsula bound for Alexandria. Timing and poor execution had foiled his efforts.[8]

Well before dawn on August 25, Jackson's troops left their camps south of the Rappahannock for a move northward. Ewell's Division led the column, followed in turn by A. P. Hill's and Jackson's (William B. Taliaferro's) divisions. The march was almost a race, with each division moving at a breakneck pace and no one stopping to rest until nightfall. They achieved the first of General Lee's goals; they quickly moved into Pope's rear—being at that moment some 12 miles north of the Union right flank at Waterloo bridge—and were ready to cut Pope's communications with Washington. General Lee, in his wildest dreams, could never have guessed that Jackson's Command would cover 25 miles in a single day. Nonetheless, Jackson was still miles away from his ultimate destination and would have to move there in the coming days over a route that was fraught with risk.[9]

Pope's watchful officers observed Jackson's move and quickly passed word of it to their commander. By midday on the 25th, Pope knew of the direction of Jackson's march and the general location of the Confederate troops threatening his right flank. But John Pope, in what soon would come to be a habit, hesitated to act. He apparently believed Jackson's move to be a feint in preparation for an attack on his left flank west of Fredericksburg. When he finally ordered his troops to respond, he ordered the Union forces on his left, not his right, to extend their position. Then Pope changed his mind and erroneously concluded that Jackson's Command—and indeed, Lee's entire army—was bound for the Shenandoah Valley. "I am induced to believe that the column is only covering the flank of the main body, which is moving toward Front Royal and Thornton's Gap," Pope wired Halleck that evening. Because of this mistaken judgment, John Pope and the Army of Virginia would remain in their now-obsolete position on the northern bank of the Rappahannock while Jackson's force marched unchecked into their rear.[10]

Jackson's Command was up once again before dawn on August 26 and moving east with great haste. Their objective that morning was to reach Thoroughfare Gap—the narrow passage through the Bull Run Mountains that contained the tracks of the Manassas Gap Railroad—as quickly as possible. Jackson knew that the Yankees would soon catch wind of his movement and time remained of the essence if he was to seize the gap. By midday on the 26th Stonewall's men had taken Thoroughfare Gap and evening found them in Bristoe Station, a stop on the Orange and Alexandria line. They had marched another 20 miles—making a total so far of 45 miles in two days time—and were poised to cut Pope's vital link with Washington. After easily overwhelming the small Federal guard force at Bristoe Station, Jackson's Command set to work tearing up the tracks. And although one returning train managed to barrel through the station before it could be stopped, by nightfall the Orange and Alexandria line was severed.

Early in the morning of August 27, John Pope was greeted by the dispiriting news that Jackson had not moved into the Valley, as he had believed, but was in fact somewhere near Manassas Junction. Pope knew his army was in a dangerous position and that failure to move quickly risked losing it, the capital, or both. Nonetheless, from the Army of Virginia's commander's perspective this news was not all bad, for in it he saw a glimmer of opportunity. He had indeed made a serious error about Jackson's destination and had lost track of Stonewall's Command for nearly two days, during which time the Confederates had marched directly between his army and Washington; for this he would certainly receive condemnation from his superiors. At the same time, if he acted quickly, the situation could be reversed and these errors covered in a sea of success. For John Pope had intelligence that James Longstreet's Command was still moving slowly toward his right flank and if he turned and struck Jackson quickly—before Longstreet and Lee could join him—he might destroy both wings of Lee's army in turn, as he had originally planned. And so it was that on August 27, John Pope ordered his army to abandon their Rappahannock position and establish a new line facing north, with his right on the Orange and Alexandria railroad line and his left on the Warrenton Turnpike. From this position Pope would be better able to defend Washington, if it came to that, as well as to hit Jackson in his exposed position.[11]

At the same time that Pope's army was shifting its focus northward, Jackson's army was on the move consolidating its position. Stonewall apparently intended to establish his force in a position from which he could repel a Union attack, should it come before being joined by Longstreet's Command, while at the same time enjoying the Union plunder he might seize. Early on the 27th, Hill's and Jackson's divisions marched to Manassas Junction to reinforce Trimble's Brigade, which had easily taken the important but lightly defended Union supply depot the previous day. Ewell's Division remained at Bristoe to guard Jackson's rear and link up with Longstreet. The movement, like everything else Jackson had tried in the last few days, went largely as planned.[12]

After routing George Taylor's New Jersey brigade, which had ridden a train right into Jackson's trap, Jackson's men quickly returned to their dining—gorging, really—on captured Union stores. "The Federal depot was vast storehouses filled with all the delicacies, potted ham, lobster, tongue, candy, cakes, nuts, oranges, lemons, pickles, catsup, mustard, etc.," boasted Private Worsham of the 21st Virginia of their booty. To the chaplain of a Louisiana regiment, however, the scene had the air of pagan revelry, "I saw the whole army become what appeared to me to be an ungovernable mob, drunk, some with liquor but others with excitement."[13]

The easy defeat of George Taylor's brigade at Manassas Junction sent shock waves through official Washington. Halleck pleaded with McClellan to rush his forces to Pope's aid and directed Pope to drive the Confederates away from the junction as quickly as possible. But General Pope already had his forces advancing on the area in hopes of finding Jackson's troops and striking them before their anticipated reunion with Longstreet. On the afternoon of August 27, Joseph Hooker's division of McDowell's III Corps advanced on Bristoe Station from the west in an effort to probe for Jackson's line. Hooker's men soon found Ewell's Brigade still on rear-guard duty at Bristoe and tried mightily to drive them in. An hour of inconclusive battle ended with Ewell's boys retreating in good order from Bristoe Station, overwhelmed but hardly defeated, and they burned the bridge over Broad Run to slow their pursuers. By evening Ewell's Division joined the rest of Jackson's Command at Manassas Junction and took part in the feasting.[14]

In his headquarters that evening, John Pope was quite confident that the next day would bring his Virginia campaign to a successful head because for the first time in several days the situation was turning in his favor. Not only had he finally found elements of Jackson's Command and driven them back, but he also had intelligence that convinced him that acting now might make good on his promise to crush each half of Lee's army in turn. Prisoners taken by Hooker's brigade at Bristoe Station revealed not only the size and condition of Jackson's force, but confirmed their exact location. Based on this heartening information, Pope ordered his widely scattered army to unite in the Manassas area early the next day. On August 28, he would "bag the whole crowd" and strike a decisive blow for the Union.[15]

At the same time that General Pope was plotting his attack, Stonewall Jackson was looking for good defensive terrain on which to fight a delaying action, should a fight come before Longstreet's Command arrived. It would take only a glance at the map for Jackson to find the ground he was looking for. North of Manassas Junction lay the unfinished bed of a railroad line, a convenient feature that clearly could serve as a set of hasty entrenchments for his troops should Pope attack from the east. To the railroad bed's immediate west and running parallel to it stood a land form known locally as Stony Ridge, a long high ridge line that would be perfect for defending against an attack from the west. Both positions ran from the Warrenton Pike on the south to the Sudley Road on the north, either of which could serve as an escape route should the situation turn against him in battle. Making the position even more attractive, a thick woods surrounded much of the area around the ridge and railroad bed, perfect cover for his men. At 9 P.M. on the 27th, Taliaferro's Division began moving north toward Stony Ridge; by morning of the next day Jackson's entire command had abandoned its unsuitable post at Manassas and was ready for anything Pope might throw at them.[16]

By midday on the 28th, John Pope had once again lost track of Stonewall Jackson's force. The first troops to arrive at Manassas Junction found a wasteland of empty boxes, crates, warehouses, and ruined train cars but no trace of the Confederate army. In fact, the only Rebels they found were a handful of stragglers who had stayed behind to sift through the remains of their comrade's revelry and been caught unaware. These prisoners quickly told their Federal captors where they believed the army was headed; intelligence that General Pope was all too eager to believe. Based on these erroneous reports, Pope now thought Jackson was headed to Centreville to await Longstreet's arrival. The time to strike Lee's divided force was quickly closing, but if his army could unite today they might yet pull off a victory. Without hesitating, General Pope ordered the Army of Virginia to change direction and march to Centreville.[17]

As daylight waned on August 28, 1862, General Stonewall Jackson propped himself against a fence post and pulled his worn Virginia Military Institute cap down over his eyes to get some much needed rest. He knew well that sometime soon his command would once again be in battle and rest would be in short supply. Stonewall had barely gone to sleep when a courier raced up to him warning of the presence of a Federal column approaching from the west. The general didn't need to ask who they were or how many of them were there, for he knew that these were John Pope's men and that the time for battle was here. Jumping on his horse, Jackson raced to the southern crest of Stony Ridge on which sat the farmhouse of the Brawner family. There, in a clearing by the house, Jackson saw the vanguard of Pope's army—Rufus King's division of McDowell's III Corps—wending their way east toward Centreville. Wheeling his horse, Jackson charged off to prepare his men for battle.[18]

The men of King's division had seen the lone rider but thought him little more than a cavalry vidette, for everyone knew the Rebels were somewhere nearby. Within moments, though, guns appeared near the farmhouse where King's men had seen the rider and shattered their quiet march, opening a fight that would later be named for the Brawner farm on which it was fought. That evening held an unusually brutal round of fighting for the men of King's division, and most especially for the westerners of John Gibbon's brigade, who bore the brunt of the fight for the Union. On the gentle slope just east of the farmhouse they fought Jackson's men at very close range for several brutal hours. When darkness finally closed the fight at the Brawner farm, 1,150 Federals and 1,250 Confederates lay dead or dying on the ground, their bodies so close that had they been alive they might have talked together in hushed tones.[19]

John Pope and Stonewall Jackson, though, knew the evening's fight, bloody as it was, had only opened a more serious contest that might well decide the fate of the entire war. Pope, for better or worse, had once again found Jackson's Command, perched north of Manassas Junction, and he now raced to bring all his massive force to bear on that point as quickly as possible. By late on the 28th, orders had gone out to Union corps commanders to unite on the old Manassas battlefield. General Pope knew that if he was to kill Jackson's force alone it would have to happen on the morning of August 29, to wait longer invited disaster. Sigel's Army of Virginia I Corps and Samuel P. Heintzelman's III Corps from the Army of the Potomac, then in the process of forming a line west of the stone house at the intersection of the Warrenton Pike and the Sudley Road, would strike the flanks of Jackson's line. Fitz John Porter's Army of the Potomac V Corps, then still at Manassas Junction, would march around Jackson's right flank and cut off both Stonewall's route of retreat and Longstreet's route to join Jackson. Stonewall was equally certain of renewed battle in the morning but this time, unlike in the Brawner farm fight, he would let Pope attack. For Jackson had found the ideal ground on which to fight and that ground was *his* ground. If Pope would oblige him by fighting once again—and Stonewall had every reason to believe Pope would—than he might well wrap up all of the Army of Virginia the next day.[20]

At 7:00 in the morning Sigel's attack got underway using a plan based more on the strength of his own force than the disposition of Jackson's line. It was poorly executed, though, and after three hours of fruitless assaults it was clear that Sigel's weak effort had failed. The Union attacking force had little choice but to fall back and regroup. At noon John Pope and his staff arrived on the field and set up headquarters on Buck Hill, within view of Jackson's line in the railroad bed. Almost immediately the general began laying the groundwork for another attack in the afternoon that would, Pope fervently believed, finish Jackson off once and for all.[21]

Unfortunately for John Pope, the moment to strike each wing of the divided Southern army had passed even before he had arrived to personally direct the battle. By midmorning Longstreet and Lee had arrived on the field and Longstreet's Command, arriving in pieces, worked quickly to build on Jackson's line. By noon Lee's overall line extended an additional three miles to the south and was ready for anything Pope might dare to throw at it. At the same time Jackson's men reinforced their position in the unfinished railroad bed and massed their artillery on Stony Ridge, from which they could rake a Union attacking force. Viewing the situation, Robert E. Lee could only feel satisfaction that his risky move— dividing his army and sending half on a dangerous route into the enemy's rear—had all paid off. He was now ready to wrap up the miscreant Pope for good.

Pope's plan for the afternoon centered on General Porter's V Corps turning Jackson's "exposed" right while Jackson was busy fending off a small attack on his center. The largely diversionary attack in Jackson's front, led by Cuvier Grover's brigade of Hooker's division, was launched at around 3 P.M. Grover's men charged directly into a gap in the Rebel line between Edward L. Thomas's and Maxcy Gregg's brigades, storming up the railroad embankment and breaching Jackson's line. But the attack was unsupported—not being Pope's main point of attack—and Grover's men were quickly driven back. Porter, meanwhile, led the main Union attacking force on a stumbling march toward what he imagined to be Jackson's flank but into what had now become the very center of Lee's extended line. Having no direct orders to press ahead—in fact, thanks to Pope's poorly worded orders, Porter had no idea that he was leading the main attack—Porter stopped and established his line after encountering a larger-than-expected enemy force. The first attack on Jackson's line conceived by John Pope—and the second such Union effort of the day—had failed.[22]

Pope followed up the failure of Grover's and Porter's attacks by trying the very same thing in miniature. He ordered General Jesse L. Reno to launch a "demonstration" in his front to occupy Jackson's attention while John Reynolds's division swept around Jackson's "flank" and threatened his exposed right. Despite reservations about the plan, Reno directed

James Nagle's 1st Brigade to throw itself at the Confederate line. Reynolds launched his drive as ordered but recalled his men upon encountering the first resistance; Reynolds had spent the morning watching Longstreet's Command deploy in his front and had no desire to conduct a suicide attack solely because the commanding general would not believe his intelligence reports. Nagle's attack, meanwhile, successfully drove Trimble's Brigade out of their position but suffered the same fate as Grover's men whose attack also lacked support at the moment of success. They abandoned their gain and retreated in haste to the Union line from which they had come.[23]

Next it was Philip Kearny's turn to launch a diversionary assault in support of Porter's allegedly impending flank attack. Even though he knew his effort was not intended to be the main attack, General Kearny planned his portion of the fight as if it were. To improve his chance for success, Kearny asked General Isaac Stevens—commanding the position on Kearny's immediate left—to assist him, and Stevens offered up Daniel Leasure's 2nd Brigade for the task. What Kearny and Stevens could not have known was that Fitz John Porter's V Corps would remain immobile throughout their diversionary attack, meaning theirs was a wasted effort even before it began. Nonetheless, as directed by General Pope at 5 P.M., Kearny's division and Leasure's brigade stormed into the left center of Jackson's position in the railroad line. Kearny's men plunged directly into the part of Stonewall's line held by Gregg's Brigade, while Leasure's New Yorkers and Pennsylvanians struck directly at James J. Archer's brigade, to Gregg's immediate right. The attack caught A. P. Hill's weary troops low on ammunition and at a point when they could least resist an attack. Kearny's swift and brutal assault broke the enemy line and for several moments it appeared that Jackson's once-strong position might break. But just as the situation appeared darkest for the South, Hill's only fresh brigade—that of Lawrence O'Brian Branch—raced into the line and halted Kearny's attack. Lacking any reinforcements to throw into the fight, Kearny had no choice but to fall back. The third Union attack on Jackson's line—and the third to breach the Rebel line—had failed for want of reinforcements.[24]

As daylight waned on August 29, Lee must have been fully satisfied with the performance of his troops that day. They had, after all, held off three Union attacks, albeit weak and uncoordinated ones. Lee, in fact, had already begun shifting men to fill gaps in his thinned line in preparation for any assault John Pope might foolishly consider throwing at him in the morning. After all, a full Federal corps—Porter's—remained unused opposite his right and they had to be constantly watched lest they turn the Confederate right. But even so, Lee had attack plans of his own and directed John Bell Hood's division forward along the Warrenton Pike to feel out the final position of the Union center and lay the groundwork for a morning offensive. At 7:00 P.M., Hood's men, supported by James Kemper's and Cadmus Wilcox's brigades, began pushing the center of Lee's line toward Groveton. At the same time that Hood's reconnaissance was preparing to move, John Pope was ordering his own advance. Pope had observed the Southern movements from his headquarters on Buck Hill and for some unexplained reason became convinced that Lee was retreating. To exploit this alleged weakness, Pope directed John P. Hatch's division to push west along the Warrenton Pike in the direction of Groveton beginning at around 7:00 P.M. Hatch's two brigades—those of Abner Doubleday and Timothy Sullivan—ran headlong into Hood's force and the fighting that erupted was as severe as it was unplanned. The outnumbered Federals were quickly overwhelmed but darkness saved them from sure defeat. Nonetheless, this fourth assault of the day failed just as miserably as its predecessors had.[25]

The repeated failures of August 29 did nothing to deter John Pope's aggressive disposition. He used the cover of night to position his force for renewing the attack in the morning, a move which chiefly consisted of pulling Porter's V Corps back from the Union left and placing them in the center of his line. Furious with Porter for failing to launch the intended main attack, Pope was determined that in the morning Porter would be given a chance to redeem himself. His corps would lead the next day's attack. And to John Pope's credit, his plan for the 30th seemed at first glance to be an effort to learn from the failure of the 29th, for he planned to launch a major, well-supported attack at Jackson's center and ignore the enemy's well-protected flanks. But Pope certainly knew that night that the only thing that mattered now—especially in Washington—was a victory on the battlefield the next day.[26]

Only a few miles away, General Lee spent his evening doing much the same as his Union counterpart. Lee, Longstreet, and Jackson carefully strengthened their respective positions, preparing for the morning's action. At 3 A.M. on the 30th, Richard Anderson's division—the last of Longstreet's units to reach the field—posted on a ridge east of Groveton. Even before the entire division was in place Anderson recognized the error of putting his command in such an exposed spot. But his men were tired and needed what little rest the night still offered; he would wait until dawn to order their retrograde move. When the move rearward came, it was spotted at first light by one of Hatch's brigade commanders, who quickly send word to General Pope. When John Pope heard of this move, he again seized the idea that Lee was retreating. It would be this poor bit of analysis that paved the road to disaster for John Pope and the Union cause on August 30.[27]

At 8 A.M. on the 30th—the third day of the as yet unnamed battle—General Pope held a conference at his makeshift headquarters to pass along the attack plans for the morning. But when the general's subordinates failed to support his plans, he was simply stunned. Pope's evident confidence at the start of the meeting had only been so much false bravado and when his subordinates did not shore up that confidence with instant agreement, John Pope caved in to their collective demands. His confidence shaken, Pope withheld ordering his planned attack and spent the rest of the morning scaling down the assault to suit the wishes of the corps commanders. To the troops in the field their inaction throughout the morning, in full view of the Rebels, confirmed the rumors that their commander had lost his nerve after nearly two days of failure. But when Generals McDowell and Heintzelman reported observing Confederates missing from their lines or moving to the rear in their front, Pope's confidence began to soar once more. Here was the proof that his corps commanders had been wrong, that Lee was retreating as he had earlier believed, and that now was the time to launch a major thrust at Lee's center.

Key to any such effort though were the fresh reinforcements that Washington had been promising for days. But General McClellan, by all appearances, had done his best to keep those forces away from Pope's control. It has been bad enough for George McClellan to have his troops—*his* Army of the Potomac—stripped from his control, but the greatest insult of all was that they were being given to a man whom McClellan considered his personal inferior and a military incompetent. Early in the morning of August 24, McClellan had written his wife Mary Ellen, "I learn that all my troops are ordered to Alexandria for embarkation—so I presume they will be merged with Pope's army. If that is the case, I will (if I find it proper) ask for a leave of absence! . . . I don't know how I can remain in the service if placed under Pope—it would be too great a disgrace & I hardly think Halleck would permit it to be offered to me." At 12:30 that same afternoon McClellan had received a telegraph message from General Halleck confirming his worst fear; Porter's V Corps and Reno's IX Corps were to move forward from Alexandria as rapidly as possible and place themselves under Pope's command.[28]

Bitter that he was being eclipsed by the "inferior" Pope, McClellan apparently now did all he could to hinder Pope's chances for success in the coming battle. At noon on the 27th, Halleck sent McClellan a telegraph message ordering William B. Franklin's VI Corps—half of McClellan's remaining command—to also join Pope's force as soon as possible. McClellan, fearing that he would soon be left in charge of no one, responded an hour later that Franklin's command was unprepared for battle, being short of artillery and cavalry, and should not be sent. Instead, he suggested, to ensure the safety of the capital Pope should be ordered to retreat to the Washington defenses. McClellan did not need to mention to Halleck that this plan, if adopted, would then place Pope's entire force under his command. Halleck, however, brushed this suggestion aside and at 12:30 the next day sent an order directly to General Franklin telling him to move rapidly to Manassas. At 4:30 on the 28th, McClellan, aware of Franklin's direct communication, interceded with Halleck in order to prevent the VI Corps movement. As before, McClellan claimed that Franklin's shortages of cavalry and artillery prevented the movement the War Department demanded. Finally, at 10 P.M. that night, McClellan telegraphed Halleck to assure him that "Franklin's Corps has been ordered to march at 6 o'clock tomorrow morning."[29]

Frustrated that Halleck had repeatedly ignored his plans to defend the capital rather than reinforce Pope, McClellan tried one last bit of subterfuge to bring the army once again under his control. At 2:45 P.M. on the 29th, General McClellan sent a message directly to President Lincoln claiming that he was receiving reports from the front that Pope's force was retreating and hinting that Pope had already been beaten. Then, building on this foundation, he suggested, "I am clear that one of two courses should be adopted—1st To concentrate all our available forces to open communication with Pope—2nd To leave Pope to get out of his scrape by himself & at once to use all our means to make the Capital perfectly safe. No middle course will now answer. Tell me what you wish me to do & I will do all in my power to accomplish it. I wish to know what my orders & authority are—I ask for nothing, but will obey whatever orders you give. I ask only a prompt decision that I may at once issue the necessary orders. It will not do to delay longer." Lincoln, however, was well aware of McClellan's grandiose vision of himself and would not rise to the bait. The president's carefully worded response demonstrates his understanding of both General McClellan and of the strategic situation at Manassas: "I think your first alternative to wit 'To concentrate all our available forces to open communication with Pope' is the right one, but I do not wish to control. That I now leave to General Halleck aided by your counsels."[30]

Although Franklin's corps was on its way to Pope early on the 29th, it moved with deliberate sloth and by late that day had only reached Annandale—some 10 miles from Pope's position on the old Manassas battlefield—where it stopped for the night. Halleck now was nearly frantic, desperately trying to avoid another Manassas disaster. Aware that Pope's forces were at least in some form of trouble at Manassas, on the afternoon of the 30th Halleck ordered both of McClellan's remaining corps to reinforce Pope at once. He noted, "They must use their legs and make forced marches. Time now is everything!" Unable to stall any longer, and well aware that Pope was already in the midst of suffering a defeat, McClellan finally rushed his troops to the front.[31]

By midday on the 30th, the vanguard of Franklin's corps was finally nearing Centreville. As they marched away from Fairfax City the men of the VI Corps could hear the booming artillery and musket volleys rolling over the parched farmland and they knew trouble lay ahead. Their senior officers had already been warned that Pope was having a rough time of it near Manassas and that they should be equally prepared to cover a general retreat or to join in the battle.

General Henry W. Slocum, commanding the VI Corps' 1st Division, was well aware of the unpredictable situation that faced his command as he rode west with his men toward Fairfax Court House that morning. Should Pope's forces have to retreat anytime soon the VI Corps likely would be left virtually alone to cover the movement and, quite possibly, to protect the capital. If this were the case success or failure would revolve on protecting the Warrenton Pike, the army's main route of retreat from Centreville and Fairfax Court House, where the bulk of the army would regroup before moving into the Washington defenses. Safeguarding the Warrenton Pike would certainly prove a most difficult task because several roads converged on the pike between Centreville and Fairfax, making it easy for the Confederates to cut off the army's retreat with cavalry. With this in mind, Slocum took it upon himself to ensure Union control of the Warrenton Pike east of Centreville. As time would soon prove, General Slocum's initiative was fortuitous.[32]

As the 1st Division was resting at Fairfax Court House midday on August 30, General Slocum considered how best to use his division to cover a retreat in light of his conflicting orders. Although they were expected in Centreville sometime that afternoon, he certainly had the latitude to detach one of his three brigades for this important task. After all, his forces would not be separated by more than a few miles and the detached brigade could be quickly recalled if the 1st Division were ordered to join an attack. For the important though thankless task of guarding the Warrenton Pike, Slocum selected the New Jersey Brigade, consisting of the 1st, 2nd, 3rd, and 4th New Jersey Regiments, now under the command of Colonel Alfred T. A. Torbert. This was Philip Kearny's old command and, perhaps because of this fact or the truth that this unit had a proven record as fighters, General Slocum must have believed that if any of his brigades was capable of singlehandedly covering the army's retreat, it was Torbert's New Jersey Brigade.[33]

Thus, while most of Slocum's division was forming up to march west to Centreville, the general directed Colonel Torbert to move his 1st Brigade two miles west of Fairfax Court House and post it on a hill overlooking the Warrenton Pike. There they would reinforce Battery A of the 1st New Jersey Light Artillery, who were then alone covering the western approach to Fairfax with their six 3-inch ordnance rifles. Colonel Torbert's role was to guard the main approach to Fairfax Court House and hold off any attack that might come down the Warrenton Pike from the west. Slocum also directed four companies of the 1st New Jersey Infantry to remain posted at the courthouse to act as a provost guard there, under the command of a Captain Baker.[34]

Late on the afternoon of the 30th, with the rest of the brigade long ago having departed for Centreville, Captain Baker was left alone to consider his position at Fairfax Court House. The small force under his command clearly was incapable of defending the large, open area around the courthouse it had been assigned to guard. Nonetheless, he had orders to be prepared to defend Fairfax Court House and would have to make the best of his circumstances. If they were forced to fight here, then preparation and advance warning would be key to any chance of success. Surveying a map of the area between Fairfax and Centreville, Baker must have observed the potentially disastrous terrain feature that somehow had been overlooked by General Slocum. Like a dagger aimed directly at the courthouse, the Little River Turnpike cut southeastward through the Virginia countryside, merging into the Warrenton Pike in front of the courthouse but behind the hill where the rest of the New Jersey Brigade was posted. On local maps this intersection was labeled simply "Jermantown." Any Rebel cavalry trying to seize Fairfax Court House to cut off a Union retreat might well use this road as a natural avenue of approach. Though he had few troops to spare, Captain Baker ordered one company of the 1st New Jersey to march immediately for Jermantown and serve as a picket guard there. They might not be able to resist a determined attack but their presence would at least serve as a trip wire to warn of an assault. Thus, by the evening of August 30, as the Union army was beginning its retreat from Bull Run, only one company—fewer than 100 men—was holding the northern flank of the army's most likely route of retreat to Washington.[35]

General Lee, too, was meeting with his subordinates shortly after dawn to plan the day's actions. But unlike John Pope, Lee decided to cancel his planned morning attack. His troops were weary, low on ammunition, and already sitting in solid works that had plenty of life left in them. Lee would wait until Pope had flung his Federal units against these works, wear the Union army down, and then attack the left with Longstreet's fresh men. For now, Lee would adopt an uncharacteristic defensive posture. But Lee knew that Pope had proven himself more unpredictable than George McClellan and so he crafted a contingency plan in the event that Pope failed to launch an attack. This backup plan called for Longstreet to stage a diversionary strike on the Union left while Jackson, abandoning his defensive works, would recreate in miniature his bold flanking march around Pope's right. Pope's army would either dissolve in confusion or run like burned dogs to once more place themselves between Lee's army and Washington. Either result was acceptable to Lee; he could capture or destroy Pope's broken army or, should it retreat to Washington, the way would be clear for his planned invasion of Maryland.[36]

At 1:00 P.M., Pope sent orders to Porter to launch the two divisions of his V Corps, in conjunction with Hatch's division, on a major attack at the Confederate center. But Porter bungled the effort nearly from the start. His command was nowhere near ready for the attack and it took him over two hours to get everything in place in the thick woods east of Groveton. Porter would later argue that General Pope had failed to offer any assistance to the drive—Porter had no reinforcements or diversionary attacks to help him—and the odds were against him even before the first shot had been fired. When the attack finally came, starting around 3:00 P.M., Jackson's men were ready for them. Most of Hatch's men, moving on the right of Porter's line, reached the eastern embankment of the railroad bed but, with no reinforcements, could go no further. Daniel Butterfield's division, holding the left of the Union attack, was under a constant and galling fire from Stephen D. Lee's artillery on Stony Ridge behind the Brawner house and so when they reached the enemy line the fight had been knocked out of them. Porter's attack stumbled on for nearly an hour and, although Jackson's line was breached several times, it finally ran out of steam. Porter lost his will to fight. He had committed his entire force and come up short, and to send more men in would only uselessly prolong the slaughter.[37]

Near 4:00 P.M., as Porter's attack was winding down, General Longstreet's flanking attack on the Union left was just getting underway. Led by John Bell Hood's brigade of Texans, the right half of Lee's line surged forward hoping to engulf Pope's exhausted army and destroy it in place. The first Federals to discover the attack were the New York Zouaves of Gouverneur Warren's brigade. Though Longstreet's veterans decimated Warren's two small regiments standing alone on Chinn Ridge, their sacrifice bought the brigade commanders collectively leading the Union left time to act. They quickly recalled units then in the process of shifting to the Union's center to support Porter and threw these recalled brigades piecemeal into a hasty defense along the ridge. Despite the heavy price paid by the men of McLean's, Tower's, and Stile's brigades, the tactic worked well enough to slow Longstreet's attack and rob him of momentum.[38]

Meanwhile, Pope threw whatever units that were free in the rear of the Union left into a hasty defense line near Henry Hill. John Pope knew that he was staring defeat squarely in the face and that his actions in the remaining hour or so of daylight would not decide between victory and defeat but rather between defeat and utter disaster. Working feverishly, the commanding general posted four brigades pulled from Sykes's and Reynolds's divisions into the Sudley Road—a sunken road that served very neatly as a defensive position—along the base of Henry Hill. To these he soon added two more brigades on the crest of the hill acting as a reserve. When Longstreet's Command finally secured Chinn Ridge, after nearly an hour and a half of severe fighting, they barely paused long enough to re-form their lines before pressing on toward their objective on the Union left. But when they encountered Pope's hastily positioned men in the Sudley Road, Longstreet's attackers found they could go no further. Even the efforts of two fresh brigades from Richard Anderson's division on the Confederate right flank were not enough to propel the tired Southern line forward. The sacrifices of the four brigades on Chinn Ridge had paid off and had saved John Pope's army for now.[39]

The men of the 21st Massachusetts had spent most of that day waiting to enter the battle, unlike most of their comrades on the field. At 7:00 P.M. they marched to the western crest of Henry Hill and, along with the rest of their brigade, halted the attack of two of Longstreet's lead brigades. As they lay under arms that evening on Henry Hill, the very spot of the first battle at Manassas, the significance of their action a few hours earlier was not lost on the men of the 21st. They all realized that they had prevented a repeat of the terrible flight that had ended the fighting on that same spot less than a year ago. For that they were justifiably proud.[40]

Around 6:00 P.M., Jackson's Command finally rose from their trenches of the last two days and pressed forward toward the Union right in their front. The attack came on with vigor, at first, overwhelming a number of Union batteries too slow in limbering up their pieces for flight. But Stonewall's men were tired, the sort of worn weariness that can only come from two-and-a-half days of nearly constant danger, and Pope's regirded defensive line north of the Warrenton Pike blunted Jackson's attack with little trouble.

Sergeant Daniel Fletcher of Company H of the 40th New York Volunteer Infantry remembered seeing the right wing of Pope's army falling back and then breaking. At almost the same moment, Fletcher's entire brigade started running for the rear. "I threw away everything I had except my musket and equipments," Fletcher remembered. They had run but a short distance when they encountered General Philip Kearny, their division commander, who immediately recognized his fleeing troops by the "Kearny patch." This symbol, a red diamond insignia worn on each man's sleeve, had been created by the general to easily distinguish his men on the field in just such a moment. Fletcher and his comrades very much loved and respected Kearny and his mere presence stopped their flight. Kearny halted the brigade by a battery and then fronted them to face the advancing enemy. Sergeant Fletcher recalled, "While we were halting near the battery a large body of men filed down near us in our front. General Kearny, thinking they were our men, rode toward them. They were rebels. The first thing he knew, he was between the rebel pickets and line of battle. He said, 'can you tell me where the --th regiment is?' naming a southern regiment he knew to be in that locality. The picket, supposing him to be a rebel officer, let him pass. So he escaped. Another of Kearny's hair breadth escapes." With their commander once more by their side, and order similarly restored to the ranks, Kearny's division stood firm to stop Lee's counterattack in their front.[41]

Shortly after 7:00 that evening, as the sun dipped toward the horizon, Lee's counterattack on the Union line came to a standstill. At 8:00 P.M., John Pope ordered his army to retreat. While the 21st Massachusetts protected the retreating army as it moved east, most of the rest of the men of the Union army made their way to the strong, entrenched position at Centreville in any way they could. Some units marched more or less intact, but most of the regiments arrived at Centreville in pieces, a few men at a time. "The night march to Centreville was a dismal one," remembered John Vautier of the 88th Pennsylvania, "all along the road, in the darkness and the gloom, the commanders tried to collect their men,

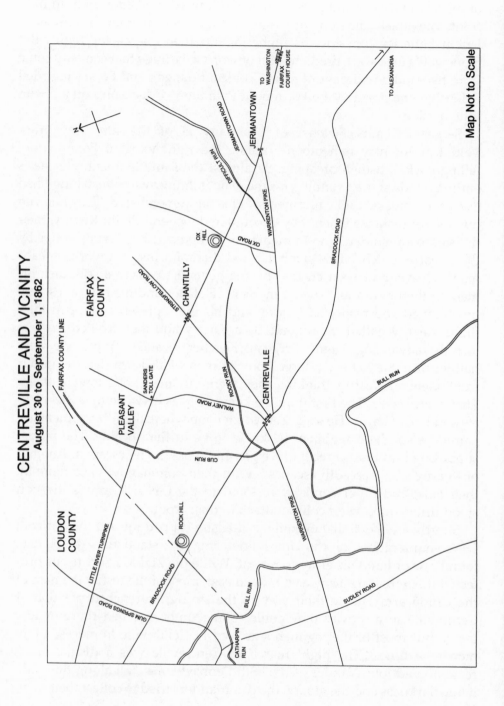

CENTREVILLE AND VICINITY
August 30 to September 1, 1862

Map Not to Scale

and the horse cries of 'This way for Tower's brigade, Fall in, 88th,' resounded through the cheerless night."

"To make our march the more gloomy," recalled Captain Lyman Jackman of the 6th New Hampshire, "a pouring rain came down before we reached Centreville, and, thoroughly drenched, tired, and hungry, we lay down on the wet ground, with sad thoughts and gloomy forebodings." By midnight the 21st Massachusetts, too, had arrived in Centreville. "Disgusted and sick at heart," remembered Captain Charles Walcott, "we continued our slow march along . . . the obstructed road to Centreville, where we arrived in a drizzling rain . . . and our hungry and wearied men, after they had looted an army wagon loaded with sugar, laid down to rest upon the ground without blankets."[42]

The men of the 51st Pennsylvania arrived in Centreville that evening dead tired, soaked to the skin by the near constant rain, and completely without food. But the regiment's mood was soon changed by the discovery of a hidden store of dry, new clothing. The delighted Pennsylvanians were soon tossing away their wet rags, that only moments before had been Federal uniforms, and donning fresh, new clothing. Soon the original owners of the confiscated goods, a predominantly German regiment, discovered their loss. Thomas Parker of the 51st recalled, "their woeful looking countenances bespoke the sad disappointment they felt at their loss, and their 'Cod fer tams' were frequent and loud." Under the strained circumstances these new Americans could do little to stop the looting going on before their very eyes.[43]

General Pope and his headquarters staff reached Centreville at around 9:00 that night. The sight that greeted Pope was one of utter confusion and disaster. Most of the small number of houses in the hamlet were acting as hospitals and the groans of men suffering under the surgeon's knife could be heard everywhere through the night. Outside of the many makeshift hospitals severed limbs were strewn about. One Pennsylvania volunteer was moved to write of Centreville that night, "It was an awful sight, and one that I have never forgotten. It had the appearance of a slaughterhouse." The constant stream of wounded men needing medical treatment that arrived in Centreville would only amplify the sense in many of the men that hell had burst forth on the Virginia countryside for a night.[44]

Although only part of the broken army had reached Centreville by 9:00 P.M., those that were there were scattered everywhere in no apparent order. Only a handful of units retreating from Bull Run arrived that night in anything resembling order. Pope knew that this disorder invited attack should it last into the morning. To combat this problem, he ordered his staff to quickly begin placing placards on trees along the ridge on which Centreville rests so that his divisions and corps could begin to restore some order during the night. Pope's crude organizational system worked better than even he could have hoped and within hours of their placement, the Army of Virginia once again began resembling an organized fighting force.[45]

With this task done, Pope began considering what to do next. The commanding general was alone in the flood of options and angles that he had to consider that dark, dreary night. In the best situation he could imagine Lee would not attack, giving him time to reorganize with an eye toward reopening his own attack in a day or two. In the worst case, Lee might attack at dawn, before his tattered force could regroup, most likely forcing him to either face another defeat or worse. Defeat was not the worst case after all, for capture of this army would bring ruin on both himself and the Union cause. But he certainly could not consider attacking the Confederates again without the reinforcements that General Halleck had been promising him for days. And if he began a general retreat to the Washington defenses now he would certainly be ruined professionally, and with his failure might come flagging public support in the North for the war. Indeed, John Pope must have felt very alone that night, with the weight of these important decisions hanging on his shoulders and without the kind of supporters that McClellan enjoyed in at least half of the army. Still, he would have to tell Washington something that evening and he could not rest until he had done so. At 9:45 P.M. Pope began to write a dispatch for General Halleck. It would be this dispatch that would frame Washington's first understanding of the outcome of three days of fighting, three days that had gone very badly for him and the Union cause. John Pope's only hope now would depend on carefully weaving this message to ensure that Washington would leave him alone long enough to somehow undo the damage that had been done.

Given the message's importance, John Pope took the only course he must have believed was available to him that night—he lied:

> We have had a terrific battle again to-day, the enemy, largely reenforced, assaulted our position early to-day. We held our ground firmly until 6 p.m., when the enemy . . . forced back [our left] wing about half a mile. At dark we held that position. Under all circumstances, both horses and men having been two days without food, and the enemy greatly outnumbering us, I thought it best to draw back to this place at dark. The movement has been made in perfect order and without loss. The troops are in good heart, and marched

off the field without the least hurry or confusion. Do not be uneasy. We will hold our own here. We have damaged him heavily, and I think the army entitled to the gratitude of the country. Be easy; everything will go well. P.S.—We have lost nothing, neither guns nor wagons.[46]

As he sealed his dispatch and directed an aide to ride it to Washington immediately, Pope must have felt confident that this neat bit of deception would do the trick. It was reassuring enough to convince old Halleck that he had things here under control and that all would be well in the end. Still, it had just enough of the truth in it to keep the letter from being considered an outright fabrication. The rest would now be up to him. Somehow John Pope would have to turn the situation around.

With this important task concluded, General Pope returned to considering his options for the morning. He had received several dispatches from Halleck during the 30th, telling him that reinforcements from the peninsula were already on their way and should be arriving soon. These men would give Pope fresh troops around which to structure his rebuilt army, an important consideration whatever might happen in the morning. If Lee appeared ready to attack at dawn—his worst case scenario—then he could certainly hold the Rebel army off here in Centreville at least long enough for fresh troops to arrive. If Lee failed to exploit his advantage, then he could consider attacking Lee again. His last order of the night was for each of his corps commanders to report to him as early as possible after dawn on August 31. Having laid the groundwork to restore order to his shattered command, and decided on his course of action for the morning, John Pope tried to get a few hours of fitful sleep.

At the same moment, on the other side of Bull Run, General Lee, too, was deciding his next move. Lee stood in the twilight of August 30, watching his weary army collect its prisoners and re-form its units, uncertain whether to chase Pope in what remained of the day or to let the men rest and renew the fight at dawn. It was getting dark and no one knew exactly how many Union troops lay beyond the run. General Lee was concerned, as he had been throughout the campaign, about the number of reinforcements that Pope might now have at his disposal. Although one of Lee's key objectives in this campaign had been to get McClellan's troops away from Richmond, at the same time he had feared they would very quickly move north to reinforce Pope. Also, Washington was only 20 miles away and guarded by some 35 infantry regiments, nearly an entire Union corps. Although the capital's guard was unlikely to leave its important prize, Pope might still have a massive number of men at his disposal, even now.

Eventually, General Lee surrendered the initiative to nature and would later report, "The obscurity of the night and the uncertainty of the fords of bull run rendered it necessary to suspend operations until morning . . ." When the next attack was launched, it would have to be well coordinated and well supported to be successful lest the gains of Second Manassas be lost. The Army of Northern Virginia would get a few hours of much needed rest before launching another blow against Pope's army.[47]

But most of the Southern soldiers on the field that night would get little rest despite General Lee's good intentions. The ground between the unfinished railroad cut and Bull Run lay littered with killed and wounded men of both sides. Broken gun carriages, dead horses, and discarded muskets and equipment added to the dismal scene. Nowhere on the field that night could one look and avoid the grim evidence of war. The men sleeping, talking, and cooking amidst the carnage were a strange juxtaposition of calm amid devastation, a scene that was by now commonplace to many of the veterans. The 55th Virginia, like most other Confederate units, had dropped in its tracks after the fighting ended and its men quickly turned to getting food and rest. The experience of T. J. McGeorge of the 55th Virginia's Company G, who hadn't received rations in three days, was typical of the situation throughout the Southern army: "I offered one of our men five dollars for one slice of bacon—he refused to let me have it, so I went across the battle field in search of something. I found a dead Yankee. I took his haversack to the fire light and found some bloody cracker, from which I scraped his life blood and ate."[48]

2

The Confluence of Two Lives

Despite the broken spirits in Pope's Army of Virginia, most men were relieved once they arrived in Centreville that dismal night, for they understood that there were few other places in northern Virginia that presented such a strong defensive position. The small village of Centreville was situated nearly atop the crest of a ridge running north-south that was a little over two miles in length. This ridge dominated the descending slope of the land around it for miles; for at least two of the five miles to Fairfax Court House to its east as well as to Bull Run, four miles to its west. From the heights of Centreville, General Pope could see all the way to the Bull Run Mountains, foothills of the Appalachians. Adding to its military value, the Warrenton Pike—the major westward route from Alexandria and a direct route to the Union capital—climbed over the top of the crest. The Confederate army had further enhanced Centreville by building an elaborate system of works and fortifications, including a star-shaped fort, facing Washington to the east. Centreville itself had seen more than its fair share of war already and few of its 14 houses and two churches remained fully intact as the Union army clambered into town that night.[1]

Philip Kearny

With the Union army that night was Major General Philip Kearny, who arrived in Centreville in the early hours of August 31. He immediately sought out the location of his command, the 1st Division of the III Corps, Army of the Potomac. Riding swiftly with his small staff to the western slope of the Centreville heights, where the III Corps had been posted to guard the eastern approach to town, Kearny ensconced himself in a small cottage just off the Warrenton Pike. Once settled in, he turned to writing his official report of the events of the last two and a half days. Kearny always liked to prepare his reports as soon after a battle had ended as the situation allowed, so that the events of the struggle were fresh in his mind.

Just in case the task this night should prove beyond even his considerable endurance though, Kearny began writing his report in the crude bed that remained in the house.[2]

After finishing his report—which he failed to sign—the general wrote a short letter to his wife:

Dearest Love,

I wrote you yesterday morning. Since then there has been a sort of Bull Run episode. It is dangerous work to fight in this army; you have to fight ten times your share; and to expose yourself to prevent the demoralizing effect of almost cowardice in others. Hooker's Division is almost the only exception. This army ran like sheep; all but General Reno and General Gibbon. As for myself I was abandoned shamefully. My only salvation depended on holding a certain hill and house in the rear adjoining me. In the darkness of twilight the enemy came and fired a few trifling shots and Stevens' people ran; we alongside never dreamed of it.

I had a staff officer taken prisoner and I was only a few yards behind him. It was perfectly ridiculous; but he was so unsuspicious that I could not help him as scouts were stealing in all around me; he was so surprised; it was very funny. I will tell you some other time.

My regiments behaved like perfect doves—so beautifully steady. I stayed for more than three hours after all the Americans but Reno and Stevens had left; and Reno was as much to the left as I was to the right behaving very handsomely. My friend, Towers, was wounded. This disaster is not Pope's fault but rather the other generals in places they are not fit for.

It is tiresome to have one's victory ignored; as at Sangsters Station and Williamsburg and in the New Market Road and to be ignored, though fighting hard and successfully; and exposing myself, as my nature unfortunately is, in other people's defeats.

Yesterday would have been ridiculous, if not so sad for our cause: Our men would not fight one bit; it was amusing to watch them. I foresaw it all three hours before it took place. But I am sorry for our cause.

Kiss the children; love

Phil [3]

Although he was a faithful correspondent with his wife, in many ways the army was Philip Kearny's first and truest love. He was born on June 1, 1815, in New York City to one of the nation's wealthiest families, ensuring that Kearny's childhood would be free of material wants. His emotional well being, however, never enjoyed the same prosperity as his financial fortunes. For Kearny's childhood was not very different from that of many of the young children of the very wealthy in early nineteenth-century America. His parents could afford an extensive staff of nursemaids and tutors, who were responsible for caring for young Phil day to day. Also typically, he would develop closer bonds with these hired servants than with his own, preoccupied parents. And when his mother, Susan Watts, died as a result of an extended series of complications from his birth, eight-year-old Philip was told of her passing by a family servant.[4]

Kearny's father and grandfather were both founding members of the New York Stock Exchange and each had profited handsomely from their efforts in the world of stock trading. Young Philip, however, longed to become a soldier, like his uncle, Stephen Watts Kearny, who was a hero of the War of 1812 and a famous western explorer. But despite his longing for a military career, Philip's grandfather John Watts—who controlled the family's wealth—wished for him to enter the ministry. When it came time for Kearny to choose between West Point and a private college, his family persuaded him—forced him, really—to attend Columbia College to study law. This career choice had been the result of a compromise with his grandfather and, while not his first choice, it kept him from having to accept complete submission to his domineering elder. Kearny graduated from Columbia in 1833 with a law degree but soon embarked on a round-the-world tour with his cousin, John Watts de Peyster. After returning to America, Philip accepted a position as a law clerk in the New York law office of Peter Augustus Jay.[5]

Before Philip Kearny could fully establish himself in a law career, however, fate intervened to lead him down the path his heart longed for still. Kearny's soul was a restless one that would never have been content in the quiet of a law practice. In 1836 his grandfather died, leaving him a one million dollar fortune and at the same time instantly removing much of the family resistance to his plans for an army career. Kearny departed almost immediately for Washington and on March 8, 1837, received his commission as a first lieutenant in his uncle's regiment, the 1st U.S. Dragoons.[6]

After proving his worth as a capable and promising young officer during two years at Fort Leavenworth, Kansas, with the 1st Dragoons, Kearny was selected by the secretary of war to join two other young officers attending the French Cavalry School at Saumur, the world's premier cavalry institution. In 1840, after only six months of study, First Lieutenant Kearny left the school to join the Chasseurs d'Afrique of the French army and campaign in Algiers, fighting nomadic Arabs who had attacked French colonists there. Kearny's role in the capture of Milianah earned him the offer of a command in the Foreign Legion and the Cross of the Legion of Honor. But as a commissioned U.S. Army officer, who could accept no foreign military awards, he was forced to refuse both honors.

After returning to the United States later in 1840, Kearny was posted to Carlisle, Pennsylvania, where he wrote a cavalry tactics manual entitled "Applied Cavalry Tactics Illustrated in the French Campaign," building on his experiences in France and Algeria. After publication of this book and another small volume of his experiences in Africa, Kearny's professional life took another boost when he began service in Washington as a staff officer to a number of senior army officers including Winfield Scott.[7]

In 1841 Kearny's life changed, as well, when he married Diana Bullitt, whom he had met years earlier during a stay at Jefferson Barracks in Missouri. Diana was a beautiful young woman with raven hair and high cheekbones, who had charmed Lieutenant Kearny with her goods looks and her strong will. She seemed to him the perfect match for his own iron will and outlook on life. In the beginning their marriage was a happy, prosperous one and Diana bore Kearny four healthy children. But Diana knew well what was in store for her as an army wife and she wanted none of it. Perhaps she had hoped that the wealthy young officer would tire of the suffering of military service and leave to enjoy his inheritance. But whatever Diana may have hoped, Kearny showed no inclination to leave the army. As the time approached for him to receive a new posting in the field, far from the comforts and social pleasures of Washington, Diana increasingly pressed Kearny to seek a new career. After repeated conflict over the issue, he relented to her wish. The tedium and political nature of staff work wasn't what he had joined the army for anyway and, disillusioned, he resigned his commission on April 6, 1846.[8]

Once again, though, fate intervened to pull Philip Kearny back where he apparently belonged—in the army. The outbreak of the Mexican War in December 1846 brought Kearny back to active duty as a captain commanding a company of dragoons during Scott's Vera Cruz campaign. In early March 1847, Scott landed his 10,000 man force on the beaches— including Kearny and a captain of engineers named Robert E. Lee—and prepared to surround Vera Cruz. Captain Lee was put in charge of positioning Scott's artillery for the siege; providing mounted protection for Lee and his men was Philip Kearny and his dragoons. Late on August 20 that same year, Philip Kearny led his company in a daring charge of the Mexican position at Churubusco, receiving a wound that would cost him his left arm. The wounded Captain Kearny was too weak to safely return to the American lines that day and was saved by a young lieutenant named Richard Ewell. The loss of his arm to the surgeon's blade ended Kearny's Mexican War service and he would spend the remainder of the war recuperating in veterans' hospitals.[9]

After the war Kearny returned home to Diana and the children, but he had tasted military life in the way that he had imagined it should be, full of adventure and danger. He now was determined to return to full-time active duty. If their married life had been difficult before the war, this decision made each day a misery for both of them. The strong wills that had initially attracted Philip and Diana to each other now set them at war. Diana made it clear to Kearny even before his service in Mexico that she would never return to the trying life of a military wife and his final decision to rejoin the army was the last straw. Diana soon left him, and taking the children went to live with her parents in Kentucky.[10]

Freed of his family connections, Kearny left in January 1851 to join his regiment at a frontier post in California. He and his men were to protect the flood of gold prospectors setting up mining operations in the area from hostile Indian attack. In one skirmish, Brevet Major Kearny and his men fought over 300 Indians of the Rouge River band and captured 40 prisoners. But fighting Indians was not what Kearny wanted in an army career. Adding to his growing frustration, he soon realized that promotion in the peacetime army came painfully slow and in 1851 he once again resigned his commission.[11]

Kearny, perhaps to escape the fact that he had lost his family for a career that he now had abandoned, once again left to tour the world. While in France, he met the stunning beauty Agnes Maxwell, daughter of the director of customs for the port of New York, at a ball in the Tuileries. Before the end of the ball, Philip and Agnes were smitten with each other. In the days after their first meeting he showered Agnes with gifts and repeatedly called for her. Despite their growing love, the relationship faced numerous hurdles. To begin with, Kearny was 38 years old while she was barely 20. Making things worse, Agnes's parents objected to the growing relationship, in part because of their age difference but mainly because Agnes had broken off her engagement with a prosperous New

York financier. But of course the greatest hurdle the two lovers faced was the fact that Philip Kearny was still a married man.

Kearny decided to return to America to ask Diana for a divorce and in February 1854, arrived once more in his home state of New York. But Diana, counseled by Philip's father, curtly refused the divorce request. Kearny realized he could never marry his beloved Agnes and broke off their relationship. He plummeted into depression over his personal affairs and went into seclusion in upstate New York.

Try as he might, though, Kearny could not banish his love for Agnes. To pass the time and begin the healing process he would take long rides through the countryside seeking escape from his own thoughts. On one of these rides, Kearny crossed over an old decrepit bridge he had ridden over dozens of times. But on this occasion the weight of horse and rider was too much for the rotten planking of the bridge and he and his horse fell through the span and tumbled to the bottom of a ravine. The fall inflicted serious injuries and for days Kearny hovered between life and death. It was during these tense, uncertain days that someone decided to send word of the accident to Agnes in France.[12]

Upon receiving the message of Kearny's condition, Agnes packed her things and immediately departed for New York. Although he had weathered the worst of his injury by the time Agnes reached his bedside, she remained with him to nurse him through several months of recuperation. And once he had fully recovered, Kearny vowed to Agnes that they would never again be separated by the talk of others.

Kearny was good as his word to Agnes. Despite his lingering marriage to Diana, he invited Agnes to move into his estate in New Jersey. The couple immediately settled into their new home—named "Bellegrove" and modeled after a medieval French chateau in Saumur—and Agnes began the process of making Bellegrove in her image. Philip and Agnes were happy at Bellegrove and fully enjoyed the love they had been denied earlier in their relationship.[13]

But New York society was less tolerant of the scandalous pairing than Paris society had been. Tongues wagged incessantly in the fashionable parlors of New York and the scandal even reached the society pages of the newspapers. When Kearny heard of the growing gossip he was outraged, vowing "to slice out the tongue of any gossip, man or woman!" But the talk proved hard to ignore and when Agnes was found to be pregnant in 1855, they recognized something would have to be done.[14]

Kearny and Agnes left their beloved Bellegrove for France, leaving the estate in separate carriages to avoid any unwanted attention. Unlike their earlier time in France, the happy pair attracted no undue attention and most people they encountered simply assumed they were married. In 1856, their daughter Susan Watts Kearny was born and the new family was happier than ever. But both Philip and Agnes knew that they could never be completely contented until they were legally married.

Kearny resolved to return home to do what he should have done years earlier, confront Diana and secure a divorce. At first Diana refused, but when Kearny threatened to take their son, John Watts, from her, Diana softened and granted him what he had wanted for so long. Kearny and Agnes were finally married in April 1858 and they soon returned to Paris. Sometime after returning to France, their second child, Archibald Kennedy Kearny, was born and their collective joy grew even greater.[15]

In 1859, Kearny was in France when that nation declared war on Austria in order to free northern Italy from Hapsburg control. Upon hearing this news, Kearny immediately contacted old friends from his days in Algeria and was soon attached to the staff of General Morris in Napoleon III's Imperial Cavalry. Once at the front, Kearny chafed to join in the action and asked the general if he might be permitted to join his old "unit," the Chasseurs d'Afrique. General Morris agreed and Kearny later wrote of the war, "I participated in every charge that took place." For his role in the charges at Magenta and Solferino, Philip Kearny was once again awarded the Legion of Honor. This time he accepted the honor and became the first American to receive France's highest honor for military achievements.[16]

The night before the battle of Solferino, Kearny had an experience that would ominously foreshadow his future. Lost in the confusion of the massing armies and darkness that night, Kearny found two cavalry guides who offered to take him safely to French lines. Kearny agreed and followed them silently for a time. After riding some distance, however, he became suspicious and soon realized that he had been tricked into riding not into French lines but rather into the enemy Austrian lines instead. Before his would-be captors could stop him, though, Kearny spurred his horse and "had a marvelous escape." This would not be his last encounter with riding into enemy lines.[17]

Back in Paris after the Austrian war, Kearny soon received word of the impending conflict at home. He had mixed feelings about the growing sectional conflict. Although he personally despised abolitionists, he also felt slavery was a vile institution that should eventually be ended. Above all else, however, he believed in the preservation of the Union and it would be to this cause that Philip Kearny would pledge himself.

Many of Kearny's friends and fellow Americans abroad, however, had other loyalties. Two of his closest such friends were John Magruder, a still-commissioned U.S. Army officer, and Robardeau Wheat, a wild soldier of fortune. The three had often talked of the sectional problems at home and all knew that these difficulties might one day test the limits of their friendship. When the three comrades parted for the last time, they stood on the steps of Kearny's Paris mansion, Magruder and Wheat leaving for home to offer their services to the Southern Confederacy and Philip Kearny bound for New York in the North.[18]

Back again in America, the Kearnys returned to Bellegrove and Agnes prepared for the birth of their third child, who was to be named Virginia after the state. But Kearny quickly turned to securing a senior commission from his native state, New York. No less a dignitary than Winfield Scott wrote his recommendation to New York's governor: "I beg leave to suggest Major Philip Kearny of New York, late, distinguished officer of the Army for a high commission in the New York Volunteers. His long and valuable experience in actual and active military service seems to commend him as a useful and valuable Commander and disciplinarian. He is among the bravest of the brave and of the highest spirit and bearing."[19]

Despite Scott's glowing praise, Kearny was rebuffed by Albany in his efforts to secure a general officer's commission. It seemed that New York valued gentlemanly qualities over military experience in their generals. Kearny's private life, he was informed, was simply too corrupt for him to qualify for such an important position. Furious, Kearny stalked away from New York and immediately offered his services to New Jersey. The Garden State had had trouble finding someone qualified to command its first brigade of infantry and Kearny was soon appointed a brigadier general in the first New Jersey brigade.[20]

General Kearny would soon discover that there was a very good reason why New Jersey had had trouble finding a commander for its brigade. The newly mustered "Brigade of Jersey Blues," consisting of the 1st, 2nd, 3rd, and 4th New Jersey Infantry Regiments, was floundering in its efforts to organize and change citizens into soldiers. The brigade had encamped near Alexandria, Virginia, by August 1861, without its new commanding officer and soon had gained a reputation for drunken, uncontrolled behavior. But all that would change with the arrival of Brigadier General Philip Kearny. Private Charles Hopkins of the 1st New Jersey remembered his first encounter with General Kearny:

> [W]e were marching through the lawn in front of Headquarters, which was adjoining a peach grove . . . [we then] broke ranks and scurried for the peaches, though they were not near ripe, pulled

down branches, broke them, in fact, became an unruly mob which their officers could not control. Kearny saw this lack of discipline and reckless destruction of the fruit trees and green, unripe fruit, and while I had heard of Kearny I was convinced that he was the real Phil when I heard some of his expletives; so rich in color, if red and blue, with a sulphury smell, were a good combination. Kearny was not in uniform, but wore a seersucker coat, bareheaded, only his pants were of his uniform. Hence, to the uninitiated, looked the civilian more than the officer of rank. This non military look deceived a Sergeant of Company D, a big burly, loud voiced fellow, who paid no attention to the demands of Kearny to stop the destruction of the trees and fruit, but in derision yelled at Phil wanting to know "who the hell he was" and denounced as an old Secesh and used some lurid terms not in a very accomplished vocabulary. "I am General Philip Kearny, you damn thieving Jersey scoundrel, you (this was not the terms the General did use) get in the ranks or I will have you shot." That noisy braggadocio was as stiff as a ramrod for a moment then wilted to dimensions to fit a pinhole, so cringing and beaten. From a dirty unshaven, long-haired misfit clothed mob we were now to have someone to make us over into disciplined, well trained, well fed, well dressed soldiers.[21]

While he was engrossed in building the New Jersey Brigade into a fighting unit, personal tragedy struck the Kearny family. On February 22, 1861, their son Archie died suddenly and, although he was a man of iron temperament and will, the unexpected passing of Archie cut his father to the quick. Making matters worse, Agnes's letters demonstrated moroseness that caused Kearny to worry about his young wife. On March 12 he wrote, "when I drop my professional duties, and turn my thoughts to you and home, oh, how sadly am I oppressed. Dearest Angel, how I mourn for you, and how I grieve for myself. Our dear angel boy, whom God gave us, but to take away. His first smile, his last look, God knows how I suffer, and you angel, how much more. God give us strength." Such sentiments demonstrate the man that few who witnessed Kearny at work in the field would dare to dream existed.[22]

In his usual fashion, Kearny buried himself in his work to avoid the pain of Archie's passing and the separation from Agnes. And if he was satisfied in the progress of building the New Jersey Brigade into a capable force, he was equally unhappy with his personal fate in the army hierarchy. In particular, he felt contempt for the many less experienced and politically appointed officers whom he was forced to serve under. Kearny routinely gave vent to this frustration in his letters to Agnes, the only safe place for such emotional release. Typical of his comments on his "superior" officers were those written to her on March 30: "McClellan is no General, but a very weak paltry individual, surrounded, and flattered and cajoled by hypocrites, who are only waiting to rise by him, and then machinate against him. Notwithstanding my war service my fate, and that of my men, is confined to this engineer Franklin, who never commanded a soldier, and in the 1st corps d'Armie, a politician, Gen. King, son of the abolitionist Charles King, a graduate of West Point, way back in '33, with only one years peace experience in the Army, without private prestige, a military experience, is given command of a division." Knowing that he was more capable at exercising higher military command than any of his "superiors" was a trying thing for Kearny to bear.[23]

Kearny had been pulling political strings in Trenton and Washington for some time in an effort to do something about his low standing in the army's command structure. These efforts focused on creating a new division comprised completely of New Jersey regiments. Such a division, Kearny and his supporters argued, could be more easily administered— simplifying mail delivery and recruiting, for example—and would still be an effective fighting force. That Kearny was the man to command the New Jersey division did not need to be stated. But the efforts failed because Washington opposed creating any more ethnic or state units, and Kearny was offered command of Sumner's former division. Kearny, considering the offer an attempt to undermine him politically and an insult, turned it down flatly. Publicly he claimed that he had turned the division and promotion to major general down because his true loyalty was to New Jersey. Privately he continued to lobby for a New Jersey division and admitted to confidants that he feared he may have overplayed his hand. Nonetheless, men in his command believed his public claims and loved him all the more for his "sacrifice."

During this time in the Washington defenses, the numerous scouting expeditions Kearny's brigade was directed to undertake by his senior officers sorely tested the general's patience and his men's physical stamina. McClellan, having seen for himself the strong works erected by the Confederates at Centreville during the previous autumn and fearing the Rebels would use the Centreville works to launch attacks on the infant U.S. volunteer force, ordered a series of probes to check any such movement. After one such expedition, Kearny exploded at a lieutenant who brought his weary and heavily laden men to attention at his approach. "You damned rascal, d'you think they're horses!" he thundered, "order them to stack arms, and take off them damned knapsacks! What! Scouting with a mule load of camp equipage on their backs! Off with them, and let the men lie down!" Philip Kearny held high expectations of his men but simply would not brook any form of abusing them.[24]

During another of these probes, early in his Civil War service, an event occurred that spoke much about the general. As Kearny and his staff rode toward Fairfax Court House midday they encountered returning scouts bearing news that a Confederate cavalry picket was guarding the road ahead. Kearny, rather than call for a cavalry platoon to drive in the pickets, suddenly spurred his horse and sped off for the scene with his staff in pursuit. The Rebel horsemen were so startled by the appearance of the party rushing at them that they took flight without ever firing a shot. But Kearny, not content with merely running the guards off, continued the chase until it was clear that the enemy's headstart would permit their escape. Throughout the coming months of campaigning, Kearny would demonstrate time and again that in battle he would act first and think later about the wisdom of exposing himself to personal danger.[25]

Sizing up the strategic situation facing the army, Kearny more than once in the early months of 1862 suggested to his fellow officers that the Union army should flank the Centreville works and attack the railroad junction at Manassas, thereby drawing the Rebels out of their works to fight in the open. But no one, especially not George McClellan—whom Kearny referred to as an "ass" in a letter to Agnes—would seriously consider such a plan. Instead, General McClellan planned to move his army down the coast to the Virginia peninsula and launch a drive on Richmond behind the backs of the Rebels at Manassas. President Lincoln and his advisors had been pressing McClellan to advance on the Rebels and put an end to the war. But McClellan held his ground and on March 8 and 9, the entire Confederate army abandoned Centreville and slipped away to the Richmond defenses. Now the hue and cry was too great for even George McClellan to ignore and the next day, March 10, the Army of the Potomac moved toward Centreville and Manassas. But when they arrived at the abandoned Rebel camps, all that was found was empty works and burning supplies. McClellan's foot dragging had avoided a fight he didn't want and now the way was clear to carry out his move to the peninsula.

On April 17, 1862, Kearny and the New Jersey Brigade boarded the steamer *Elm City* for the journey south. Within the week they were moored near Yorktown on the Virginia peninsula and Kearny was champing at the bit to fight. But McClellan's army remained on the boats for several more days until all was ready for their arrival; a position that frustrated Kearny mightily. The Confederates, predictably, used the time to prepare a strong defensive line across the width of the peninsula from Yorktown westward. And when Union forces finally disembarked, McClellan settled down to a siege of the Yorktown position, preferring to avoid a direct attack. Kearny, not surprisingly, criticized McClellan's inaction.

If there was any consolation for General Kearny, it was that on May 1, he was offered command of the 3rd Division in Heintzelman's III Corps of the Army of the Potomac. This time he accepted the offer without hesitation, even when his request to take the New Jersey Brigade to his new command with him was denied. His earlier and ongoing efforts to press for a New Jersey division clearly were going nowhere. In Kearny's view, this state of affairs existed largely because New Jersey officials in Washington would not more actively back his scheme and he was determined not to suffer a personal setback for New Jersey's sake again. At the same time, he knew that accepting the appointment meant abandoning his men and, perhaps more importantly, publicly abandoning principles he had championed. In his letter telling Agnes of the appointment he stated, "People have forgotten that my position among Generals is very high, and that whilst in command of a Brigade, I was quite under the surface, that the moment I take a Division (and leave Jersey interests to the keeping of those who never sustained me) that I immediately assume my place, and become one of the highest officers, in command of Divisions, in this Army." Kearny's decision proved a wise one, for it finally placed him in a position he believed worthy of his experience and capabilities and, in any case, there was little negative reaction to the appointment in the ranks of the New Jersey Brigade.[26]

On May 3 the Confederates, convinced that they would be unable to withstand the overwhelming Union force building before them and fearing a flanking attack over water, abandoned the Yorktown defenses. The Rebel retreat moved slowly over the only two roads toward Richmond, roads that were rain-soaked and muddy, making their movement even more difficult and time consuming. On May 5 Hooker's and W. F. Smith's divisions pressed forward in search of the retreating Southern line, a move which convinced General James Longstreet that he would have to fight to protect the army's rear. He chose to make his stand outside of Williamsburg, Virginia's colonial capital. The two Union divisions had taken different roads to reach the enemy defenses Longstreet had prepared and, when the fighting started, found themselves isolated and facing the threat of being flanked. Unable to find Smith's division for support,

Hooker called for reinforcements. But before these reinforcements could arrive, Longstreet's line pressed around Hooker's flanks, threatening to envelop the division and many of Hooker's regiments broke for the rear. Once again the Union had squandered its numerical superiority and faced another defeat at the hands of the Rebels. But into this situation charged Kearny's division.

Though he had commanded them for less than a week, the men of Kearny's command had gained almost overnight respect for their dashing new leader and now anxiously followed him into battle. As they moved up Lee's Mill Road toward the sound of the fighting, Kearny encountered one of the New Jersey regiments from his former command running to the rear. As his column continued on to the front, General Kearny stopped to ask where their officers were that they were falling back in such a disorderly fashion. When told they had no officers, Kearny called out to them, "Well, I am a one-armed Jersey son-of-a-gun, follow me," and with that the Jerseymen rallied and joined Kearny's division into the fight. Kearny spurred his horse and raced to the front of the column. Ordering the men to march at the double-quick, Kearny seized his horse's reins in his mouth and swung his sword over his head with his only arm, urging the men into a battle line opposite Longstreet's formation. The swiftness and determination of the move stopped Longstreet's advance in its tracks and saved Hooker's division and the entire Union left flank in the battle of Williamsburg. And Kearny's bravery when under fire—he several times had ridden directly in front of the Rebel line to show his men exactly where to fire—only added to his legend as the most fearless of field commanders. Kearny was so proud of his men, and of himself as well, that late in the day he bragged to his corps commander, "General, I can make men follow me to hell!"[27]

Kearny's satisfaction in his personal performance and the actions of his division in the battle of Williamsburg was muted, however, by the accounts of the battle reaching Washington and the Northern press. In these official statements it was General McClellan who had saved the day by directing the fight while General Hancock and his brigade had been the key to saving the threatened Union line. Kearny was furious that his efforts and those of his men were being overshadowed for the political and person gain of his less-capable superior officers. On May 15, Kearny wrote both to Agnes and a friend expressing his anger at having his achievements ignored. In both of these letters he spared Hancock, whom he termed "a charming officer and gentleman," but noted that Hancock's action on the Union right flank, though not insignificant, cost fewer casualties and was less important to the outcome of the battle than his fight on the Federal left had been. It is General McClellan who bore the brunt of Kearny's anger for manipulating the facts to protect himself from charges of failed command ability. "General McClellan is the first Commander in history who has either dared or been so unprincipled as to ignore those under him," Kearny blared, "he fears to admit the services of my Division, lest he, thereby, condemns himself for want of Generalship, which gave rise to the crisis." In response to his friend's observation that he was bitter over McClellan's action he replied, "It is true that I feel most sadly embittered against McClellan, for he has most ungenerously robbed me of a soldier's dearest rights." While Kearny's anger over this professional slight apparently would dissipate with time, his judgment of McClellan's inability to successfully command would only grow in the coming weeks.[28]

Meanwhile, having slowed the Federal chase at Williamsburg, Johnston's Confederate army continued to retreat to the Richmond defenses. Moving apace behind them came McClellan's Army of the Potomac, pressing but not attacking the retreating foe. By the end of May 1862, the Rebels were arrayed on the eastern approaches to their capital along the southern bank of the Chickahominy River and the Union forces were deployed on the opposite side. McClellan's line along the Chickahominy formed a fishhook shape and Philip Kearny's division, in the center of the III Corps line, was posted at the center of the hook, guarding the Union left flank. McClellan's line was a strong one save for one point; the III Corps' "hook" was on the opposite side of the river from the other three Union corps. And when a terrific rainstorm flooded the Chickahominy fords and crossings, Johnston knew the time to strike this isolated enemy corps had come.

The attack on Casey's and Couch's divisions on May 31 was weak and poorly coordinated but enough to break them. Into this disaster rode Kearny's division, once again acting as the reserve rushing in to save the main Union line. They plowed up the Williamsburg Road until they reached the tiny village of Seven Pines, where they formed their main line. Once again Kearny tried to rally the fleeing Union troops, exhorting, "This is not the road to Richmond, boys!" But the disorganization of Casey's retreating troops and the swiftness of the Rebel attack overwhelmed Kearny's line and they were forced to fall back and re-form near Orchard Station. There, Kearny's and Hooker's divisions of the III Corps, along with Israel Richardson's division of the II Corps, finally stopped the Rebel advance. And in the early morning hours of June 1, the fighting of what the Union would call the battle of Fair Oaks and the Confederacy would label the battle of Seven Pines ended.[29]

Kearny's division had performed well, but not with the success they had attained at the battle of Williamsburg. "This was not victory," he wrote to Agnes in two letters during the early morning hours of June 1. Kearny's explanation for this shortfall was simple: "McClellan's injustice has changed my men. They follow me after a fashion, but were cold and slow." Yet in Kearny's own view his division had saved the day once again by appearing at the moment the Union line was breaking to serve as the foundation of a new line. And once again he had placed himself at the head of his troops, exposing himself to enemy fire so often that his horse was wounded once and finally shot from under him. Although he subsequently overstated the role his division had played, at the same time it was not wholly inaccurate to say they had been key in saving the Union from a complete disaster. But Kearny's hope that McClellan might make amends for the slight his command had endured after Williamsburg was dashed that evening when the commanding general, finally appearing on the field for the first time since the fighting started, flatly ignored him. "Just to think," he complained to Agnes, "General McClellan was over here today, and never asked for me at all, and yet, I have twice saved him from irretrievable disgrace."[30]

In the wake of the battle of Fair Oaks, McClellan shifted his line south and formed his new position where the recent battle had ended. Facing McClellan's army, the Confederates began digging in to defend their capital under the command of a new general, Robert E. Lee. In late June, McClellan finally began taking the offensive against Lee, sending Porter's V Corps north of the Chickahominy to turn Lee's left flank at Mechanicsville. The series of battles this move triggered, the Seven Days' Campaign, were fought mainly on the Union right and well away from Kearny's position on the Federal left flank. But when Lee tried a flanking move of his own around the Union left, Kearny's division was once more in the thick of the fight.

On June 30, fifteen brigades belonging to Longstreet and A. P. Hill pressed east on the Charles City and Long Bridge roads to break through the left of the Union line. By the time they arrived outside of the crossroads town of Glendale, on a patch of cleared ground known locally as the Frayser's Farm, Federal divisions belonging to Hooker and McCall had deployed on Kearny's left to create a solid if quickly formed defensive line. Kearny adjusted his own line to fit his new role as the right flank of the Union line by deploying Birney's and Robinson's brigades just east of the Charles City Road, with Berry's brigade posted to their center-rear on the road itself. Once his division was in place, General Kearny informed his men ominously that they were "the rear guard of all God's creation!" As the day would soon prove, his description of their role was only slightly overstated.[31]

Lee's main attack got underway on the afternoon of the 30th, and struck directly at the line Hooker and McCall had formed. Three of Longstreet's brigades plunged directly into the Federal center, straight at Glendale itself, in hopes of punching a hole there and then reinforcing that gain with whatever brigades might remain behind them. The attack, executed with precision and swiftness, broke the center of the line and McCall's men were soon streaming to the rear, a sight that had become all too familiar for McClellan's officers. With the center breaking before him, Longstreet now proceeded to try to turn the enemy flanks by sending three brigades into Kearny's front. Kearny's men held the line with valor but their casualties quickly mounted and for a time it seemed they would have to retreat or be slaughtered in place. But just as things looked darkest, General Slocum rushed the New Jersey Brigade, Kearny's old command, to his aid. The Jerseymen plugged the right of Kearny's line and his position held. When the fighting of the battle of Glendale—or Frayser's Farm, as the South would name it—ended, Kearny's division had suffered terrible losses, some 1,017 men, but had held the line for the Union.

During the confusion of the fight at Glendale, Kearny was as usual out front of his men reconnoitering the enemy position when he rode into the middle of some Confederate skirmishers. The moment he realized his error, an inexperienced Confederate captain approached him and, unaware of Kearny's allegiance, asked, "What shall I do next, sir?" Without missing a beat Kearny calmly replied, "Do, damn you, why do what you have always been told to do!" and he rode quickly and safely back to the Union lines. Once again General Kearny had escaped capture and death.

Lee had no intention of letting this tactical stalemate stop his flanking move and tried once more to press around the Union left on July 1. The resulting fight at Malvern Hill was poorly executed by Lee's lieutenants and this final battle in the Seven Days' Campaign cost Lee dearly. McClellan, in spite of his weak personal efforts, had finally won an important battle. As dark enveloped the weary Union lines that night, nearly everyone expected to renew the drive to Richmond in the morning. But George McClellan had already decided that his Peninsula Campaign had reached an impasse and that more fighting would pointlessly risk his army. Against all common sense, General McClellan ordered a retreat.

Philip Kearny was furious when he heard the orders to retreat. "I, Philip Kearny, an old soldier, enter my solemn protest against this order for retreat. I say to you, such an order can only be prompted by cowardice or treason," thundered the general to his fellow officers. Kearny was certain that a well-coordinated attack could break through all the way to Richmond but he also knew that McClellan would never launch such a daring strike. His personal disdain for George McClellan now had reached new heights, pushing his thin temper to it limits, and he began almost openly referring to his commanding officer as a traitor. He confided one such outburst against his commanding general to Agnes: "McClellan's want of Generalship, or treason, has gotten us into a place where we are completely boxed up."[32]

The army, of course, followed McClellan's orders, slogging its way back to Harrison's Landing and their new "base of operations." As they marched, disheartened as never before, Kearny and his division were in a foul mood. Making matters worse, the rainy weather turned the normally poor roads into quagmires of mud and muck. When they finally reached their destination, most of the troops dropped on the first patch of high ground they could find. One incident, recounted by the men of the 11th Massachusetts with glee through later years, demonstrates the foul mood of the entire army in general and General Kearny in particular that awful night. Apparently the 11th Massachusetts had discovered a patch of nearly dry high ground in a thick pine woods near Harrison's Landing and had posted several men to guard the place. But before the rest of the regiment could arrive, a German-born colonel from another regiment approached and ordered the Massachusetts men to leave "mine woots," so his men could "bitches mine dents,"or risk being shot. Before they could respond to the colonel, a piercing voice barked from the woods, previously unseen to any of the men. "So this is your 'woots' is it you infernal Dutch skulker? Bitch your dent here, will you? Drive out these fellows who are worth a whole regiment of such cowardly sneaks as you are? Threaten to shoot men, too, who've been doing the fighting, while you have been dodging behind trees and stumps, eh? I'll hang you, you damned puppy! If you and your infernal sour-crouts don't cut out of the neck of timber on a double-quick, I'll 'bitch your dents' for you, in a way you won't relish! I'll swing you, you miserable coward, to a limb with one of your own dent cords! Double-quick! Off with you lager-loafers!" While such outbursts of colorful language were hardly unusual for Phil Kearny, threatening to hang a fellow officer was not. But the suffering of the army, at the mercy of George McClellan, had driven Kearny beyond even his own sense of decorum.[33]

Throughout the rest of July and most of August, the Army of the Potomac remained scattered over the southern end of the peninsula, awaiting their next orders. This idle period gave the men many opportunities for mischief, testing their officers' abilities to control their troops. What tested Philip Kearny's patience most, though, was the fact that he was still only a brigadier general. He had commanded a division for nearly three months now and had not seen any indication that he would be given the rank of major general that accompanied his post. When a promotion list for general officers arrived in July, Kearny was dismayed to find his name missing. On July 11 he complained to Agnes, "Would you believe it, that in a List of promotions of Generals, that I have been left out." But this time it was to his close friend, Cortlandt Parker, that Kearny unloaded the full weight of his frustration. "I am the first General officer, whose feats in arms have been ignored by all," he complained. "Cheated of prestige by the falsity of McClellan, thanked not by Congress, passed over in promotion, and yet the petty nameless skirmish of Ord at Dranesville obtained him a Major Generalship for a nothing." Making matters worse, many of those whose names were on the list Kearny considered his inferior. In another letter to Parker, Kearny lamented, "My name is not on the List. Here is Heintzelman's, but since he had the good luck to have Hooker's and my Division under him, be it so. But here is Keyes, with no Mexican prestige, . . . here too is Porter . . . who lost the fight on the Chickahominy, by his bad arrangements. Here is noble old Sumner, who never has done a thing yet. But, when they passed me over, and also Hooker, it is an insult that I will not submit to." The frustration of this situation soon grew to the point that he promised Agnes that he would soon resign his commission rather than suffer at the hands of "McClellan and his parasites."[34]

Kearny's mood grew increasingly melancholy during this time of inactivity, spurred no doubt by his anger over being passed over, and he sank into a period of depression. His letters to Agnes and Cortlandt Parker during these weeks increasingly shifted from anger about his professional stagnation to disgust at the course of the Union cause. And soon he was lamenting the fact that he was fighting so many of his old friends. "I have such devoted friends of old times in the Southern army, Lee, Jackson, Longstreet, Beauregard, etc. etc.," Kearny wrote to Parker on July 24. "Gen'l. Lee released specially all my sick and wounded prisoners, captured by McC's cowardly abandonment of his communications. In Europe, McC—would be shot for treason, or cowardice, or unpardonable incapacity." These regrets over the nature of his enemy must have been magnified when he learned of the death of his friend Robardeau Wheat, who had fallen in the battle of Gaines' Mill. "You know that that noble fellow, Wheat, was recently killed. It is truly sad. I so well remember our parting on the stairway of our noble apartments."[35]

Kearny's thoughts also turned during this idleness to how he might remake the Union army to ensure its success. In addition to hiring French officers to lead the army, he advocated arming the "native" black population, a radical thought for any high-ranking American officer of the day. "The idea of black adjuncts to the military awakens nothing inhuman," he wrote to Parker on July 31. "It but permits the slave, the runaway, abandoned to us, from becoming a moneyed pressure upon us. It eventually would prepare them for freedom. For surely we do not intend to give them up to their rebel masters. Send there [the Western frontier] a Black Regiment on trial." Clearly, to Phil Kearny what mattered most was not the color of a man's skin but his temperament when under fire in battle.[36]

By August 1, Kearny and his division were finally on the move again, this time boarding steamers for the journey north to join General Pope's army in central Virginia. And if Kearny was heartened to be moving once more, he must have been ecstatic when a few days later he received word that he had been promoted to the rank of major general dating from July 4. These facts lifted the cloud of depression that had hung over him for weeks and his letters north now reflected this renewed vigor and improved outlook. After an uneventful trip to Alexandria, Kearny's division was hurried to the field to join Pope's ever-growing force. Kearny's troops were rushed to the front and what he found there lifted his spirits even more, for he was clearly glad to be away from McClellan and serving under a general who would fight. "Gen'l. Pope is quite active in his measures, and that suits me," Kearny wrote to Agnes on August 30, after their first full day of fighting in several weeks.[37]

Kearny may well have been hiding from Agnes the desperate nature of that day's fighting for his command. He had led his division gallantly in an attack on the extreme left of Stonewall Jackson's position in the unfinished railroad cut. The assault had been intended only as a diversion to support the intended main attack farther left in the Union line. Kearny, true to form though, had fought as if his was the Union's only attack and had succeeded in breaching the enemy line. But because it was intended to do no more than prevent the Southern foe from reinforcing the intended point of the main attack, Kearny's success was not reinforced and his division was forced back. Despite the Union's failure at Second Bull Run,

Phil Kearny had once again proven that he fully deserved his reputation as one of the best—if perhaps the most hot tempered—generals in the Union army.[38]

ISAAC STEVENS

Also with the Union army on that fateful night in August of 1862 in Centreville, Virginia, marched Brigadier General Isaac I. Stevens at the head of the IX Corps.

Isaac Stevens was born on March 25, 1818, in Andover, Massachusetts, the third of Isaac and Hannah Stevens's children and their first son. The Stevens family was one of the oldest and most respected in the Bay State, having arrived from England in 1638. Twelve men of the Stevens family served in the American Revolution and Jonathan Stevens—Isaac's grandfather—had fought at the battle of Bunker Hill. By the time of Isaac's birth, Isaac Stevens Sr. had built a prosperous living for his young family by converting his farm into a tavern, serving travelers journeying from Andover to Haverhill, Massachusetts. After a bumpy start, Isaac Stevens Sr. had worked his family into a solidly middle class status.[39]

Isaac Sr.'s upbringing and business interests led him early on to adopt the political stance of a staunch Democrat in the Jeffersonian model. An ardent admirer of President Andrew Jackson, he similarly loathed the Whig party as the protector of privilege and class distinction, a view he passed to young Isaac. As Isaac Sr. aged, though, the heart of his political views shifted from mere partisanship and economic self-interest to focus on what he believed to be moral rightness, especially decrying the evils of slavery. With time, Isaac Jr. would come to adopt his father's strong belief that slavery was a moral evil and must be abolished from the United States, as well as his elder's devotion to the Democratic Party.

Even while a young boy Isaac Jr. demonstrated such a remarkable talent for learning in general and mathematics in particular that his parents soon determined he would be the family intellectual. At age five he was enrolled in his first school and rapidly mastered those tasks given to him by his instructors. The school's focus on mathematics, algebra, geometry, and surveying was well-suited to Isaac's natural talents and as he entered his teenage years, Isaac was soon searching for an outlet to expand his interest in mathematics and surveying. His search quickly settled on the United States Military Academy, which in the nineteenth century dedicated itself to creating engineers to settle the frontier rather than on molding soldiers to fight wars.

In 1835, at the age of 17, Stevens entered West Point. Perhaps to compensate for his short stature and stocky physique—his four-foot, eleven-inch height and large head suggested to some contemporaries a mild form of dwarfism—young cadet Stevens excelled in wrestling and other physical activities. His classmates, however, remembered his gift for mathematics and the intensity with which he approached any task to which he set his mind. This education paid off early on in his military career and Stevens spent part of his last two years at the academy as an assistant professor in mathematics. When he graduated, Isaac Stevens was first in the class of 1839.[40]

Shortly after graduation, Stevens was commissioned as a second lieutenant in the Corps of Engineers and was soon assigned to direct construction of forts along the New England coast. The government was trying to rebuild the string of old forts built after the War of 1812, partly in anticipation of another round of hostilities with England. In 1840, Stevens was promoted to the rank of first lieutenant—a very rapid promotion pace for a peacetime army officer—based on his excellent work supervising the improvement of those forts under his control. The posting gave him duties well beyond his rank, including control of sizable sums of money and direction of hundreds of workers. Perhaps most importantly, they gave Stevens a chance to utilize his education in a practical way.

What would prove most significant about this assignment to the course of Stevens's life was its location in Newport, Rhode Island. Living in this modern city of high society exposed him to polite company and socializing, something for which he had previously had little time. It was during one of the many parties in Newport that he met Margaret Hazard, daughter of a prominent lawyer. One year older than Stevens, she was a slight woman with long dark hair done up in long ringlets, in the style of the day. Stevens was smitten at once and he courted Margaret with the same intensity he brought to all tasks he tried. On September 8, 1841, Isaac and Margaret were married in a quiet ceremony. After honeymooning at West Point, the happy couple returned to Newport, where Stevens found that in his absence his duties had expanded to include rebuilding additional forts.[41]

Like many other army officers of his day, Stevens longed for battle but consoled himself that at least he continued to receive postings in the East, where his wife could join him and he was near to family and friends. So far in his short career he had avoided assignment to one of the army's numerous remote western posts that broke the spirits of many of his young counterparts and ruined promising military careers and marriages.

In the summer of 1844, Margaret gave birth to their first child, Virginia, and Stevens's frustration with his posting was offset by his happy home life. Their joy increased in June 1845, with the birth of their first son, whom they named Hazard after his maternal grandfather. This joy would be shortlived, however, for young Virginia died suddenly in December 1845. Her tragic death, coming on the heels of the deaths of Stevens's sisters in 1840 and 1843, convinced Stevens that life was indeed too short to remain complacent with work and he began casting about for new postings.[42]

With the outbreak of war with Mexico, Stevens—like so many other young military men of his era—believed he had finally found an opportunity to distinguish himself in battle. But as the first U.S. troops were departing for Mexico, it began to appear that he would be left behind. His service rebuilding the New England fortifications, he was told, was more important to the army than service in Mexico. At first Lieutenant Stevens stoically endured this disappointment, but he quickly turned to lobbying his superiors for a chance to join the Mexican campaign. Finally, less than a week before Christmas 1846, Stevens was ordered to place his forts in the care of subordinates and prepare to deploy to Mexico. So excited was he about his opportunity that he borrowed $500 to purchase a new outfit for the campaign, complete with India rubber leggings. Once ready to depart on the barque *Prompt*, the young lieutenant ran directly into another roadblock: a quartermaster corps captain insisted the ship sail to Chandeleur Island near New Orleans before departing for Mexico. Stevens insisted that his orders superseded the captain's and the two began a duel of competing orders that delayed the voyage a full week. In the end, Stevens won the day and in early February 1847 the ship finally reached port at Brazos Santiago.[43]

Stevens soon learned that he was to be part of a team which included his former West Point roommate, Zealous Tower, and his longtime friend, James Mason, and was tasked with organizing General Scott's supply train prior to laying siege to the Mexican city of Vera Cruz. Once situated around the city, Stevens supervised a company building infantry trenches to support the siege, work which was performed under nearly constant Mexican artillery fire. His efficient work under these difficult circumstances earned Lieutenant Stevens the respect and admiration of his superiors including General Scott.

The siege of Vera Cruz lasted only four days, in large part because the shelling of the city was so intense that its defenders could hold out no longer. Once inside the city walls, Stevens caught his first glimpse of the harsh effects of war. Most of the city's once beautiful buildings had been leveled by the intense shelling. But what had the greatest impact on Stevens were the dead and wounded strewn throughout Vera Cruz. Though he had no trouble accepting the deaths of soldiers, he was genuinely depressed by the "many inoffensive people [who were] killed." Nonetheless, Stevens supported the war because he believed the United States was on "a rapid march to greatness;" Mexico had failed to understand this and had to surrender Texas in recognition of Washington's "natural" superiority.[44]

During the two weeks the army remained in Vera Cruz, Lieutenant Stevens shared quarters with his friend Mason, John L. Smith, and Robert E. Lee. The young engineer officers enjoyed this respite in the campaigning but worked hard at the same time, routinely putting in 14-hour days. This time built special bonds between the men, but most especially so between Stevens and Lee. On August 22, 1847, Stevens wrote to Meg of his newly acquainted friend, "Captain Lee is an officer of engineers of whom I have before alluded, and one of my messmates. He is one of the most extraordinary men in the service. In the very prime of manhood, of remarkable presence, and address, perhaps the most manly and striking officer in the service, of great manner and personal beauty, he has established an enduring reputation. His power of enduring fatigue is extraordinary, his strength of judgment and perfect balance are conspicuous. For counsel, General Scott relies more upon him than upon any other man in the service." These words of praise are all the more genuine because Isaac Stevens was never one to lavish praise on anyone, even if they might deserve it.[45]

When the army finally left Vera Cruz to besiege and attack Mexico City, Stevens was in sole charge of the huge train of stores, ammunition, and supplies. This was a task so great that Stevens nearly worked himself into complete exhaustion, having thrown himself into this task like all others he put his hand to. But within two days the army stopped at the Rio Del Plan; in a high mountain pass ahead lay Santa Anna and his army waiting for the Americans to walk into his strongly fortified trap. General Scott, lacking adequate maps or ideas about how to proceed in the attack, tasked his nine engineering officers to reconnoiter a route to strike the enemy force. Stevens, Lee, Tower, and P. G. T. Beauregard led this effort to find a suitable route to strike the Mexican flank. Probing through the rough underbrush and rocky mountain passes led the scouts to a hill known locally as Cerro Gordo. Climbing up to this hill the party found they had a clear view of the enemy camp, so clear that they could count the shiny brass field guns there. After two hours making sketches of the camp and collecting what intelligence they could, the group returned to pass their findings on to General Scott.[46]

They reported to Scott that if he were to seize Cerro Gordo, he could completely outflank Santa Anna's strong position in the mountain pass. Lieutenant Stevens went even further, suggesting that they were assured a victory and, if this were the case, that the entire enemy force might be captured if they could seal off their route of retreat to Mexico City. Scott was clearly intrigued by the idea and authorized Stevens to lead a reconnaissance party to map the route of the national highway behind Santa Anna's position. Stevens set out the next day at dawn and soon discovered that the route they would cross required them to climb and descend very rough terrain. In the very midst of this mission, he felt a searing pain in his midsection; within moments he knew that an old groin injury— which had been dormant for many years—had suddenly returned. Once back at camp, he was immediately confined to bed. Stevens would have to watch the next day as the army attacked Cerro Gordo along the very route he had reconnoitered. Once again, Isaac Stevens had been denied military glory.

Although the United States was victorious at Cerro Gordo, Santa Anna's army slipped away through one of the routes Stevens had been trying to find before the battle. Scott's army would have to continue on toward Mexico City and as it went Lieutenant Stevens was forced by his injuries to ride in a supply wagon rather than on his mount. General Scott knew that he would need a larger and better-rested force to successfully attack Mexico City and so he ordered the bulk of his force to stop at Puebla to await reinforcements from the States. Stevens welcomed this pause in the action because it allowed him to fully recuperate and return to duty. This idle time also permitted him to begin collecting thoughts and ideas for a book he had decided to some day write on the fight at Cerro Gordo and the Mexican campaign.

On August 8, the American army finally resumed its march to the Mexican capital and, 11 days later, reached the city's outskirts. Scott's first assault on the city failed but Stevens performed well in the action, once again driving himself to the point that he actually collapsed while leading the 9th U.S. Infantry into position. The next day Scott renewed his attack on Santa Anna's army in the village of Coyoacan. A lightning-quick attack by the Americans drove the Mexican troops back to a fortified church and convent at Churubusco, where they prepared a solid defense. When General Twiggs, in command of the assault, asked for options from his officers, Lieutenant Stevens suggested placing a battery in front of the church to strike it directly while at the same time launching flanking infantry assaults. Twiggs adopted Stevens's plan and the attack subsequently was successful. But the American force lost nearly 25 percent of its men in making the assault, a cost that would weigh heavily on Stevens's conscience over the coming days because of his personal role in the fight. Knowing that it had been his plan that had caused many of these men, some of whom were personal friends, to lose their lives pulled mightily at his peace of mind.

After a failed round of peace talks, the drive on Mexico City was renewed on September 12. Scott had determined to take a fortified hill known as Chapultepec and opened his attack with a day-long artillery bombardment. Following this, an infantry assault the next day stormed up the hill, taking the fort following a brutal, desperate round of fighting. After the American victory, and on what would become the last day of fighting, Stevens was ordered to reconnoiter the surrounding area for any remaining Mexican batteries. While on this duty a rifle ball struck Stevens's foot, cutting a swath from his little toe to the center of his instep. Doctors cut the ball from his foot and initially feared they would have to remove the injured appendage. But after four days of intense pain, they determined that the foot was beginning to heal and that such a drastic step would not be necessary. Ultimately, Stevens regained full use of his foot, although he would ever after wear a specially made shoe to ease pressure there. Stevens would, however, remain in the hospital until December, after which he was ordered to return to the United States exactly one year from his departure for the seat of war. His Mexican War service was over.

Although it may not have been exactly what he expected, Stevens's Mexican War experience had proved valuable and rewarding to the young lieutenant. He had finally experienced combat and had proven himself up to the challenge that experience presented. Though he had not come home a "hero," he had at least distinguished himself in battle. And for his efforts, Stevens had gained two brevet promotions (though Colonel Totten had recommended him for three), his first to captain dated from August 20, 1847, and his second to major dated from September 13, 1847. Perhaps more importantly, from a postwar perspective, Stevens had gained the notice and confidence of General Scott and other senior officers who could help advance his career in returning to the peacetime army.

These connections, the lack of which Stevens had often blamed for his earlier "unappealing" postings, soon proved to be less useful than he had hoped. Though the engineer corps had gained a great reputation for their exploits during the war, the bloom was quickly taken from their rose by the return to prewar army politics. When the postings were announced, Stevens was disappointed to discover he had once again been assigned to rebuilding forts on the New England coast. This disappointment was eased somewhat, however, when Colonel Totten approved his request to remain at home in Newport to convalesce from his wound. Not only did this give his foot a chance to heal but also he could spend time at home with Meg. The rest of 1848 was a happy time for Major Stevens, who must have relished his time with his wife, son Hazard, and newborn daughter Susan.

Professionally, Stevens consoled himself that other officers of his station—George McClellan and P. G. T. Beauregard included—suffered similar professional fates. But even as he was once again taking up his post in Bucksport, Stevens was casting around for a better assignment. On August 7, 1849, he finally hit pay dirt; the chief of the U.S. Coast Survey asked Major Stevens if he would consent to serve as his assistant. The job took him out of the army mainstream but placed him in Washington, D.C., where he threw himself into the largely bureaucratic job with the same vigor he had previously applied to his job in New England. The chief drawback to this job—once again being separated from Meg and the children, including his newest daughter, Gertrude Maude—was removed in October 1850, when the entire Stevens family moved into Mrs. Kelley's rooming house near Lafayette Square in Washington.

Stevens's presence in the nation's capital and his official duties with the Coast Survey brought him once more into contact with the world of politics. As second-in-command of the Coast Survey it was his task to lobby the Congress for more funds and manpower for the organization. To do this job effectively, Stevens soon learned, he had to develop strong political ties within the Congress, and he naturally turned to the Democratic Party to build these relationships. He also found that if his army career were to advance further he had to build political ties to senior officers who might help him in the future. One key step in this effort came to fruition in 1851 with the publication of *Campaigns of the Rio Grande and Mexico*, which Stevens paid for out of his own pocket. He had written this book as a response to an earlier book by Major Ripley that Stevens believed had given undue credit to General Pillow—"a contemptible egoist and a consummate ass," in Stevens's opinion—at the expense of his hero, General Scott. The book was generally well received by his fellow officers. General Scott, though, was less than pleased; apparently he felt slighted that Stevens had not been sufficiently glowing in his praise of the general's exploits in Mexico. Though Stevens was largely unaware of Scott's ire, the effort had clearly backfired and General Scott would no longer help the major in advancing his army career.[47]

The presidential campaign of 1852 brought Isaac Stevens fully into the world of partisan politics. The Whig Party chose to nominate none other than Winfield Scott, while the Democrats offered Franklin Pierce. The choice presented a personal problem for Stevens; although he still believed he had ties to Scott, he knew his personal views were more closely in line with those of Franklin Pierce. When the time came to make a decision, Stevens chose to stand with his party. And not only did he stand with Pierce, but he became an active campaigner for him as well. This news came as welcome support from Pierce's campaign staff, for the candidate's lackluster military record was becoming a weapon that Scott was regularly using against him on the stump and in Whig-aligned newspapers. The open support of Major Stevens—perhaps the only active duty military officer to support Pierce—was a big step in their effort to blunt these attacks. When Stevens took the additional step of publishing a pamphlet titled, "Vindication of the Military Character and Services of General Franklin Pierce," the Pierce camp was ecstatic. General Scott, predictably, was not.[48]

Fortunately for Stevens, his gamble in partisan politics paid off; Franklin Pierce defeated Scott in the 1852 presidential race. Friends jokingly asked the major if he was to become the next secretary of war in return for his risky political stand. But President Pierce did, indeed, remember his friend in the army, offering him the governership of Washington Territory. Although governerships of the Western territories were appointed posts, they carried a great deal of power in their own right and Stevens saw it as just the place to test his own ability to administer higher political office. On March 17, 1853, Isaac Stevens resigned his commission in the United States Army to become the first governor of Washington Territory. Because he would be heading to the northwest, he also applied to lead an engineering and survey team to explore a northern route for a transcontinental railroad. On his 35th birthday Stevens received word that Secretary of War Jefferson Davis had accepted his application to lead this group.

On May 9, Stevens and most of his party left Washington, D.C., for St. Louis, from where they traveled north on the Mississippi to St. Paul, Minnesota. Heading west from there the group was guided at first by a cartographic survey prepared by then-Lieutenant John Pope in 1849 and then was largely on their own to scout the new railroad route. Assisting

Stevens as his second-in-command on this exploration was none other than Captain George McClellan, whom Stevens had specifically requested for the task. Relations between the two Mexican War messmates were cordial until November, when McClellan returned from scouting one of several routes through the Cascade Mountains. Stevens was furious that McClellan had come back declaring the route impassable and the region uninhabitable. When Governor Stevens learned from some members of McClellan's party that he had not personally reconnoitered the routes but had instead taken the word of native Indians, he flew into a rage. Thereafter he would not trust Captain McClellan with any command responsibilities, second-guessing his every move. McClellan became so frustrated with the situation that he once snapped to a friend, "I will not consent to serve any longer under Governor S unless he promises in no way to interfere—merely give me general orders and never say a word as to the means, manner, or time of execution." Though this statement reveals much about George McClellan's inability to take direction, it also demonstrates the level of animosity that had developed between the two men. Stevens went so far as to openly criticize McClellan's performance in his official report to Washington, a move he well knew might damage an army career. His impatience with those he considered to be less-than-competent had earned him another enemy, one that would quite soon come to haunt him.[49]

On November 25, 1853, Governor Stevens finally arrived in the territorial capital at Olympia. He jumped immediately into the key tasks before him—finishing the railroad survey and speeding construction of a northern transcontinental railroad route; resolving an ongoing boundary dispute with Great Britain over San Juan Island and the rights of the Hudson Bay Company south of the 49th Parallel; and dealing with the local Native American population. After five months on the frontier Governor Stevens journeyed back to Washington to lobby Congress for an appropriations increase for the territory. His arrival there in May was a joyful reunion with his family, made all the more special because he met his newest daughter, Catherine, who had been born about the time he had arrived in Olympia. Stevens also used this opportunity to enroll 12-year-old Hazard in the Philips Academy in Andover, Massachusetts. This time in the nation's capital was a happy one and, when he departed for Washington Territory again in September, Meg and the children traveled with him.[50]

Of the problems facing the governor on his return to Olympia, dealing with the Native Americans was perhaps his most vexing and troublesome concern. Like many Americans of his era, Isaac Stevens considered the local Indian population little more than savages whose very presence unsettled the growing white population. However, at the same time Stevens respected their ability to fight and, most importantly, to make trouble for him. Governor Stevens tried very hard to placate the local native population and convened a series of councils to mediate the myriad disputes at hand. In October 1855, the work of these various councils unraveled with the opening of the Yakima War, which started as a series of skirmishes between the local U.S. Army forces and Native Americans that quickly spread throughout the region. Stevens then tried a carrot and stick approach—continuing the war while using money from Washington to buy the aid of friendly Indian tribes—but this new policy quickly proved to be a failure. When a series of raids and murders by Native Americans highlighted this failure, Stevens used his position as commander in chief of the volunteer militia to declare martial law in the territory in February 1855. Although a subsequent court challenge by local citizens determined that the governor lacked the power to declare such a state of emergency, most white settlers in the Washington Territory credited Stevens with singlehandedly restoring control of the native population. And while the move earned him rebuke in Washington, D.C., it gained him important political points at home.

In the autumn of 1856, Stevens declared his intention to run for Congress as the delegate from Washington Territory. He had clearly thought out this decision, for the result of the martial law experience convinced him both that he had the requisite political support in the territory and that officials in the Pierce administration would not reappoint him as governor. Stevens won the election handily and by December 1857 the Stevens family was back east in Washington, D.C. His first term as territorial delegate was spent largely on territorial issues, including lobbying for increased funds for developing infrastructure in the territory and trying to mediate the growing dispute with Great Britain over control of San Juan Island. In 1859, Stevens was returned to Congress for a second term, winning 61 percent of the vote. Unlike his first term in Congress, his second term was marked by his increasing focus on national, rather than territorial, politics. This change was driven by the convergence of two factors: Congress had amended its rules to permit territorial delegates to vote on national issues at the same time that the growing sectional crisis over the expansion of slavery was coming to a head.

Stevens played a key role in the intense political maneuvering that preceded the 1860 presidential election. His scheming behind the scenes of the Democrat's nominating process was designed to foster a split in the party between north and south that would force party leaders to turn west for a compromise candidate. In the end, Stevens and other like-minded westerners were only partly successful; they got the split they wanted but backers of Stephen Douglas stacked the nominating process to ensure their man would get the nod. Dissenters like Isaac Stevens left the convention to form the new Democratic National Party and nominated John C. Breckinridge and Stevens's good friend, Joe Lane, to run on their ticket.

Recognizing his leadership abilities and drive, the more senior politicians in the new party appointed Stevens as chairman of the Democratic National Party Executive Committee. His chief duties in this post were to lead the Breckinridge and Lane campaign, coordinating rallies and mass demonstrations of support for the two candidates—who followed the custom of rarely appearing themselves in public—and creating and distributing posters. The new party's leaders knew they had little chance of winning the popular vote and hoped instead to have the decision thrown to the Congress to resolve. With this goal in mind Stevens crafted a campaign strategy that focused on winning a few key northern states like Pennsylvania and New Jersey. But when the final votes were counted in the 1860 election, Breckinridge and Lane failed to win any of the key states they needed and the election went to Republican Abraham Lincoln.

Isaac Stevens returned to Washington Territory almost immediately after the 1860 election to prepare his own campaign for a third term as delegate to Congress. But his absence from the territory and his prominent role in the failed national race—which many locals believed had come at their expense—cost him the nomination. Isaac Stevens's political career was clearly stalled and it must have appeared to him at that moment that it may even have come to an end.

Disappointment in his political fortunes was shortlived, though, because the outbreak of war in South Carolina rekindled his dreams of a military career. At the same time that he realized the convention would not renominate him to run again for delegate, Stevens prepared to travel east to offer his services to fight for the Union. In early July 1861, he journeyed to Washington from New York with high hopes that an appointment would be waiting for him upon arrival in the capital. He had already written to Secretary of War Simon Cameron that "this succession movement must be put down with an iron hand," probably in an effort to allay any concerns the secretary might have had about Stevens's politics. But his efforts proved to be in vain; Secretary Cameron was unwilling to give a coveted Union general's star to the former head of the Breckinridge campaign, and General Scott, still angry over his published criticisms, blocked his way as well. Even a meeting with President Lincoln in late July failed to yield a commission. Lincoln, too, was more attuned to Stevens's recent political alignments than to his sterling military career.

Stevens was crushed by his failure to secure a command. He was particularly angered that a man like George McClellan, whom he considered talentless, had already attained a high rank, and for a few days he wallowed in self-pity and considered returning home to Newport for the duration of the war. But in the wake of the Union disaster at Bull Run, the various state governments, eager to secure qualified officers, began calling on Isaac Stevens. Massachusetts and Rhode Island both offered him positions as a colonel of volunteers. Stevens was heartened by the offers but still preferred to have a commission from the Federal government if possible. And then Washington came back to his door; Secretary of War Cameron offered Stevens command of the 79th New York Volunteer Infantry, which had lost its famous colonel—the secretary's brother James—at Bull Run. Though it was a volunteer regiment, the position carried a Federal commission and Stevens took it. On July 30, 1861, Colonel Isaac Stevens assumed command of the 79th New York Infantry Regiment.

The nucleus of the 79th New York was a prewar militia unit called the "Highland Guard," which was composed of immigrants from Scotland who proudly demonstrated their heritage by wearing kilts while on dress parade. After the firing on Fort Sumter, the Highland Guard was brought up to a full regiment with the addition of two battalions, composed mainly of native-born Americans and immigrants from nations other than Scotland. This regiment, the 79th New York "Highlanders," under the command of Colonel James Cameron was quickly moved south to defend Washington and its men eagerly longed for battle. When the regiment finally "saw the elephant" near the banks of Bull Run on July 21, 1861, the results were disastrous. Though the regiment would acquit itself nobly in battle, its success came at a terrible cost, losing its colonel, 11 officers, and 187 men.[51]

In the wake of the disaster at Bull Run, Secretary of War Cameron promised the dispirited and broken men of his dead brother's regiment that they would soon be allowed to return home to rebuild their unit and visit family and friends. But when General McClellan, the army's newly appointed commander, heard this order he immediately countermanded it. And when word of the retracted promise of leave reached the 79th's camp, the Highlander's reacted with anger at what they perceived as betrayal. To make matters worse for Stevens, they inaccurately blamed their new colonel for the turn of events. The news pushed the more disgruntled men in the regiment over the edge; they had had enough of the army and, aided by liberal amounts of liquor, talked openly of mutiny.[52]

Colonel Stevens tried first to remove those officers leading and fomenting the discontent. After only two days in camp he asked for resignations from the regiment's second in command, Lieutenant Colonel Samuel Elliott, as well as several other unhappy officers. But by now the discontent had spread down into the ranks and, when the colonel ordered the Highlanders to move their camp, they refused. The first test of Colonel Stevens's leadership skills would come not from the enemy but from his own men.

With the situation about to spiral out of control, Stevens moved swiftly to restore order, surrounding the Highlanders' camp with cavalry, infantry, and several artillery pieces. Once these were in place, he entered the regiment's camp on foot to address his men. As he and his staff walked to the center of the camp, men crawled from their tents and abandoned their card games to get the measure of their new commander. Stevens, clearly sensing that his actions in the next few minutes were critical, lifted his voice:

> I know you have been deceived. You have been told you were to go to your homes when no such order was given. But you are soldiers, and your duty is to obey. I am your colonel, and your obedience is due to me. I am a soldier of the regular army. I have spent many years in the frontier fighting the Indians. I have been surrounded by the red devils, fighting for my scalp. I have been a soldier in the war with Mexico, and bear honorable wounds received in battle and have been in far greater danger than that surrounding me now. All morning I have begged you to do your duty. Now I shall order you; and if you hesitate to obey instantly, my next order will be to those troops to fire upon you. Soldiers of the 79th Highlanders, fall in![53]

The men reluctantly moved to their place in line and, to Colonel Stevens's relief, the rebellion—at least the one in his camp—had been crushed. The Highlanders were forced to surrender their colors in punishment and were marched under guard to their new camp. But the worst of the trouble was over. Throughout the course of the next few weeks, Colonel Stevens would almost singlehandedly restore the unit's discipline, morale, and pride. And soon the regiment's colors were returned, clearing away the last vestiges of the shameful uprising. For his leadership during this troubled time the Highlanders of the 79th New York thanked Isaac Stevens with their enduring admiration and devotion. From this moment on he, and no other, would always be their greatest commander.

On September 28, 1861, Stevens's military abilities were finally recognized by the army's higher command and he was commissioned as a brigadier general from Washington Territory. General Stevens was placed in charge of the 2nd Brigade—that at General Stevens's request soon included his beloved 79th New York—and assigned to the newly formed Department of the South. The department, which comprised some 13,000 men, was assigned to regain control of the states of South Carolina, Georgia, and Florida. To achieve this objective, General Thomas Sherman planned to use U.S. Navy ships to quickly insert his infantry force on the Sea Islands of South Carolina and, once secured, use the islands to launch further attacks inland. On October 29, 1861, Stevens and his 2nd Brigade boarded a steamship for the journey south and, on November 7, after a fierce naval battle between the Union fleet and Confederate Fort Walker, they stepped ashore on Hilton Head Island, South Carolina.[54]

The ease with which Sherman's force had seized the islands caught the entire department's command staff by surprise. Their instructions from Washington were only to seize the islands; with that task completed they lacked direction. But almost immediately upon establishing his brigade headquarters in Beaufort, South Carolina, General Stevens began planning a campaign to strike at Charleston. Charleston, some 35 miles northeast of Beaufort, was connected to the outside world only by the sea and one railroad line, belonging to the Charleston and Savannah Railroad. Stevens knew the Charleston defenses well, having led an 1848 inspection tour of the region during his Coastal Survey days, and understood that the city could more easily be taken if it were isolated and its defenses limited to those few troops already stationed there. Since the navy already was blockading the coast, he proposed that the army should move with all haste to cut the city's only railroad line. Once this was completed, the Union forces would have a number of options for taking the city by land. But General Sherman, cautious by his very nature and with the support of the other two brigade commanders, rejected Stevens plan, even while declaring the idea strategically sound. Stevens was aghast at the wasted opportunity but accepted the decision of his superior officer.

While General Stevens cemented his control of Beaufort and the rest of Port Royal Island, the Confederates were busy building an earthen fortification across the Coosaw River. Stevens, under orders not to cross the Coosaw or attack the mainland, had little choice in planning offensive operations but to reduce the enemy works with artillery fire. Though this proved effective, the Confederate builders simply moved one mile farther upriver and out of the range of Stevens's guns to continue their building. Stevens eventually persuaded General Sherman to allow him to lead a joint army-navy force to reduce this threat to Port Royal Island. In the early morning hours of January 1, 1862, Stevens's brigade boarded flat-boats formerly used to haul cotton to cross the river five miles from the Confederate fort. Once on the South Carolina mainland, Stevens's men re-formed their lines and swept south along the riverbank, aided in their advance by Commodore DuPont's gunboats, which provided a covering fire ahead of them. Upon nearing the fort they encountered some resistance from the small band of Confederates inside but they were soon scattered without much of a fight. All in all, the Port Royal Ferry fight had been a success, and Stevens wrote General Sherman gleefully, "I hope the general commanding may be gratified with our celebrations of New Year's Day." It also had given most of the men in Stevens's brigade their first taste of battle.[55]

Following the action at Port Royal Ferry, the Confederates retreated from the area and Sherman's entire command settled into a routine of drill and work details similar to those of the men's first days in the army. The situation in Beaufort was so calm that Margaret arrived to join her husband, and the time they had together there was a pleasure for both husband and wife. Less pleasing for Stevens, however, was that the relative calm brought no end of administrative duties that taxed his patience mightily. One source of problems were the thousands of Black "contrabands" that entered Stevens's lines seeking safety and freedom. Stevens initially tried to ignore these refugees, hoping this strategy would both palm off a potentially huge problem on the local inhabitants while at the same time buying their support by appearing to be trying to disrupt their lives as little as possible. But the locals would have none of this and the Black contrabands kept coming in greater numbers each day. To resolve this problem, Washington dispatched scores of abolitionist teachers, preachers, and other well-meaning young people to educate and assist the Blacks. This group, labeled "Gideon's band" by their detractors in the army, was initially perceived as an impediment, but, after finding their niche in Beaufort, solved many of General Stevens's problems with the Black community. Another problem were the Treasury agents sent to the island to supervise the harvest and shipment north of the huge and now-unowned cotton crop. These numerous agents, armed with the equivalent of an officer's rank, for a time threatened to overrule the military command structure on the island. But after clarification of their role from Washington, the agents backed down and concentrated on their cotton business, leaving the army to govern Port Royal Island.[56]

General Stevens endured his administrative command as best he could but made no secret of longing for the field of battle. He used his free time writing letters to his political friends in Congress, advising them on the conduct of the war and urging them to more actively direct its course. Stevens also used these letters to attack his old adversary, George McClellan, whom he labeled as being too cautious and having "too much tenderness for the battlefield." He followed these letters with a "Brief Memoir in Relation to the War," which he mailed to Senator Henry Rice of Minnesota prior to publication. With this manuscript he openly criticized the Lincoln administration's strategy of attacking on multiple fronts, urging instead one major push in one of the Confederacy's many vulnerable areas. He also advised against the single-minded focus on seizing Richmond, which he argued should be the last of the Union's strategic goals. It would take the Union leadership years to take Stevens's advice— intentionally or not, General Grant eventually adopted Stevens's strategy—but in early 1862, few senior officers in Federal service would listen to the counsel of a "War Democrat."[57]

In March, Major General David Hunter replaced Sherman, renewing Stevens's hopes of taking the offensive once again. The new department commander quickly angered his subordinates by declaring that all Blacks under Federal control in his department instantly were free. In May, Hunter made matters even worse by ordering Stevens to collect any able-bodied Black men he could find and form them into an infantry regiment. Although Stevens doubted any of these men would serve—most told him they feared execution should they be caught bearing arms against the Confederacy—he obeyed and collected some 600 Black men for Federal service. But before any of them could be trained as soldiers, the treasury agents demanded they be sent to harvest the cotton crop. Hunter reluctantly assented and Stevens was spared having to further implement what he viewed as an unpleasant task. His concerns about Hunter's aggressive abolitionist actions finally were assuaged on May 20, when President Lincoln reversed Hunter's emancipation order on the grounds that it was undermining local support for the Union.

Stevens saw this change in climate as the right time to once again float his plan to strike the Savannah-Charleston rail line. Hunter, however, rejected his suggestion as too difficult to conduct and adopted instead a plan conceived by Brigadier General Henry Benham. Benham's plan called for an amphibious landing by Stevens's brigade on James Island, while Wright's brigade would cross the nearby swamps and marshes to reach the island over land. Once united, these two brigades, under Benham's overall command, would establish a Union presence within striking distance of Charleston. Hunter warned Benham, however, to "attempt no advance on Charleston" lest they bring on a fight Hunter's small command was ill-prepared to handle.[58]

On June 2, 1862, Stevens's brigade sailed for James Island. Their landing was barely resisted by the Charleston battalion and other Confederate militia units and after a brief skirmish Stevens established his base and waited for Wright's brigade to arrive. Although as Stevens had predicted it took days for Wright's command to slog its way through the swamps, six days after leaving they finally arrived on James Island. With the Union forces now united, General Stevens counseled Benham to quickly begin his attack. The task force's commander, however, was unmoved. Benham argued he needed time to get all the Union forces in place and for reinforcements to arrive before moving. This delay allowed Benham to reorganize his force into two divisions—one of which General Stevens would command—and one brigade. Although this was a promotion in one sense, Stevens was once again left frustrated by the seeming endless delays in taking to the field.

Benham's reluctance to move did more than just test Stevens's patience, however. It also allowed the Confederates to reinforce their position on James Island with troops brought by rail from Savannah, and to build a series of defensive works. For over a week the Rebels labored unhindered by any Union opposition and completed Fort Lamar. The earthen fort was well-suited to defense, even by a small number of men. Its 16-foot-high parapet controlled the field of fire over the cotton fields and swamps surrounding its location. In addition, the only dry route to reach the fort was a narrow strip of land, surrounded by thick swamps and open water. At the base of the fort was a deep ditch, another obstacle to any attacking enemy. Inside these strong works was placed the 1st South Carolina Artillery and several Confederate infantry regiments. On June 15, General Benham, though well aware of the terrain surrounding the Rebel fort, ordered a frontal assault on the Confederate works. Stevens's division was to lead the assault on the Confederate center, aided by Wright's division and William's brigade on each of his flanks. Though Stevens openly opposed the plan, arguing the obvious difficulties presented by the terrain, he was overruled and left with no option. He would try his best to make Benham's attack work.

At about 1:00 A.M. in the dark morning hours of June 16, Stevens's men moved through the dense woods and toward the Confederate works, pushing back grey-clad skirmishers as they went. Benham earlier had rejected Stevens's advice to use an artillery barrage to weaken the Confederates prior to the infantry attack, arguing that a surprise attack was needed. But by the time the first Union troops arrived in view of the fort, enemy guns and sharpshooters were already well aware of their presence and waiting for them. Only two regiments at a time could cross the narrow path to the fort, and General Stevens selected the 8th Michigan and his own beloved 79th New York Highlanders to lead the charge. As the two regiments surged toward the fort they were exposed to a murderous fire from the Rebel artillery. The effect of this fire was devastating; by the time the surviving men reached the fort, where the Confederate infantry opened on them, they could do little but die or retreat. They simply didn't have enough manpower left to breach the fort's walls. Though other regiments were thrown into the fight, Benham compounded his errors by committing his forces to the battle piecemeal. By nightfall the battle had finally ended and Stevens's men returned to their camp. The battle of James Island was a major Union defeat and the first significant battle for many of General Stevens's men. Although their losses were appalling—Stevens's command alone suffered 529 men killed and wounded while the entire Confederate force lost only 202 men—Stevens and his troops had acquitted themselves nobly, doing the best they could with a very bad situation.[59]

At the end of June, General Stevens and his command returned to Beaufort and routine duty. Stevens was made second-in-command to Rufus Saxton and quickly became frustrated at being once more faced with the problems of Blacks, Treasury agents, and abolitionists, rather than Rebels. Frustrated to the breaking point, he wrote a letter directly to President Lincoln advising him to remove all troops from the department on the grounds that they were too few in number to be of any military value there and that they were certainly needed in either McClellan's or Pope's armies. He probably hoped that the letter, with its "view from the field," would be just the thing that would move him and his command closer to the center of the war's action in Virginia.

Time soon proved General Stevens correct. On July 13, Isaac Stevens and his brigade boarded the transport *Vanderbilt*, departing forever the Department of the South, and steamed to Virginia to reinforce McClellan's army following its withdrawal from the peninsula. On July 16, he led his men ashore at Newport News, Virginia, and awaited their new orders. On

July 20, the War Department issued an order creating the IX Corps, merging the commands of Generals Reno, Stevens, and Parke together under the command of Ambrose Burnside. This order also formalized Isaac Stevens's position as a division commander.[60]

Isaac Stevens, though the least experienced division commander in the corps, had already proven his abilities, both to the men and the army's senior commanders. In fact as he entered Centreville on the evening of August 30, 1862, there was talk in both the officer's corps and in the ranks that he had already been pegged for corps command, should the war last long enough for the opening to appear. Stevens, aware of the talk, certainly was fully confident that he was ready for this challenge. In fact, he probably felt such a promotion was long overdue. His performance in the recent battle near Manassas had been good and perhaps, if the Rebels would cooperate and attack again soon, he could truly demonstrate his ability for higher command. In any case, Stevens was secure in the knowledge that having quickly re-formed his men and deployed them for battle without the benefit of a full night's rest, he had performed well at Centreville on August 30.

Neither Isaac Stevens nor Philip Kearny knew that rainy morning in Centreville that their respective lives were about to converge. Because neither man wrote his personal thoughts about the other, it is likely they had little more than a passing acquaintance prior to the campaign in which they were now both engaged. Certainly each man had long known of the other, both having served in Mexico. But it is quite possible that they had never even met until the battle opened near Manassas on the 29th of August, when General Pope's deployment plan threw Kearny's and Stevens's divisions together on the right of the Union line. And whatever view Stevens might have held of Kearny before the latest fight, it is doubtful Kearny would have thought much of Isaac Stevens; he had regularly written his wife disparaging the engineers and other support service officers he found himself serving under in combat. But Kearny had now seen Stevens at work in battle on the 29th and 30th, and knew that Isaac Stevens, whatever his background, was a fighting general like himself.[61]

In many respects Generals Kearny and Stevens were two very different men with little in common. Isaac Stevens's politics and Democratic Party positions defined him in the eyes of official Washington, while Philip Kearny's politics were so private that a colleague later remarked that he never knew to what party Kearny belonged. Kearny came from one of the nation's wealthiest families and lived a personal life that flaunted conventional morality. Isaac Stevens's family was of modest economic standing and he always was proud of the fact that his life was a model of decorum and Christian behavior. Nonetheless, the two men also had much in common. Both were devoted family men who, despite the fact that their careers took them away from home for long periods, often wrote their wives and in these letters demonstrated genuine concern for the well being of their children. But perhaps the most noticeable trait that bound these two together was their aggressiveness in battle and their sometimes reckless propensity to expose themselves to enemy fire. Both men had demonstrated time and again that they believed the only way for a senior officer to really lead men into battle was to be willing to physically lead them into the fray. There would be no directing the fight from a rear headquarters tent for these fighting generals. They would always be found at the point of action, directing their divisions within range of the enemy's fire. No one would ever question the personal courage of Isaac Stevens or Philip Kearny. And on the last day in August of 1862, as the rain fell lightly over the army encamped at Centreville, it was this trait that would soon intertwine their eternal destinies.

3

MOVEMENT AND MACHINATIONS

★————————————————★

SUNDAY, AUGUST 31, 1862; DAWN TO MIDDAY

As day dawned on August 31, most of the Union army was congregated in Centreville, though men continued straggling in throughout the morning. Few of the men felt any comfort in the arrival of the new day. William Todd of the 79th New York, Company B, remembered, "Rain began to fall at daylight and our condition was, to say the least, uncomfortable. No supper the night before, no breakfast or prospect of any; defeated in battle; wet to the skin, and covered with mud from head to feet, we presented a rather demoralized appearance." But despite the dampened spirits of the men, and the similar nature of the weather, the army gradually began shifting itself once more into a fighting force.[1]

As the morning wore on, Centreville and Pope's army alike began to hum with life once more. Wrote Major Evan Woodward, Adjutant of the 2nd Pennsylvania Reserves:

> The houses in the town were crowded with our wounded, and the road thronged with soldiers of every arm of the service, trying to find their respective commands. Wagons were moving to and fro, Generals, aides, and orderlies were galloping about, and squads of prisoners were sent to the rear, and long trains of ambulances were pushing toward Washington. Omnibuses, carriages and other vehicles lined the roads and covered the fields in every direction, the Government . . . having sent them out for the wounded. Large droves of horse, tied to long ropes, were also sent from the Government employees, and many citizens also came out, and emptied their pockets of all the tobacco and postage stamps they had, as those articles were in great demand among the soldiers.[2]

For many of the men, the kindness of the residents of Washington was the only joy they had experienced in several weeks. For some, the morning of August 31 even brought special pleasure. One of these fortunate few

81

was Lieutenant Ford of the 101st New York who recalled, "Morning broke. Some hundreds of hacks and carriages with supplies and comforts for the sick and wounded . . . arrived, and, meeting a former schoolmate, then an employee of the Treasury Department, who had charge of one of the carriages, I made myself known to him. His look of surprise, and hearty shake of the hand, convinced me that he had not forgotten his old schoolmate and friend." After some time spent reminiscing, the weary lieutenant coaxed from his friend the secret of his cargo. "I have a few bottles," his friend stated in hushed tone, "[T]hey are for the benefit of the sick and wounded, but I guess I can spare you some." Parting from his schoolmate once more, Lieutenant Ford returned to the 101st New York and shared this bounty with his fellow veterans. "[S]oon more than one of our comrades," he would comment years later, "had a pleasant and congenial feeling for the rest of mankind."[3]

For some in Pope's army, the break from regular duty presented by the circumstances of August 31 was an opportunity to forage from the local inhabitants, a favorite sport of soldiers since the dawn of time. Those unfortunate locals who were the target of this activity, though, would more likely have described it as nothing more than thievery, which in most cases it was, in light of the numerous orders from above prohibiting such unauthorized foraging. Typical of the experiences of northern Virginia farmers this day was that of the Machen family. Their small but prosperous farm was situated about one mile from Centreville, sitting astride Walney Road which derived its name from their farmhouse. Until this day the war's effects had seemed remote. In fact, its greatest impact to date was that the army had taken away the hired help on which Lewis Machen, ailing and too old to work himself, had depended to keep the farm running. But now the war would literally come knocking at their door. Caroline Machen described it to her brother Arthur in a letter:

[W]e had a constant succession of soldiers around and in our house, robbing us of everything they could lay their hands upon. They broke open the stone house, your father's secretary, the closet in the entry, and took from them whatever they pleased—broke in the meat house, and took six or seven hundredweight of bacon, took off the cellar door and robbed that, stole every fowl that we had, and even took iron and tin articles from the kitchen. Our barn and stable fared no better; they broke open both, took from the barn all the tobacco and threshed wheat, ten bushels of corn I had just bought for family use—from the stable, all our horses and our carriage—both pair of oxen—killed one cow and two yearlings, all our hogs, all our potatoes and other vegetables. Every peach and apple was threshed off the trees and carried away.[4]

That such destruction and robbery did not elicit harsh words about the Union army from Caroline is perhaps due to an incident that occurred on the afternoon of September 1. "One thing, however, that the kind providence of God prevented their accomplishing was [to] break into the house where your father was lying sick," she continued. "On Monday afternoon they were battering two of the doors at least twenty or thirty of the worst looking men I ever saw, in and around the house. I was outside with my back against the door leading from a passage with eight or ten in front of me. I told them they could not enter. I felt assured they would be prevented; the words were scarcely spoken, when Captain Cowen of a New York Battery rode to the door, and soon relieved us from our unwelcome visiters." Cowen would further endear himself to Walney's residents by appointing a guard to stand at the Machen's door to prevent more looting or threats to the family's safety.[5]

Waking before dawn that day, Pope's staff had set to work immediately, continuing the reconstitution of the shattered army. Their most immediate task was to ensure that the army formed itself around Centreville in the manner the commanding general had dictated the night before. The size and flexibility of Pope's force would have made any army commander jealous. Indeed, he had two entire corps in his reserve and yet still had a solid defensive line. McDowell's III Corps, Army of Virginia, would deploy two miles east of Centreville on the Warrenton Pike to cover the army's retreat, should it become necessary. Heintzelman's III Corps, Army of the Potomac, was placed on the eastern slope of the Centreville heights, to serve as a reserve should Lee attack directly. Pope's main defensive line, when fully formed, would provide a six-corps-large arc around the Centreville position. Forming the extreme right of Pope's main defensive position, facing Lee to the west, was Edwin V. Sumner's II Corps, Army of the Potomac, which would post north of town astride Walney and Stringfellow Roads. To their left was Porter's V Corps, Army of the Potomac, facing northwest on Braddock Road, and pinned on Franklin's VI Corps, Army of The Potomac, which was posted on the northern side of the Warrenton Pike west of town. Banks's II Corps, Army of Virginia—when they arrived from Manassas—would deploy on the southern side of the Warrenton Pike west of town. On their left were Sigel's I Corps, Army of Virginia, and Reno's 2nd Division of the IX Corps. Deployed two and a half miles in front of the main line and posted on the eastern bank of Cub Run, was Stevens's division of the IX Corps, acting as skirmishers.

The IX Corps likely had been selected to serve as skirmishers for the army in part because they were the smallest corps present that day. What they lacked in overall firepower they made up for in flexibility. Only two divisions of the IX Corps had arrived in time to participate in the recent battle, the rest of the corps was still enroute with its commander, Major General Ambrose Burnside, from the Fredricksburg area. The two divisions present, Stevens's 1st and Reno's 2nd, moreover, were small divisions by the standards of the rest of the army, having only two to three brigades each versus the standard four or five. The corps' acting commander, Major General Jesse L. Reno, also had not served long as a corps commander and retained at the same time command of his division. But he had proven himself able in stopping Jackson's effort to counterattack on August 30 and was considered by many of his fellow officers as a rising star in the Union command hierarchy.

For whatever reason that General Pope had chosen the IX Corps for picket duty that morning, most men and officers of the small corps resented having to return to frontline duty so quickly. While other units in the army got some much needed rest, the men of the IX Corps would have to remain alert and could get no sleep. Oliver Bosbyshell of the 48th Pennsylvania remembered angrily, "It was 4 o'clock in the morning of the thirty first, when the Forty-eighth reached [Centreville], soaked to the skin, a heavy rain having closed the scenes of the day . . . the endeavor to secure some rest proved futile for back over a portion of last night's road trudged the regiment . . ." Being assigned this tedious duty without any rest only hardened the poor attitude the men of the IX Corps had held about General Pope and his Army of Virginia since joining Pope's expedition in late July.[6]

Covering the ground overlooking the Cub Run valley, they formed a heavy skirmish line to protect the army at Centreville. The line was considered heavy because it was supported by artillery—posted in the main line—as well as cavalry to guard its flanks. Standing atop the ridge in the rear of the line, Brigadier General Isaac Stevens could view the results of his morning's work with satisfaction. He had posted the IX Corps in the best possible way to screen the army's position using the terrain he had been given. His satisfaction must have been made even greater by the fact that this was his first action as an acting corps commander, as General Reno, having taken ill late on August 30, had turned over direction of the corps to Stevens.[7]

Even as General Stevens and his men were watching Confederate pickets in their front, reinforcements from the Army of the Potomac were arriving in growing numbers in the Centreville works. The first units to arrive belonged to Major General William B. Franklin's VI Corps, some of whom had appeared at dusk on the 30th, too late to help the Union cause that day. These fresh troops must have been a great relief to Pope for they would be better able than his own weary men to halt a Confederate thrust at his center that could come at any time. Key parts of Major General Edwin V. Sumner's II Corps—Pope's other major source of reinforcements—were still on the march from Alexandria that morning and would arrive at Centreville by noon to take up their place on the far right of Pope's defensive line.[8]

As the unseen sun climbed higher behind the clouds of Sunday morning, the Union's hold on Jermantown was slowly growing stronger. Before dawn on the morning of August 31, Colonel Torbert had relieved Captain Baker's small command with six companies of the 2nd New Jersey. In repositioning his troops, the colonel apparently agreed with Captain Baker's view of the importance of Jermantown; he redoubled the brigade's picket force and extended its right to cover the Little River Turnpike, a mile in front of that intersection. Once they had completed their move, Torbert's picket force extended in an arc from south of the Warrenton Pike running northeast to the eastern side of the Little River Turnpike. This move not only relieved the provost guard at Fairfax of the responsibility of guarding the Jermantown intersection, but also gave the Jerseymen a better chance of responding to any threat that might come at them from either of the two roads they were guarding.[9]

While the 2nd New Jersey was moving to its new post, the cloud-filled sky opened and let a steady rain down on the weary troops. Resting within the Centreville works, George Lewis of the 1st Rhode Island Light Artillery morosely observed that "our battery lay . . . in a cheerless rain, thinking over the fortunes of another retreat and wondering what next in the line of misfortune was in store for us." Seven miles west, the Confederate veterans of another Southern victory were also soaking in the rain. J. Shoemaker of Pelham's Battery, part of Stuart's Horse Artillery, recalled, "We rested as much as it was possible for us to do, considering the weather. It was raining hard and there were no living Yankees in sight, but plenty of dead ones."[10]

When General Lee first opened his eyes before dawn on August 31, he in all likelihood already knew what he wanted his army to do. They must regain the offensive, before a unique opportunity to inflict what could be a devastating blow to the Union cause was lost. If the Northern army was as badly beaten as their defeat in the recent fighting suggested—and

Pope's morale as a commander was equally low—then Pope would certainly remain in the Centreville works for the immediate future. Lee must have understood that the Centreville position was a double-edged sword; its invulnerability to frontal assault made it equally vulnerable to a flanking attack that pinned the defender in his works. If Pope's army remained there, a frontal attack would be pointless and futile but a move against either of Pope's flanks might deal his force a deadly blow and cut him off from Washington. However, Lee could not rule out a Union attack, which could easily come if McClellan's troops had arrived during the night. One thing was certain, the general would need more information about the enemy's condition, positions, and intentions before he could fully formulate his plan of attack.[11]

The dark skies overhead were only just beginning to lighten as General J. E. B. Stuart climbed atop his mount for the journey to inspect the Union lines west of Centreville. He had received orders from General Lee the night before to scout the enemy's position and determine their condition, intelligence that was critical to determining the course of Lee's plans for the hours and days that lay ahead. Once his brigade commanders were assembled, Stuart dispatched Colonel Thomas Rosser and his cavalrymen to recapture Manassas Junction and clear out some small force of Yankees who were reported to be there and who might threaten the Southern right flank. Then Stuart personally led the rest of his command east along the Warrenton Turnpike and across Bull Run. Once within view of the new Federal position on the Centreville heights, Stuart and his men must have considered what to make of the scene before them. Abandoned equipment littered both sides of the Warrenton Pike but few Federal units remained outside the Centreville works. There was still confusion in evidence inside the fortifications but, most troubling of all, there were fresh troops clearly in evidence in the center of Pope's line. These reinforcements were no doubt from McClellan's Army of the Potomac; Richmond previously had warned Lee that these units had left their positions facing the Southern capital, and only two days prior, Stuart himself had reported to General Lee information from Fitzhugh Lee's reconnaissance of Fairfax Court House that the Army of the Potomac's II and VI Corps were beginning to arrive. To their right, looking south toward Manassas, the Union line extended beyond their view, and artillery could be seen moving in that direction. To their left, looking north, the Federal line also appeared strong and disappeared over a sloping ridge, leaving open the question of what road or land form Pope had pinned his right on. What was clear to the Southern cavalry commander was that Pope's army was not the devastated, beaten force he certainly had hoped to find when setting out that morning.[12]

Once the reconnaissance party arrived at Lee's headquarters, Stuart quickly apprised his commanding officer of his morning's findings. For General Lee this information settled what had been weighing on his mind for hours. The arrival of reinforcements in the already strong Centreville works made a direct assault futile. Even if the left of Pope's defensive line did not extend all the way to Bull Run, a flanking move on the Union's left would have little room to maneuver once the fighting began. The Union right was probably an easier target and, though they could not be sure where it ended, it could be flanked by using any number of good roads. The Confederate army would move north around Pope's right.

Declining breakfast, probably in an effort to get things moving early, Lee mounted his horse Traveller and rode off, with General Stuart in tow, to find Generals Jackson and Longstreet. Encountering the two near the remains of the stone bridge over Bull Run, Lee passed on his orders. Jackson would lead his command on a flanking move around Pope's right, moving north on Gum Springs Road and then east on the Little River Turnpike, with their ultimate goal being the intersection with the Warrenton Pike at Jermantown. Longstreet's Command would initially remain west of Bull Run—to convince Pope that Lee's army was still in his front—and then follow Jackson by half a day to reinforce him at Jermantown. Stuart and his cavalry were to cross Bull Run and move north to the Little River Turnpike. Once on the turnpike Stuart would move east, clearing the way for Jackson's force and feeling out the location of any sizable Union formations that might block their way.

If they moved quickly enough Stonewall and his men could take Jermantown and place themselves between the Union army and Washington, then move on Centreville and trap Pope's army in their own works. Even if Pope tried to retreat, Jackson could fight him on ground of his own choosing and still deliver a crushing blow to the Union cause. In the worst case Lee might imagine, the fight would end inconclusively and the Southern army could resume his long-planned campaign into Maryland. Time remained of the essence, for if Pope and his army retreated to the Washington defenses before Jackson could cut him off, the move would have been for nothing and Jackson's weary command would be in a very dangerous, exposed location. At the end of the brief commander's meeting, Jackson reportedly muttered only "Good! Good!" of the plan and stalked off to prepare his command for the movement.[13]

Despite the potential payoff of Lee's plan, it was not without risk. Lee

ROUTE OF JACKSON'S FLANKING MARCH
12:00 P.M. August 31 to 3:00 P.M. September 1, 1862

KEY:

XXXX
POPE
Federal
Army

XXX
JACKSON
Confederate
Infantry
Corps

Map Not to Scale

certainly understood that another way of looking at his "grand turning maneuver" was that he would be dividing his force in the face of a numerically superior enemy and sending half of it deep into that enemy's territory. The chief danger was that if Jackson moved too fast or Longstreet too slow, Pope might use his sizable number of reinforcements to cut the Confederate army in two. This risk, however, could certainly be reduced by General Jackson making sure that his lines of communication with Lee and Longstreet remained open throughout the march. In the end, Lee's course of action suggests he believed that the potential strategic gain was worth the tactical risk.

The other risk involved was in choosing Jackson's Command as the leading element of this march. General Lee selected Jackson's force because it was already on the left of his line and closest to the Bull Run fords at Sudley Springs, minimizing any unnecessary movement of troops that might warn the Yankees of the maneuver. But Jackson's men were worn nearly to exhaustion by the past week's forced march and three full days of fighting. Captain James Garnett of the Stonewall Brigade's staff remembered: "The men were so tired and nervous from the continual marching and fighting that the pop of a cap would start them off, but they would soon rally." Adding to their fatigue was the fact that many of Jackson's men had not eaten in over three days. And Stonewall also had to carry out Lee's plan without two of his three seasoned division commanders. Brigadier General William B. Taliaferro had been wounded in the recent fighting near Manassas and Brigadier General William E. Starke was now commanding Jackson's former division. Major General Richard S. Ewell too had been wounded near the Brawner farm on the 28th and Brigadier General Alexander R. Lawton now led Ewell's Division. Of Jackson's original immediate subordinates, only Major General Ambrose Powell Hill remained at the helm of his division.[14]

At the same time, though, the morale of Jackson's men had never been higher, despite their physical discomfort and limitations. They recognized they had borne the brunt of the fighting at Second Manassas and justly had earned the lion's share of glory, all due in large part to the leadership of Stonewall Jackson. Their individual and collective pride in serving in Jackson's Command is evident in the remarks of a wounded soldier that Jackson encountered crawling from the unfinished railroad cut on the 31st. Upon finding the man, Stonewall asked if he were injured and he replied, "Yes, General, but have we whipped them?" Jackson, touched by the veteran's dedication, dismounted and asked the man what unit he was with and the soldier replied, "I belong to the 4th Virginia, your old brigade, General. I have been wounded four times but never before as bad as this. I hope I will be able to follow you again."[15]

Following the officers' meeting, Lee gathered a cavalry escort and rode off to see for himself the state of his army. Throughout the morning General Lee rode along the Confederate lines, and perhaps conducted reconnaissance trips forward of the main line as well, attending to the details of his army. During one of these trips someone, probably startled by the presence of a large body of Union troops that in reality were prisoners, shouted out "The enemy's cavalry!" throwing everything nearby him into pandemonium. In the confusion, General Lee's horse, Traveller, rose up, throwing the general violently to the ground. After being helped to his feet, it became clear that Lee was injured and in some pain. Despite his staff's concerns, General Lee insisted that he continue to ride the Southern lines unaided to plan his flanking move. When the pain refused to subside, though, Lee was persuaded to let a surgeon look at his wrists. The doctor's examination revealed that this accident had severely sprained both of Lee's wrists and that several bones in his right hand were broken. But the army's commander would allow the doctor to do little more than bandage his hands and wrists, for he had work to do. Victory would not wait for his wrists to heal.

As the day wore on the injury proved increasingly painful. By late morning General Lee was completely unable to ride a horse—or use his hands at all—and was forced to abandon his normal routine of personally seeing to details of his army's movement from the saddle. Major Walter H. Taylor, Lee's adjutant general, recalled, "He had no use of either hand, and for some days each arm had to be carried in a sling. He could not ride his horse, and for some time thereafter moved in an ambulance. This was a sore trial to the general's patience. The ambulance could not go into many places where a horse would have carried him, and so his movements were greatly hindered. . . ." This impediment to Lee's usual style of command—along with the constant pain—would soon nearly take the Army of Northern Virginia's leader out of the command picture, testing both the skill of Lee's immediate subordinates as well as Lee's informal style of command.[16]

General Pope rose early on August 31 in his headquarters in Centreville and began considering just what to do next. He knew Washington expected him to somehow regain the offensive posture he had promised to maintain at the start of his Virginia campaign—to do any less risked his command position and, perhaps, the Union cause. But the general's confidence was clearly shaken from his experiences of the day before. Not only from the army's retreat but more importantly from the knowledge that he no longer commanded the support and confidence of his men. During the march to Centreville, General Pope had been forced to endure the bitter remarks and taunts of men who blamed him personally for the latest defeat at Bull Run. "Go west, young man, go west!" a soldier had shouted at him from the safety of the ranks, throwing Pope's earlier boast about his success in the western theater back in his face. A man in General Gibbon's "Black Hat Brigade" remembered that "open sneering at General Pope was heard on all sides." A soldier in the 3rd Wisconsin would later write, "the feeling was strong in the army against Pope . . ."[17]

Since Pope now lacked the self-confidence to attack, and knew that to order a further retreat without Washington's approval was professional suicide, he decided to lay the groundwork for taking either action. At 8:30 A.M., he issued a circular to his corps commanders ordering that ammunition be brought forward and distributed to their commands. About the same time he issued another circular to these same commanders directing them to send all their wagons—except those needed to bring ammunition forward—back to Alexandria. Along with the wagons would go the thousands of wounded who populated Centreville's temporary field hospitals. Just how quickly to evacuate the wounded must have weighed on the general's mind for some time and he had directed that the personal wagons of some 60 War Department clerks, who had ventured too close to the fighting the day before and been captured, be pressed into service as ambulances. Moving all the wounded, in any case, would take some time and was a prudent move whichever way Washington ordered—attack or retreat.[18]

Whatever Henry Halleck and Washington might have been considering that 31st of August, the arrival of the army's immense wagon train, bearing thousands of wounded, could not help but give Halleck and the other bureaucrats in the capital some hint of the army's beaten condition. Perhaps General Pope hoped this development would be enough to convince Halleck to order a retreat. In any case, Pope's utter lack of any preparations for an attack suggests that on August 31 he favored ordering a retreat.

Pope grew increasingly frustrated as the morning wore on with no sign of any direction from Washington. The general finally decided to take an unusual tack to see if he could prod the Union's senior army commander into ordering a retreat—he would finally reveal the truth about the army's condition. At 10:45 that morning he wrote:

Our troops are all here in position, though much used up and worn out. I think it would perhaps have been greatly better if Sumner and Franklin had been here three or four days ago; but you may rely on our giving them as desperate a fight as I can force our men to stand up to. I should like to know whether you feel secure about Washington, should this army be destroyed. I shall fight it as long as a man will stand up to the work. You must judge what is to be done, having in view the safety of the capital. The enemy is already pushing a cavalry reconnaissance in our front at Cub Run, whether in advance of an attack to-day I do not yet know. I send you this that you may know our present position and my purpose.[19]

Having blatantly lied in his previous message to Halleck, Pope now spun a carefully woven tale of shaded truth. He admitted to Halleck that the army was, in fact, "used up and worn out," an accurate assessment of the army's state that morning. His comment on the tardiness of the II and VI Corps was a not-too-subtle way of laying blame for the recent defeat squarely at McClellan's doorstep. He then suggested—in a moment of unbridled temerity—that, if ordered, he was prepared to fight on even though the men may not be up to it. The truth, as Pope surely knew, was that the men were up to a fight but might not fight for him, though he could never admit this to Washington. Then he cleverly placed the suggestion of retreat in Halleck's mind by asking how the general viewed the safety of the capital in light of the army's sorry state. Pope knew well that he need not raise the threat directly, Halleck's personal responsibility for protecting Washington would certainly be great enough to forestall any orders for an attack. Once this message was completed, General Pope ordered his dispatch quickly conveyed to Washington. With any luck Washington would respond before General Lee could determine the course of the day's events.

With the groundwork laid for a retreat, Pope turned to gaining the support of his immediate subordinates. At 11:00 A.M. he convened a meeting of his corps commanders at his headquarters, ostensibly to consider the army's next move. As each of the leaders entered the room, Pope posed the question—stay and fight at Centreville or retreat to the Washington defenses? In turn, Reynolds, Heintzelman, Franklin, Porter, and Sumner each answered that the army was in no condition to fight and unprepared for offensive action. They agreed that Lee would likely try a flanking move rather than attack Centreville directly, with his goal being either an attack on the army's rear or a move into Maryland. In any case, the corps commanders agreed remaining at Centreville would be pointless at best or disastrous at worst. Retreat was the only viable option.

Pope now had covered all the political angles needed before ordering a retreat. But as the meeting was winding down a message from Halleck in Washington arrived. Written at 11:00, as the corps commanders meeting had been starting, Halleck wrote, "My Dear General: You have done nobly. Don't yield another inch if you can avoid it. All reserves are being sent forward. Couch's division goes to-day. Part of it went to Sangster's Station last night with Franklin and Sumner, who must be now with you. Can't you renew the attack? I don't write more particularly for fear dispatch will not reach you. I am doing all in my power for you and your noble army. God bless you and it. Send me news more often, if possible."[20]

Pope's demeanor changed the minute he read the dispatch. Now having clear orders from Washington, he immediately undid his morning's work. The general abruptly dismissed his corps commanders, telling them he had been "ordered" by Washington to remain at Centreville and that he "was glad of it." Pope's subordinates wandered from the meeting stunned by their commander's sudden change of position and his obvious lack of military judgment. They all understood what had happened but none could fathom why Pope would so easily adopt a strategy that could lead to disaster for the army. "The decision was foolish if not criminal," wrote General Porter years after the war. "Each felt that the government was not truly informed of the condition of affairs—perhaps deceived."[21]

Pope now had what he had wanted for days, direction from above absolving him of at least some responsibility for whatever might happen next. Whether it made military sense to remain at Centreville or whether the army was really prepared for attack no longer mattered. Washington had issued its orders and General Pope now had only to determine how best to make those orders happen.

Responding to Halleck's directive to attack, General Pope returned to a tactic that had already served him well in his correspondence with Washington—lying. Shortly after noon, he wrote, "Your dispatch of 11:00 A.M. has been received, and I thank you for your considerate commendation. I would be glad to have it in such shape that the army might be acquainted with it. I had a letter from Lee this morning. Ewell is killed. Jackson is badly wounded, and other generals of less note wounded. The plan of the enemy will, undoubtedly, be to turn my flank. If he does so he will have his hands full. My troops are in good heart. I need cavalry horses terribly. Send me two thousand in lots, and under strong escort. I have never yet received a single one." That General Pope had received Halleck's late morning dispatch and that he was woefully short of cavalry were the only accurate statements he made in this reply. And despite the confidence Pope displayed earlier with his corps commanders, his request for Halleck to disseminate his praise of Pope to the entire army suggests that the army's leader knew that he still commanded only the bodies, but not the respect, of his troops.[22]

4

Stuart's Salutation

★————————————————————————★

Even as John Pope was reading General Halleck's latest dispatch, Jackson's Command was beginning its arduous flanking march around the Union's right. Around noon Jackson issued the orders to his division and brigade commanders to have the men fall in a column on the Sudley Springs Road and march north. A. P. Hill's Light Division would lead the movement, followed by Jackson's remaining two divisions. The rain that had started early that morning had grown to a steady drizzling rain, turning the already mud-choked roads to an oatmeal-like mush in many places, making a difficult march even worse. For Dr. Spencer Welch, surgeon of the 13th South Carolina Volunteers, the annoyance of the rain was overshadowed by a much more depressing aspect of the scene: "[W]e started away and I passed where Groggans's body lay. Near him lay Captain Smith of Spartanburg. Both were greatly swollen and had been robbed of their trousers and shoes by our own soldiers, who were ragged and barefooted, and did it from necessity."

After going nearly three miles, Jackson's Command crossed over Catharpin Run at an unnamed ford some 200 yards north of Sudley Springs Ford, and turned onto Gum Springs Road, still moving north. While marching along Gum Springs Road that afternoon General Jackson, whether he knew it or not, passed within miles of a place known locally as "Peach Orchard Farm" where his mother, Julia Neale, had been born in 1798.[1]

Moving ahead of Jackson's column was the cavalry brigade of Brigadier General Fitzhugh Lee. Their task was an important one, for neither Jackson nor Lee yet knew the exact location of the Union left flank. They would be the force to feel out that position. By 2:00 that afternoon, Lee's brigade turned right onto the Little River Turnpike and headed east without finding any sign of Federal soldiers. For several miles they rode on with no evidence of the Union right, passing several roads that might easily have held Federal troops. As they neared the turnpike's intersection with Stringfellow Road, however, Fitzhugh Lee's pickets sighted a Yankee cavalry patrol resting astride the turnpike. The Southern pickets quickly

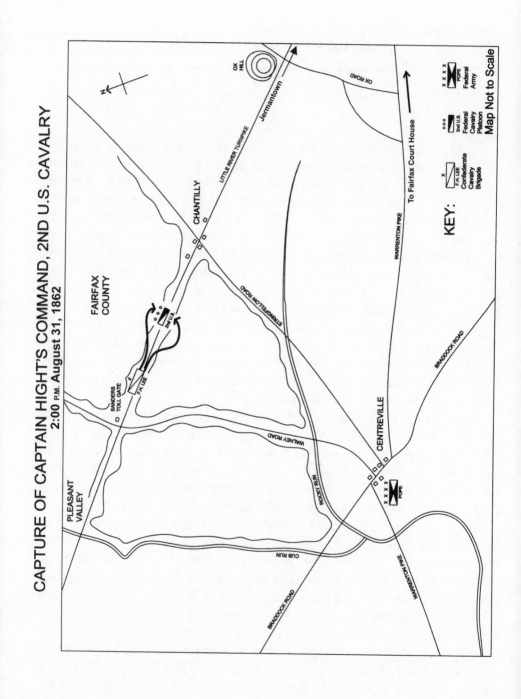

CAPTURE OF CAPTAIN HIGHT'S COMMAND, 2ND U.S. CAVALRY
2:00 P.M. August 31, 1862

but quietly brought their mounts about and raced to bring this important bit of intelligence to their commander.

What Lee's troopers had discovered was a squadron from the 2nd U.S. Cavalry Regiment. Under the command of Captain Thomas Hight, they had been sent from Alexandria to Centreville on August 30 in response to General Pope's urgent demand for cavalry. The platoon had spent the morning of the 31st scouting the road north and west of Centreville for any signs of a Confederate flanking move but had found no evidence of the Rebels by midafternoon. After reporting this fact to General Sumner at Centreville, they departed with orders from Sumner to scout the route to Jermantown. Shortly before 2 P.M., Captain Hight halted his small command just west of Chantilly to rest and feed their horses. Most of Hight's men immediately dismounted and scattered about the roadside to boil coffee and get some much needed rest out of the saddle. With no apparent danger about, Captain Hight let his men rest where they would on both sides of the road, with no order to the formation. The captain, apparently relaxed by the absence of an enemy, posted only one mounted sentinel each in front and to the rear of the resting patrol. This nonchalant attitude about his forces' security would soon come to haunt the captain and his men. About 15 minutes into their rest break, the sentinel on Hight's western flank reported the presence of horsemen on the road they had just covered. But because the captain had seen numerous stragglers on the route, he dismissed this report as nothing more than that— and their rest break continued.[2]

Once his pickets had returned, Fitzhugh Lee ordered an immediate attack on the unprepared Federals. Lee's troopers charged down the road in a column and were on Hight's men before they knew what was happening. Those of Hight's troopers closest to the charging Confederates scattered, running for any cover available, but were quickly captured without offering any form of resistance. Those in the rear of the column scrambled to form a defense, offering a scattered and ineffective fire, but they too were quickly overwhelmed by Lee's charging troops and likewise captured. Two or three of Hight's men charged from the road into the woods, racing for any place that was away from the scene. Though their actions might have appeared cowardly to their comrades, at least one of these men, Lieutenant Harrison, would soon play an important role in the unfolding events east of Centreville. The other men of Hight's squadron of the 2nd U.S. Cavalry, along with 20 or so infantry stragglers Lee's men had rounded up like so many cattle, would remain guests of Stuart's cavalry until the next morning.[3]

As Fitzhugh Lee's brigade was regrouping from its capture of Captain Hight's squadron, General Stuart and his remaining two brigades—Robertson's and Hampton's—arrived on the turnpike. As General Robert E. Lee had instructed, Stuart and his men had started early that morning by crossing Bull Run near where the Warrenton Pike crossed it and ridden north across country along the western bank of Cub Run. They had attracted the attention of Federal pickets along the way, as General Lee had certainly intended, convincing their Union observers that the Confederate cavalry was merely carrying out a probing reconnaissance to find weaknesses on their immediate flanks. Those Union pickets never imagined that the cavalry they were watching so closely was diverting their attention from the movement of half the Confederate army that was then well underway a few miles to the west. With his entire cavalry division reunited, Stuart renewed his eastward march along the Little River Turnpike to discover the strength of the Federal position—if such a thing existed—at Jackson's Jermantown destination.

Ahead of Stuart at Jermantown, the massive Union supply train was already rolling its way eastward. The number of wagons moving through the intersection there seemed endless, part of a line stretching for miles beyond the sight of any of the men in Torbert's command who were guarding them. Colonel Torbert well knew that these slow-moving wagons were the army's most vulnerable asset and guarding them from Confederate cavalry raids was a nearly impossible task. When the colonel, then at Fairfax Court House, received word late in the afternoon of the 2nd U.S. Cavalry's skirmish with the Rebels, he became justifiably worried. His brigade could reasonably hold off an attack by a similar-sized unit, but a determined attack by a large cavalry force might overwhelm his command. Once again, warning of an attack would be key, allowing Torbert to call for reinforcements from Fairfax Court House or Centreville. Mounting his horse and dashing toward Jermantown, Torbert stopped only long enough to gather Lieutenant Harrison of the 2nd U.S. Cavalry and the few others who had escaped capture by Lee's men, who provided the colonel with important firsthand intelligence of the threat then coming his way. Once at Jermantown, Torbert took the only reasonable course of action available, moving five companies of the 4th New Jersey Infantry forward to bolster his picket line northwest of the Jermantown intersection.[4]

Throughout the afternoon, General Pope appeared to be blissfully unaware that Stuart and his men already had flanked the Union right and were moving ever closer to the rear of his army. If Pope knew anything of the capture of Captain Hight's command, the general's actions suggest he wasn't worried by the presence of Confederate cavalry on his right flank. At 5:00 P.M. Pope ordered General Marsena Patrick to select two regiments of infantry to escort the wagon train from Centreville to Fairfax Court House, to which Patrick responded by sending the 21st and 23rd New York. Fearing that these two regiments alone might be inadequate to the task, Pope sent another dispatch late in the afternoon, this time to Colonel Torbert, ordering him to detach two of his infantry regiments and two artillery pieces to Centreville to assist in escorting the wagon train back to Alexandria. Torbert must have had mixed feelings about this order. He now knew that Confederate cavalry was operating near his position and that to obey this order meant cutting his force nearly in half at the same time that the enemy might be at his doorstep. And yet the order had come from General Pope himself, the very top of the command structure, and he would resist it at his own peril. In the end, perhaps lacking compelling evidence for resisting the order, Torbert responded to Pope's orders by sending the 1st and 3rd New Jersey Infantry Regiments and two guns, as ordered. The result of this decision was that Colonel Torbert was left with only two infantry regiments and four artillery pieces to defend the critical junction at Jermantown that afternoon.[5]

As Stuart's cavalry division continued its probe late in the afternoon, Jackson's lead division was just turning east onto the Little River Turnpike, eight miles to their rear. Jackson's men had made uncharacter-istically slow progress that entire afternoon, having moved only eight miles or so the entire day. The men, for their part, marched on with no idea why they were moving or where they were going. "There is much specu-lation but no knowledge of our destination," wrote William Jones later that evening. Jackson, however, clearly wanted his command to move slowly. A. P. Hill—commanding the march's vanguard division—was try-ing to set a brisk pace, probably assuming that Jackson would want to get to the Jermantown intersection quickly. Late in the day, however, Jackson sent Hill a message reprimanding him for setting too rapid a pace and ordering him to slow down. In fact, the only thing characteristic about Stonewall's actions that afternoon was that he gave Hill no reason for wanting to slow the pace. Typically, Jackson's desire to do so would have to suffice as motivation enough for his division commander.[6]

Meanwhile, at the rear of the expanding Southern position, Longstreet's Command was finally beginning its own march northward, following Jackson's earlier route. Longstreet's Command had taken longer than expected to prepare for the day's march because they were

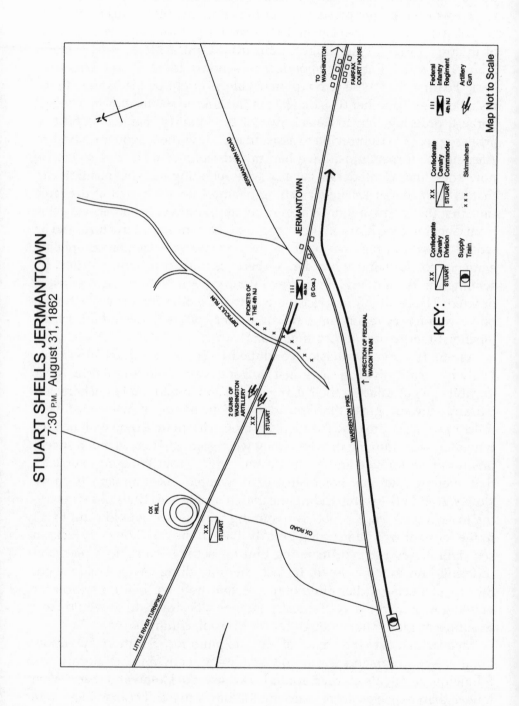

STUART SHELLS JERMANTOWN
7:30 P.M. August 31, 1862

KEY:

x x Confederate Cavalry Division STUART	x x Confederate Cavalry Commander STUART
Supply Train	x x x Skirmishers
III 4th NJ Federal Infantry Regiment	Artillery Gun

Map Not to Scale

TO WASHINGTON
FAIRFAX COURT HOUSE
JERMANTOWN ROAD
JERMANTOWN
4th NJ (5 Cos.)
PICKETS OF THE 4th NJ
DIFFICULT RUN
2 GUNS OF WASHINGTON ARTILLERY
x x STUART
WARRENTON PIKE
DIRECTION OF FEDERAL WAGON TRAIN
OX ROAD
OX HILL
x x STUART
LITTLE RIVER TURNPIKE

saddled with all the extra duties Jackson's Command had avoided by their hasty departure—burying the dead, guarding and moving the thousands of prisoners from the recent battle, and guarding the army's wagon train. Once they had left, however, these arduous tasks fell to General D. H. Hill's Division which finally had arrived from Richmond by midday. They would remain behind not only to guard the trains but also to preserve the illusion that the Southern army remained largely in place. As his men were forming up in columns and facing left to begin their march, General Longstreet engaged in a bit of subterfuge. The general ordered Roger Pryor's brigade, in the rear of his column, to march directly east on the Warrenton Pike to give the impression of an impending assault on the banks of Cub Run, hoping they would push just far enough to convince the Yankees that at least some portion of the Confederate army remained in their front.[7]

At about 6:30 P.M., Stuart and his cavalry force reached Ox Hill, just north of the Little River Turnpike and three miles from Jermantown. Scouts had already alerted Stuart to the presence of the Union wagon train moving east in front of them. The general knew this meant Pope's army in all likelihood was still in Centreville and that Jackson still might interpose his command between them and Washington. Now he had only to determine just how many Federals were there to contest Jackson's taking the intersection the next morning. Before proceeding eastward, Stuart posted two guns from the Washington Artillery on the crest of Ox Hill to cover their advance and then began his reconnaissance. Riding slowly toward the intersection, they came within shouting distance of the Union picket force posted along the western bank of Difficult Run, one and a half miles from Jermantown. Although it was getting dark and hard to see, from this point Stuart nonetheless could see all he needed to of the Yankees facing him and decided not to press the issue. Heros Von Borcke, riding with Stuart, recalled, ". . . The shades of night were just closing in on us when the heavy rumbling of the convoy, which was several miles in length, became distinctly audible. As the escort protecting this train consisted of several brigades of infantry, General Stuart did not regard it as prudent to hazard a direct attack, and concluded to pay them only a distant salutation."[8]

Stuart and his staff returned to Ox Hill around 8:00 P.M., where the rest of his division was waiting, and prepared to give his "salutation" to the Yankees. He ordered the two guns of the Washington Artillery moved off Ox Hill and led them forward to a ridge overlooking Jermantown. From this point the guns' captains could clearly see the Federal wagon train, trapped conveniently on the road like a sitting duck. Firing their shells into this ripe target was almost too easy for these experienced artillerymen. On General Stuart's command, they opened fire on the unsuspecting wagons.[9]

The Union teamsters slogging through Jermantown had no idea they were in Confederate sights—or even within view of the enemy—until the first shells rained down on them. After the first two shells hit, causing little damage themselves, the once orderly train disintegrated into chaos as the heavily laden wagons careened madly in an effort to escape further danger. Teams ran headlong into each other while others struck from the road, driving in any direction that might offer them protection. Some of the drivers even abandoned their wagons where they were and ran for cover. In the midst of this, soldiers of Torbert's command dashed about, trying vainly to restore some order. For a few minutes—the time it took Stuart's gunners to fire six rounds—Jermantown was in a state of sheer pandemonium.[10]

Heros Von Borcke, along with the rest of Stuart's staff, enjoyed a safer view of the scene: "The confusion in a few minutes became bewildering, as balls from our guns went crashing through the heavily-laden vans, and the loud cries of the drivers vainly endeavoring to get out of range commingled in tumultuous din with the disorderly commands of the officers of the supporting force, who did not seem to know from what quarter to expect the attack, or how to meet it."[11]

Colonel Torbert, meanwhile, was doing what he could to regain control and meet the Confederate threat on the turnpike. The colonel later recounted his efforts that evening: "My guards, stationed on the road to arrest stragglers, by great exertions stopped the train and restored order, forced men to take charge of wagons and drive them to Alexandria and toward Centreville. I immediately advanced a portion of my picket line opposite the artillery, which retired; prepared my own artillery for action; sent the Second Regiment, New Jersey Volunteers, up the Centreville Pike opposite the point where the train was shelled, then sent a staff officer to report to General Pope the state of affairs."[12]

By the time the 2nd New Jersey Infantry was moving to meet Stuart's guns, however, the cavalry general and his artillery were long gone. "[B]y the time they had formed their line of battle, and were pushing bravely forward upon our position," wrote Von Borcke, "we had proceeded already several miles upon the back-track towards the small village of Chantilly . . ." Stuart's cavalry division returned there and spent the remainder of that evening and night in bivouac.[13]

Stuart and his staff, though, had grander plans in mind than remaining on the cold ground with the other men. Heros Von Borcke described their evening's activities:

> Some six miles distant from Chantilly lived on their plantation a family who were old and dear friends of Stuart. Finding himself in the neighborhood, and not having seen them for a considerable time, our General could not resist the opportunity afforded by our night's halt in bivouac of paying them a visit, and the members of his Staff determined to keep him company. A brisk canter through the dark woods brought us about midnight to the mansion, where all were fast asleep. . . . Stuart proposed that we should arouse the slumbering inhabitants with the dulcet-notes of a serenade; and the serenade was attempted; but the discordant voices that joined in the effort . . . persuaded [the proprietor] that his peaceful residence was surrounded by a party of marauding Yankees. . . . His surprise and delight, when at last he recognized "Jeb" Stuart's voice, cannot be described. In a few minutes the whole household, young and old, were aroused, and we remained talking with our kind friends until the morning sun, stealing through the curtains of the drawing-room, reminded us that it was time to be off. And so, after a hasty but hearty breakfast, we took leave of the hospitable family and rode back to our command.[14]

Stonewall Jackson probably did not know it, but General Stuart had failed him twice that evening. J. E. B. Stuart—Jackson's "eyes and ears," who was to be scouting Jackson's risky route deep behind Union lines for the presence of Federals—initially had done his job. As ordered, he had reconnoitered Jackson's route of march and discovered the chief Southern objective at Jermantown to be only lightly guarded. But then he had offered the Union his artillery "salutation," unnecessarily exposing the Confederate presence and virtually ensuring Pope would reinforce his small post there before Jackson's troops could arrive—his first failure. His second came shortly thereafter. At the very time that Colonel Torbert's staff officer was wending his way back to Centreville to alert General Pope of the attack in his rear, General Stuart and his staff were on their way to visit friends rather than report to Stonewall and apprise him of the situation facing him. Had Jackson been aware of these failings, he most certainly would have been furious.

At 8:00 P.M. Stonewall decided the men had endured enough marching for one day and ordered his command to halt near Pleasant Valley. Jackson had good reason to be concerned that evening. His "foot cavalry" had covered only 11 miles since leaving their position on the Manassas battlefield at noon. But even so, as Jackson looked west up the Little River Turnpike he could see his command strung out all the way to Gum Springs Road, some four miles in all. This dispersed position made the command an easy target for Union attacks and Jackson remained mindful that Pope, who now had at least two fresh corps of seasoned veterans at his disposal, might strike his weary half of Lee's army. Making matters worse, Longstreet's Command was nowhere in sight, meaning that the army was divided, probably by many miles. Had Jackson known that Longstreet bivouacked his men for the night after having gone no further than Sudley Springs, he would have been even more concerned.[15]

While General Jackson worried about the state of his command and its flanking move, his men were more worried about their stomachs. The truth was, there simply was no food to issue them that night after a hard day's march. The wagons carrying what food the Southern army had remained well to the rear—even behind Longstreet's Command—with no prospect of reaching Stonewall's hungry men. Once word spread that there would be no food that night, the men did what came naturally. They wandered off in large and small foraging parties to find what little food was available in the surrounding countryside. "The soldiers were very bad," wrote Jed Hotchkiss in his journal that evening, "stealing everything they could lay their hands on, after trying to buy it. They were also very thirsty, water being very scarce." Most of the men, though, would sleep in the rain that night with no food at all to sustain them.[16]

At the same time that many of Stuart's men were settling down for the night, and their general was off to his party, a platoon from the 10th New York Cavalry was engaged in a different sort of mission. They had been sent out from the Washington defenses that morning along with other cavalry regiments to reconnoiter the area north of Pope's right flank in the area around Dranesville, Herndon, and Frying Pan Road. They also had been sent to find the band of Confederate irregulars known as "the Commanches," who were periodically terrorizing the local Unionist populace. One platoon of the 10th New York Cavalry, about 30 men under the command of Captain Pratt, was assigned to ride southeast, going as far as Fairfax Court House, before rejoining the regiment at Frying Pan. Sometime late in the afternoon, Captain Pratt led his party south along a road that crossed the Little River Turnpike. While they rode, the men talked of the late battle that they had all regrettably—at least in their view—missed and of the fact that this road would lead them right to the battlefield where they could view the carnage at Bull Run for themselves. Since they had nearly completed their assigned missions—without having found the Rebels—and were already very close to the battle scene, the captain agreed there would be no harm in a little sightseeing. After all, he had wide latitude to follow whatever route he chose during the reconnaissance and the chances of finding any of the Commanches were growing slimmer as the sun began to set. With that, the small party turned west toward the battlefield on the Little River Turnpike—rather than east toward Fairfax Court House—moving along at a leisurely pace.[17]

As the party neared the small hamlet of Chantilly they unexpectedly encountered a lone cavalry picket. Captain Pratt halted his men and called out to the picket to identify himself. Without hesitation, the picket called back through the darkness that he belonged to the 1st Pennsylvania Cavalry. Having no reason to doubt the picket, Captain Pratt ordered his first sergeant to ride forward and talk to the man to see if they could continue on toward the battlefield or at least to Centreville, where the rest of the army was encamped. The sergeant ventured forward in the dark until he was within a few feet of the picket. Suddenly, the woods around the lone Union sergeant were alive with carbines—all pointing at him.[18]

The sergeant discovered himself in the midst of not the 1st Pennsylvania but rather the 12th Virginia Cavalry of Beverly Robertson's Brigade, under the command of Lieutenant Colonel R. H. Burks. Having little choice, he immediately surrendered and was quickly and quietly led off the road and into the woods. As he was being led away, the rest of the 12th Virginia Cavalry charged Captain Pratt's unsuspecting patrol, taking them all prisoner without a struggle. Unlike his fellow cavalrymen of the 10th New York, the first sergeant's luck would improve during the night. For while his Rebel guards were otherwise occupied, he slipped away into the wet, dark woods and spent the rest of that lonely night searching for the safety of the Federal lines. Despite his efforts, the sergeant would not reach Union lines until late on September 1, missing any chance of warning General Pope of the Confederate threat facing him on his right flank.[19]

As darkness descended over the men of Pope's army in Centreville that evening, they could rest easier knowing that their units slowly were approaching a state where they could once again fight, should the situation come to that. But for now most soldiers would find comfort in whatever form they could. For many of the men that meant sleep, and for most it would be the first good night's sleep they had had in over a week. Others were anxious to send word of their continued existence on Earth to family and friends back home. "As we had not for the last two weeks had time to write to our friends at home," wrote George Lewis of Battery E, 1st Rhode Island Light Artillery, "our leisure hours were spent in that agreeable service." Still other men were thankful just to have the time to enjoy food once more, after having had fresh food issued too rarely, and several days of wolfing it down cold from their haversacks while under fire or threat of renewed action. "[C]offee and crackers were issued, and we soon got our fires burning," recalled Evan Woodward of the 2nd Pennsylvania Reserves. "This was a perfect godsend to us, every mouthful of coffee we drank seeming like so much life passing into us."[20]

Colonel Torbert's Jerseymen spent the night trying to get some fitful sleep while laying on their arms at Jermantown. Their evening encounter with Stuart's guns had shattered any illusions of safety that being in the rear of the army's main position might have earlier provided. They knew the Confederates had been on their flank and that more than likely they would be back. One mile to their east, the men of the 21st and 23rd New York were encamped outside Fairfax Court House after escorting part of the wagon train there in the late afternoon.

During the early evening Brigadier General John Reynolds and his Pennsylvania Reserves arrived on the eastern bank of Cub Run to replace Isaac Stevens's two divisions on the picket line. Surveying the IX Corps' line, General Reynolds chided Stevens that he had allowed the Rebel picket line to come too close and that his position was not well prepared to absorb an impending attack. General Stevens quickly dismissed Reynolds's concerns. "I think it most probable that the enemy will move around and strike us under the ribs," he commented. Finally relieved from their day's stressful duty, Isaac Stevens and the men of his two divisions wearily marched back to the heights of Centreville, where they camped for the night one mile south of town.[21]

General Philip Kearny had spent the day reorganizing his division from the disaster of the recent battle and by evening pronounced his command once again fit for battle. The evening of August 31 found the general finishing some paperwork and looking forward to getting some well deserved rest in his temporary headquarters. Late in the night, Kearny called to his room his young orderly, who later recalled: "I found him in bed; he gave me some official documents and a letter addressed to Mrs. Kearny, which I believe was the last letter he wrote, and three or four old dollars and some silver to defray my expenses and told me to post them in Alexandria. He gave me a pass through the lines."

That letter to Agnes Kearny was brief, but opens a window on Philip

Kearny's heart that evening. It read, "Dearest Love, Yesterday I held my position. Again I am a little disgusted at having to fight for other people. In the night about two in the morning I had two pieces of cold chicken and a bottle of Claret; and all because my man James ran away. Phil."

The general's letter was brief but seems to be intended to let his wife know that he was all right despite the hardship of life in the field. Kearny may well have believed that the battle would be renewed in some form in the morning and that if a letter were to reach his wife, it would have to be posted that morning. Kearny, with all his years of experience in the field, well knew the uncertainty of army life.[22]

General John Pope was not yet considering sleep during the waning hours of August 31. He had spent most of the latter part of that day preparing to regain the offensive Washington had earlier ordered. He could feel confident that his efforts to move the sick and wounded back to Washington and out of the way had gone well enough. By nightfall most of the makeshift hospitals that had populated Centreville since the end of the fighting late on the 30th were gone and with them the thousands of wounded men whose screams of pain had served as a constant reminder to those still able to fight of their recent defeat. Gone, too, for the most part was the army's huge wagon train of supplies, which was then still in the process of retiring to Alexandria. He also had been successful in getting Washington to deliver equipment and support he would need to carry out an attack. The few wagons that were arriving in Centreville mostly bore food and ammunition that the army would need when they finally took the fight back to Lee.

Considering his day's efforts, General Pope could finally feel his confidence returning after the deep doubt that the defeat at Bull Run had plunged him into during the last two days. He had clear orders to attack and preparations for his next move were well underway. The men no doubt still were blaming him for their recent failure but they would certainly fight for him if ordered, that much was certain. And once he had led them into victory, as he had his Western troops, these Eastern boys would see him for the leader he really was. The only thing left to do that night was to plan the attack while Lee's army was still weakened from the recent fight and in a known position. So, as the remaining minutes of the month of August 1862 wound down, John Pope prepared his next attack on Lee's Rebel army, which he knew with great certainty to be resting comfortably five miles to his west.

5

THE GATHERING STORM

September 1, 1862, was only minutes old when an event occurred that would once again undo General John Pope's efforts to steer his Union army in a clear direction. Colonel Torbert's staff officer finally arrived at Centreville shortly after midnight and went immediately to the commanding general's headquarters. He was escorted in and apprised Pope of both the capture of Captain Hight's command—probably passed to Torbert via Lieutenant Harrison—and the recent clash at Jermantown. After hearing the officer's account, General Pope must have known that his plans to regain the offensive were in jeopardy. A cavalry raid on his flank was one thing but Torbert's staff officer was reporting an attack on the army's rear. The fact that artillery had been used certainly did not rule out that it could have been cavalry and not infantry making this attack, but in any case such a blatant and bold strike would not have been an accident. To make matters worse, the attack had come on one of only two roads the army could use to withdraw to Washington and safety if things fell apart at Centreville.[1]

Following the departure of Torbert's staff officer, General Pope began reassessing his plans in light of these two reports. The news the officer had brought would not preclude his plans to attack Lee's army but they did raise the specter of the Confederate flanking march that had first been suggested during yesterday's corps commanders meeting. Incidents such as those just reported would be expected if Lee were planning or carrying out a move around his right flank. But if a large body of Confederates was moving around his right—or already in his rear—some other reports would almost certainly have reached headquarters before now. Still, he had insufficient cavalry to protect his flanks and it was possible that Lee had stolen a march on him during the confusion of restoring order to the army. The potential that such a thing had occurred, though, was certainly not enough to risk the political capital he already had staked on regaining the offensive; for the time being General Pope decided to continue to plan for an attack. But to be safe a reconnaissance force would be conducted to check the army's right flank, just to make sure these incidents were only cavalry probes and not preparations for a major Confederate attack.

At 3:00 A.M. on September 1, General Pope sent a message to General Sumner directing him to conduct a reconnaissance of the army's right flank at dawn. Pope cautioned Sumner: "It is essential that your right be carefully watched. I desire you at daylight to push a reconnaissance of not less than one brigade, supported, if necessary, by a second, towards the north of your position, to the Little River turnpike and beyond. The direction of your reconnaissance should be as nearly due north as practicable, and should be pushed not less than five miles. It is of great importance that this reconnaissance should be made at an early hour in the morning." Although the commanding general did not openly indicate any great concern about the army's position to Sumner—nor did he in a similar message to General Porter—the tone of this dispatch belies a growing worry that Lee really might be flanking his right.[2]

In conjunction with probes by the II and V Corps on the army's right, General Pope moved to reinforce his position at Jermantown. Pope was well aware that there were then only two regiments at that location and the artillery bombardment of last night certainly could be viewed as an indication of Lee's plans for a larger attack. But his plans called for launching an attack in the near future and if he was going to do so, he would have to avoid committing too many troops to any defensive redeployment, especially when it wasn't clear that any such move was really needed. Consequently, he directed Colonel Edward W. Hinks—commanding Dana's 3rd Brigade, 2nd Division, II Corps, Army of the Potomac—to take five of his regiments and two batteries and quickly repair to Jermantown. Colonel Hinks wasted little time in carrying out his orders and well before dawn he had his brigade moved east down the Warrenton Pike.[3]

Pope then took steps to reinforce the safety of Fairfax Court House as well. It would be hours before Sumner and Porter could begin their reconnaissance moves and even more time before he could expect to receive any word of their results. Indeed, Lee might already be around his flank or in his rear and could even be planning to seize Jermantown at dawn, the same time that his two corps commanders would just be starting their probes. If Jermantown were taken, Fairfax Court House would be next and it, too, remained lightly guarded. The safest course, given the shelling of Jermantown a few hours ago, would be to further reinforce the Fairfax Court House position, and sending another brigade there would hardly hinder his attack plans. For this task he chose General Marsena Patrick's 3rd Brigade, 1st Division of the III Corps, Army of Virginia. At dawn,

Patrick marched half his brigade—the 21st and 23rd New York were then already encamped at Fairfax Court House—east toward Jermantown, following closely behind Colonel Hinks's men.

As dawn neared, Pope apparently became increasingly concerned that the alleged Confederate flanking march might well be genuine and that, if so, his position at Centreville would be in serious trouble. His concern focused on genuine fear that the reconnaissance probes by Porter and Sumner might stumble into a fight and bring on an unwanted larger battle before he and the army were prepared for it. That had been just how the recent Second Battle of Bull Run had begun and he certainly had no wish to be put in that position again. At 5:45 the commanding general penned a follow-up message to Sumner that both clarified his earlier order—directing him to go only as far as the Little River Turnpike—and clearly ordered him not to bring on a battle. "I do not care that the brigade shall be pushed further than the Little River turnpike, . . . in order to ascertain whether the enemy is making any movement towards Jermantown and Fairfax Court-House. I do not wish any engagement brought on at present on that ground; but where the information required shall have been obtained by the brigade, withdraw it."[4]

At dawn on September 1, 1862, rays of sun poked through the broken, heavy clouds over the Union and Confederate armies, offering some promise of better weather. But men on both sides who followed the weather—nearly everyone did and with great interest—knew that despite the sun, the dark clouds scudding rapidly by overhead promised even more rain. In spite of this, most of the men of the Union army in Centreville enjoyed another morning of relative leisure. The men of the 21st Massachusetts, along with the rest of their brigade, cooked breakfast and then moved to a new campground, where all expected they would remain for an extended period. The Bay Staters pronounced their new location "a pleasant spot" and immediately began the process of turning the empty field into a comfortable new "home." Nearby, the 79th New York Highlanders were welcoming the return of the regiment's popular second-in-command, Lieutenant Colonel David Morrison, who had been missing since being wounded during the action on James Island in June. Over in the bivouac of the 13th Massachusetts the regimental band was mustered out early in the morning. Charles Davis remembered: "[W]e enjoyed the presence of our band. It was one of the best in the service, and afforded us daily entertainment that was highly appreciated." All in all, it was a much-needed return to the mundane duties of camp life after several days of hellish fighting.[5]

At the same time that most of the army was rising for the day, Porter's and Sumner's reconnaissance parties were leaving Centreville to look for any signs of the suspected Confederate movement around their right flank. The two generals earlier had agreed on a three-pronged movement—using easily traversable roads—as the best way to determine if such a move was actually underway. Porter's force would take the western-most of the three roads, moving almost directly northwest along Braddock Road. Sumner selected Howard's 2nd Brigade of the 2nd Division to cover the other two roads, Walney Road in the center and Stringfellow Road in the east, both running almost directly north from the Warrenton Pike to the Little River Turnpike.

As the men of Torbert's brigade posted at Jermantown awoke early that day, each was aware that with the dawn came the prospect of more action. They could expect nothing less than another attack from the Rebels—the artillery firing of the previous evening must have had a purpose, after all—but they knew this time General Lee would strike in larger numbers and probably with infantry. Throughout the morning the men of Torbert's command continually scanned the western horizon looking for any sign of Confederates. Much to the relief of the New Jersey volunteers, though, no Rebels appeared to harass them that morning.[6]

What did arrive in Jermantown, however, were the reinforcements that they all had been awaiting since last night. Beginning around 8:00 A.M., the men of Hinks's 3rd Brigade began reaching the rear of the Federal position and were quickly thrown into the line. Colonel Hinks immediately sent the 20th Massachusetts and 42nd New York Infantry Regiments forward to replace the tired men of the 4th New Jersey on the picket line in front of Jermantown. He further posted the 19th Massachusetts and the 7th Michigan on his main defensive line, running from Flint Hill Road, one mile north of Jermantown, to the Warrenton Pike. By midmorning of September 1, Jermantown was finally being manned by a force that had some hope of defending this strategically important intersection.[7]

Stonewall Jackson's men, too, were up early and once again moving east shortly after dawn. For this day's march Jackson ordered that his command reverse its position from the orders of the day before; Starke's Division would lead the way, followed by Ewell's Division, and Hill's Division would bring up the rear. Whether this change was intended to reign in A.P. Hill's speed or for some other reason, Jackson never recorded. In any case, unlike their Yankee counterparts only a few miles away, they did not enjoy a leisurely breakfast that morning because most of the Southern volunteers had nothing at all to eat. The little that could be scavenged from the countryside had been collected the night before and the army's supply wagons remained miles away, near Sudley Ford, behind Longstreet's men.[8]

The hungry men of Jackson's Command weren't the only ones concerned with the whereabouts of General Longstreet that morning. Stonewall, too, looked anxiously to the west, longing for the other half of the army to join him. His anxiety was made all the greater considering how difficult it had been for his command to reach this point. Longstreet's men would have the added difficulty of trying to march through the morass the turnpike had been turned into by thousands of feet, hooves, and wheels. Ever since he had begun this movement Jackson must have had concern about the army's ability to carry out Lee's ambitious plan. Lee's plan was a good one, which he had fully endorsed, but it depended on the entire army—not just a portion of it—attacking Pope in his Centreville works or on ground of Lee's choice. And with the men hungry and tired, Jackson knew it would take everything Lee could muster to fight Pope, who had the fresh troops reported from yesterday's reconnaissance near Cub Run. The longer Longstreet delayed, the greater the chance that Pope would discover their flanking march and attack the divided army, one part at a time. But Stonewall would look in vain for Longstreet that morning, for while Jackson and his men were marching ever deeper into Union territory General Longstreet's command was still crossing the fords north of Bull Run, 10 miles and nearly a day's march away.

Shortly after resuming their march, Jackson and his men entered Fairfax County, which most men in the ranks marked by crossing the rude bridge over Cub Run. The entire command resumed the languid—or, perhaps more accurately, sluggish—pace of the day before and by 8:00 the van of the column had progressed only two and a half miles. At about that time Jackson encountered General Stuart and his staff, the first time the two commanders had met since receiving their orders from General Lee early on August 31. What exactly Stuart told Jackson during this encounter remains uncertain. Most probably the cavalry commander informed Jackson of the results of the last evening's reconnaissance of the Union position at Jermantown, particularly the strength and disposition of Union forces there. If he told Stonewall of his "salutation" to the Federal wagon train, neither officer ever made mention of it. Had he informed General Jackson of the small, largely pointless artillery attack, however, Jackson would very likely have been furious that Stuart had risked exposing the Confederate flanking move for a mere show of force. In any case, Stonewall did not adjust the speed or direction of his march to account for whatever intelligence Stuart may have told him.[9]

Jackson did make one change after the meeting with Stuart, however, asking him to order a cavalry force ahead of the command to give warning of an impending Federal attack, should one come. Stuart responded by ordering Beverly Robertson's cavalry brigade to move south along Walney Road while Fitzhugh Lee's cavalry brigade would press ahead of Jackson's column to feel their way along the Little River Turnpike. While this bolstered cavalry screen may have been ordered up in response to Stuart's information, it may just as likely have been a result of Jackson's understanding of the new terrain he was encountering. As his command pushed farther east into Fairfax County they would have to pass three roads before they could strike Jermantown, each of which ran directly north from the Warrenton Pike to the Little River Turnpike. A glance at the map and an understanding of the position of both forces made the danger of these roads apparent—Pope could use any of them to launch a flanking attack on Jackson's tired column with little warning. Jackson would have to worry about what might lay down each of these roads until the command was past them and the army safely united.

Around 9:30 A.M. Jackson halted his column at a small collection of houses clustered around the junction of Walney Road and the Little River Turnpike, identified on maps as Sanders' Toll Gate. Although the renowned foot cavalry had been marching for several hours, for all their effort they had moved just three miles closer to reaching Jermantown. Jackson apparently ordered the stop here for both practical and military tactical reasons, though. The strain of the morning's march had pushed many of the men beyond their ability to keep up and correspondingly his column was stretched out nearly over the entire route of the morning's march. He knew that if he was to retain order he literally had no choice but to stop and let the stragglers catch up.[10]

Jackson's men were not the only ones who were feeling the physical strain of the last few days, for their commander himself must have been feeling groggy and tired. He had slept but little the previous night and needed rest if he was to continue to perform at his best. So while waiting for the stragglers to show up, Stonewall Jackson stretched out on the ground under a nearby tree. Pulling the old, worn Virginia Military Institute slouch cap that he wore down over his eyes, Thomas Jackson grabbed some much needed, and much deserved, sleep.[11]

Meanwhile, the weather had taken a noticeably ominous turn for the worse. The bright sunshine of early morning had given way to a parade of ever darker clouds overhead, urged on by wind that seemed to grow stronger and swifter by the hour. Everyone who was awake at Sanders'

Toll Gate could see that a storm of unusual proportions was approaching.[12]

After awaking from his nap, Jackson took this break as an opportunity to dash off a letter to his wife, Mary Anna. In this first letter since the recent fighting at Manassas, Jackson wrote:

> We engaged with the enemy at and near Manassas Junction Tuesday and Wednesday, and again near the battle-field of Manassas on Thursday, Friday, and Saturday; in all of which God gave us the victory. May He ever be so with us, and we ever be His devoted people, is my earnest prayer. It greatly encourages me to feel that so many of God's people are praying for that part of our force under my command. The Lord has answered their prayers; He has again placed us across Bull run; and I pray that He will make our arms entirely successful, and that all the glory will be given His holy name, and none of it to man. God has blessed and preserved me through His great mercy. On Saturday, Colonel Baylor and Hugh White were both killed, and Willie Preston was mortally wounded.

It certainly must have pained Stonewall to pass on to his wife the sad news of Hugh White and Willie Preston's deaths, for both young men were sons of longtime family friends and members of the same Lexington, Virginia, church the Jacksons attended.[13]

Once all his men had arrived at Sanders' Toll Gate, Jackson reordered his command's formation before proceeding any further into Pope's rear. He directed his division commanders to deploy their brigades on each side of the road, positioning themselves in a two-man-deep line of battle facing either north or south rather than their original four-man-across column formation facing east. In the center of this formation Jackson posted the command's artillery reserve, maximizing protection of his vulnerable, slow-moving guns and speeding their deployment for battle along a wide front. This new order offered greater flexibility to respond to whatever situation they might face. To resume the command's eastward march to Jermantown, each unit would simply face right or left without doubling and proceed forward; to prepare for battle, officers would only need to face their units to the front. Repositioning his troops in such a way was taking a risk of no small proportion, though. Its chief drawback was that Jackson's force was now stretched out over nearly three times the area they had covered while in a column, making it nearly impossible for him to direct the entire command personally. And whatever his intent, Jackson was sacrificing ease of marching and speed to gain readiness, suggesting he was ever more worried about protecting his command from a Union

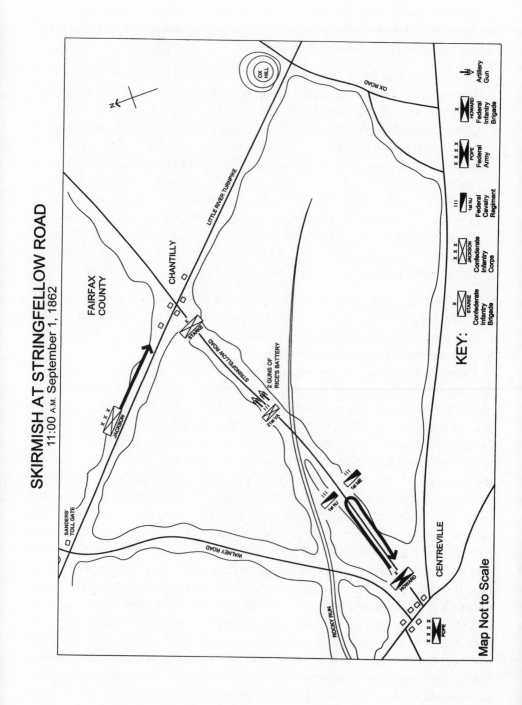

SKIRMISH AT STRINGFELLOW ROAD
11:00 A.M. September 1, 1862

KEY:

Artillery Gun

HOWARD
Federal Infantry Brigade

POPE
Federal Army

1st NJ
Federal Cavalry Regiment

JACKSON
Confederate Infantry Corps

STARKE
Confederate Infantry Brigade

Map Not to Scale

flanking attack from one of the three roads ahead. Once Jackson was fully satisfied that his command was properly "closed up" and repositioned to his liking, its eastward march toward Jermantown resumed.[14]

Riding safely past Walney Road after leaving Sanders' Toll Gate, Jackson could consider that at least one obstacle was now behind him and he could focus his attention on the second of the three roads his force would encounter before reaching Jermantown. Having no more cavalry to spare, though, Stonewall detached Starke's 2nd Brigade, commanded by Colonel Bradley T. Johnson, of Jackson's Division to push ahead of the command and guard the junction of Stringfellow Road and the Little River Turnpike, a place known locally as Chantilly.

Upon arriving at the head of Stringfellow Road, Colonel Johnson posted the bulk of his brigade—including the 1st Virginia Battalion, 42nd Virginia, and 48th Virginia Infantry Regiments—in a line astride the road and facing south. In front of this main line Johnson posted the 21st Virginia Infantry and two guns from Rice's Battery to act as skirmishers. Captain William Witcher advanced the 21st in skirmish order—a formation in which the regiment deployed in a single line with each man about 10 yards apart from his nearest comrade—to a small, sloping hill that overlooked Little Rocky Run. After reaching this point he advanced one company of his men even farther forward as pickets. This formation was well-suited to the 21st's mission as the brigade's skirmishers, for although it did not give the captain much depth it did permit him to extend his control to cover a wide area with a small number of men. With his infantry in place, Witcher then posted his two guns in the roadway itself. From this position he could command a field of fire for several hundred yards down Stringfellow Road. It might not be a good enough position to singlehandedly stop a Yankee advance, but the captain certainly could hold out there long enough to give Colonel Johnson warning of an attack.

By midmorning Porter's and Sumner's Union reconnaissance forces were nearing their objectives. As directed, Porter's men pushed out Braddock Road for five miles or so, remaining in place to search for any evidence of a Confederate flanking move. One of these patrols posted itself on top of Rock Hill, a steep rise just west of a ford across Cub Run. From this vantage point they could see for several miles around, including a raised portion of the Little River Turnpike some two and a half miles to their north. Around 9:30 or so the men posted there spied a body of infantry and artillery moving east on the turnpike. From their location and direction of march, it was clear they could only be Confederate troops. Although the Union boys could not determine the exact size of the force they were observing, an officer was quickly dispatched back to Centreville to report the movement to General Porter.

At around 11:00 A.M., Brigadier General Oliver O. Howard's brigade of Sumner's reconnaissance force was turning north on Walney and Stringfellow Roads. Twenty minutes later the portion of Howard's "Philadelphia Brigade" probing Stringfellow Road encountered Captain Witcher's pickets of the 21st Virginia. General Howard ordered his men to continue forward without firing until "they gave way; then we came in sight of his skirmishers, who opened fire on us at once." Howard returned the 21st's fire, dressed his line, and pressed his men even closer to the Confederate skirmishers.[15]

The 21st Virginia's Captain Witcher, meanwhile, worriedly watched the Federals inch ever closer to his skirmish line on the hill. His concern was not only for his own position but for the safety of Jackson's entire command, who were already beginning to pass the junction with Stringfellow Road a mile or so to his rear. Knowing that the 21st alone was no match for the Yankees, he ordered the two guns of Rice's Battery under his command to open fire. Rice's guns seemed to have greater effect than Captain Witcher could have hoped for, for immediately after the first few shells burst in front of them, the Union line withdrew back to their original position.

Howard, however, was simply following the orders passed on to him from General Pope to avoid a general action. The general remembered, "When we pressed them more closely we succeeded in drawing the fire of their noisy batteries. My purpose was now gained, and I fell back slowly and steadily to my place in the general line." Once back on the Warrenton Pike, General Howard quickly dispatched his own staff officer to alert General Pope of his discovery and ordered forward several regiments from Bayard's cavalry brigade. These men, the 1st Maine and 1st New Jersey Cavalry Regiments, were soon in place and would trade intermittent shots with the men of the 21st Virginia the rest of the afternoon.[16]

By the day's end the fight on Stringfellow Road would appear little more than a skirmish and would barely be mentioned in the various official reports. But to the Machen family, in whose fields the fighting occurred, it was anything but small. Once again, the sting of war was being felt literally in their back yard. Emma Machen described the scene to her brother Arthur in a letter written the day after the skirmish: "We have been almost in the midst of battles. Indeed a cavalry charge was made in our corn field. The uncertainty whether cannon balls and shells might not be falling about us at any moment added not a little to our unpleasant situation, especially after the theft of our horses and oxen left us entirely without means of moving if the danger to life had seemed so imminent." The fighting at their very doorstep scared the Machens greatly and, when the bodies of those who fell in the fighting in their cornfield lay unburied for days, the family decided to leave their home at Walney and stay with Arthur Machen in Baltimore.[17]

The late morning skirmish on Stringfellow Road must have magnified Stonewall Jackson's earlier concerns about the safety of his command. Although the Yankee infantry had retreated and cavalry had come up in their place—meaning that this was unlikely to develop into a larger confrontation—Stonewall now could be certain that his position was no longer a secret from Union commanders. And if Pope knew about this Confederate flanking move he could be expected to follow up this small infantry and cavalry reconnaissance with a more forceful effort to block Jackson's advance. It was increasingly important now that Longstreet's Command join up with him soon, for Jackson had to expect that he would be engaged in some sort of larger battle with the Federals before the day was out. Unfortunately for Stonewall, by late morning the van of Longstreet's Command was only just beginning to turn east on the Little River Turnpike, still at least half-a-day's march behind them.

Colonel Johnson, responsible for securing the right flank of Jackson's Command as they passed Stringfellow Road, checked the position of his brigade to make sure they were prepared to meet any additional Yankee attacks. It would be his job to hold off an attack long enough for General Jackson to prepare the command for a larger battle, should it develop here. But as time passed and Federal cavalry alone remained in their front, Colonel Johnson could breathe a sigh of relief—probably the Yankees would not attack Jackson's left flank, at least not for now and probably not on Stringfellow Road. In any case, Colonel Johnson and Starke's 2nd Brigade would remain there for the time being, reinforced by Robertson's Cavalry Brigade which had just arrived from completing their reconnaissance of Walney Road.

At the same time that Beverly Robertson's men reached Jackson's Command near Stringfellow Road, Robertson rode off to find General Stuart. He had just finished scouting Walney Road with his brigade, as Jackson had ordered, and was wondering what his next orders might be. Finding Stuart, Robertson got the directions he needed and quickly rode off to rejoin his brigade. As General Robertson understood it, he was to remain at Chantilly to support Colonel Johnson and Starke's 2nd Brigade in their ongoing skirmish with the Federal cavalry. To Stuart's mind, however, Robertson had been given the important responsibility of ensuring the safety of Jackson's Command's entire right flank. Six months later, in his official report of Second Manassas and Ox Hill, Stuart would state for the record that Robertson had been given this job. Whatever actually transpired during the brief meeting of these two cavalry generals, the fact was that Robertson's Cavalry Brigade would remain at Chantilly for the rest of the day while Jackson's Command forged ahead east, ever deeper into the Union rear, without any cavalry whatsoever covering its exposed right flank.[18]

The optimism that had gripped General Pope at sunset the night before had completely vanished by dawn on September 1, replaced by the uncertainty that apparently had pervaded the general's mind late on August 30. Knowing that he had reinforced the positions at Jermantown and Fairfax Court House and sent out reconnaissance patrols to scout the army's right flank were little comfort to him as he once again tried to consider what the army should do now—attack or retreat. The report he had received at midnight certainly increased the chances that the Confederates were moving around his flank and that his army should begin a general retreat to Washington. If the Confederates cut off their route of retreat and trapped them here, the result might be nothing short of disaster. But he had promised General Halleck and Washington in his latest dispatch to renew the attack as soon as possible. To abruptly change his mind now would certainly risk his position as commander of the Army of Virginia and he simply didn't have time to re-create the political and personal groundwork to support retreat in the thorough way he had done yesterday before Halleck's message had arrived.

By midmorning General Pope's uncertainty had been replaced by the growing realization that retreat was the army's only realistic option. Although time was short, he might still be able to send a message to Halleck suggesting retreat and receive a response before being forced into action by the coming day's events. At 8:50 A.M., General Pope drafted a message to Henry Halleck that clearly was intended to prepare the commanding general and Washington for the eventual full retreat of the army. The dispatch began innocuously enough with an honest appraisal of the army's condition and a reiteration of the promise to attack soon:

All was quiet yesterday, and so far this morning. My men are resting; they need it much. Forage for our horses is being brought up. Our cavalry is completely broken down, so that there are not five horses to a company that can raise a trot. The consequence is that I am forced to keep considerable infantry along the roads in my rear to make them secure, and even then it is difficult to keep the enemy's cavalry off the roads. I shall attack again to-morrow if I can; the next day certainly.[19]

This done, Pope quickly turned to laying blame for failing to regain the offensive. Though he must now have believed an attack impossible, clearly Pope could not yet bring himself to admit so to Halleck. The cause of this failure, he would argue, lay at the doorstep of General McClellan and his supporters in the Army of the Potomac:

I think it my duty to call your attention to the unsoldierly and dangerous conduct of many brigade and some division commanders of the forces sent here from the peninsula. Every word, and act, and intention, is discouraging and calculated to break down the spirits of the men and produce disaster. Their constant talk, indulged in publicly and in promiscuous company, is that the army of the Potomac will not fight; that they are demoralized by the withdrawal from the peninsula &c. When such example is set by officers of high rank, the influence is very bad amongst those in subordinate stations. You have hardly an idea of the demoralization among officers of high rank in the Potomac army, arising in all instances from personal feeling in relation to the changes of commander-in-chief and others. These men are mere tools or parasites, but their example is producing, and must necessarily produce, very disastrous results. You should know these things, as you alone can stop it. Its source is beyond my reach, though its effects are very perceptible and very dangerous. I am endeavoring to do all I can, and will most assuredly put them where they shall fight or run away.[20]

Then the general got around to the real reason for writing this dispatch, laying the groundwork for the army's retreat:

My advice to you—I give it with freedom as I know you will not misunderstand it—is that, in view to any satisfactory results, you draw back this army to the entrenchment's in front of Washington, and set to work in that secure place to reorganize and rearrange it. You may avoid great disaster by doing so. I do not consider the matter except in a purely military light, and it is bad enough and grave enough to make some action very necessary. When there is no heart in their leaders, and every disposition to hang back, much cannot be expected of the men.

What Pope cast as advice in this message was not so much that as a plea for permission to retreat.[21]

Pope's assessment of the danger his army was in was certainly genuine—and accurate—but he knew as well as anyone in Centreville wearing shoulder straps that morning that it was not the McClellanites who were really to blame for the army's current sad state of affairs. Certainly they had greatly contributed to the men's crumbling morale and General McClellan himself had actively added to Pope's troubles. But the Army of Virginia's commanding general had only himself to blame. His own dashed morale and inability to make key command decisions had allowed this poor tactical situation to fester until it had reached the brink of disaster. As midday neared, it would be John Pope's task alone to somehow bring the bulk of the Union's eastern armies out of this mess intact.

6

DUEL AT JERMANTOWN

★————————————————————★

Late in the morning, around 11:00 A.M., two cavalrymen dismounted in front of the house serving as the Union army's field headquarters in Centreville. They demanded to immediately see General Pope, claiming they had vital information that he needed to hear directly. Once in the presence of General Pope the cavalrymen told their story. They had been out foraging north of Centreville during the morning and had spotted a large body of Confederate infantry, artillery, and cavalry moving east on the Little River Turnpike. They recounted clearly that they had been in the vicinity of Chantilly when they had found the Confederates.[1]

In an instant, all of General Pope's planning and scheming and all of General Halleck's orders sent from Washington during the past two days had been undone. The intelligence these men had brought meant Lee was not on his flank, as he had earlier feared, but was already in his rear. And Pope didn't need to look at a map to know the Confederate objective for this march—Jermantown and Fairfax Court House. If they reached Jermantown, the strong defensive position at Centreville would be irrelevant at best and dangerous at worst. But at the same time, retreating without Washington's approval would be career suicide. As worrisome as the cavalrymen's report was, John Pope was not yet ready to sacrifice his army career on the basis of one piece of intelligence.

Considering all the factors he had to weigh in making a decision—the new intelligence, the army's condition, and a myriad of political factors— Pope chose to play a dangerous game that, if successful, might permit him to preserve both the army and his career. He would mount a defense of Jermantown to stop Lee from interposing his force between the Union army and its capital. At the same time, he would prepare Henry Halleck and Washington for the increasingly inevitable retreat and hopefully coax Halleck into issuing the retreat order himself. The key variable in this plan was time; by choosing this path Pope was betting both that Lee would move slowly—attacking later rather than sooner—and that Halleck's reply would come quickly and contain the retreat order he wanted. Pope was inviting disaster if he proved to be wrong on either of these critical factors. But if he was right he might just be able to pull off this delicate balancing act.

Once General Pope knew clearly and decisively what he had to do, for the first time in at least several days he acted swiftly to make those decisions become reality. The first act of his plan consisted of sending news of the Confederate threat to Washington, with a view to prodding Halleck into ordering a general retreat of the army. This message read: "The enemy is deploying his forces on Little River pike, and preparing to advance by that road on Fairfax Court-House. This movement turns Centreville, and interposes between us and Washington, and will force me to attack his advance, which I shall do as soon as his movement is sufficiently developed. I have nothing like the force you undoubtedly suppose, and the fight will be necessarily desperate. I hope you will make all preparations to make a vigorous defense of the intrenchments around Washington." As in his earlier message suggesting retreat, this carefully worded dispatch avoids asking directly for a retreat order but uses facts in an effort to force Halleck's hand. Pope gambled that if he was guessing correctly about Lee's current location—he had reports confirming that at least some Confederate troops were still on the Bull Run battlefield—Halleck would have just enough time to respond before the situation got out of hand.[2]

Even as the rider carrying Pope's dispatch for Halleck was leaving army headquarters, the commanding general began preparing his army to stop Lee's advance, the second component of his risky plan. Pope significantly reinforced the weak line northwest of Jermantown, further boosting their guard force at the key intersection. At noon, he ordered Major General Irvin McDowell to march his entire III Corps of the Army of Virginia to Jermantown, and "assuming command of the two brigades now there, . . . immediately occupy Jermantown with your whole force, so as to cover the turnpike from this place to Alexandria. Jackson is reported advancing on Fairfax with twenty thousand men. Move quickly." Once in place, McDowell's command would give the Union a full corps with which to defend the Jermantown intersection. And placing General McDowell in charge of the troops there would not only put in place a senior officer to lead and coordinate the defense but would also give General Pope a single point of contact for his orders.[3]

Pope next turned to doing what he could to quickly bolster the existing Jermantown line until McDowell's corps could arrive. The only way to do this rapidly was to consolidate the few troops already posted in the

Fairfax Court House–Jermantown area in a forward position. At 12:30 P.M. Pope wrote Colonel Torbert, "Move your brigade at once to Jermantown and join it to the one under Colonel Hinks at that place. Major General Hooker is assigned to the command of the forces arriving at Fairfax Court House from Washington, together with those stationed at Jermantown."[4]

If the dispatch to Torbert demonstrates Pope's decision to finally act, it also proves that he had a less than perfect grasp of the army's disposition. Apparently General Pope had forgotten that Colonel Torbert and half his brigade were already at Jermantown and had been there for two days. After all, it had been one of the colonel's staff officers who had brought Pope word of the Confederate shelling of the army's train late the night before. So while Pope's order gave Torbert the authority to recall the other half of his command from Alexandria, the order was largely moot and in reality did less than the general may have believed it would to bolster the Union's Jermantown position.

To further reinforce Union control of the Jermantown position, Pope ordered General Hooker to leave his division and take command of the Jermantown–Fairfax area. At 1:00 P.M. General Pope sent a communication to Hooker telling him to ". . . at once proceed to Jermantown, assume command of the troops at Fairfax Court-House, together with the brigades now under the command of Colonels Torbert and Hinks." By taking this step Pope provided a senior commander who could oversee placement of the arriving troops and take command until General McDowell could arrive. And Major General Hooker also would have the rank and authority to pull other troops into any fight that might appear at Jermantown.[5]

If General Pope finally understood that a threat existed on his right, he apparently did not appreciate the full extent of the threat or that time was beginning to turn against him as the day wore on. Pope summoned Major General Samuel P. Heintzelman and Major General Edwin Sumner to his headquarters to inform them of their role in reinforcing the Jermantown line and stopping Lee's advance. As General Heintzelman remembered, "On the 1st of September, at 1 P.M. I learned from General Pope that the enemy was threatening our rear, and he detached General Hooker from his division to take command of some troops near Jermantown to hold the enemy in check, advancing on the Little River turnpike. General Sumner and I were ordered to march at daylight the next morning across the Little River turnpike in the direction of Chantilly to aid in this movement." That General Pope would permit the Army of the Potomac's II and III Corps—units that would be vital in stopping Lee's advance—to remain undeployed for another 12 hours indicates just how poor a grasp Pope had of the tactical situation that was evolving around him at an ever more rapid pace.[6]

Having primed Washington for a retreat order and prepared for the defense of the Jermantown line, John Pope now turned to the third component of his defense and retreat plan—guarding against a Confederate flanking attack west of Jermantown. While Jermantown still was the most obvious place for Lee to insert his force between Pope's army and Washington, another avenue of approach existed that could not be ignored. Two and a half miles west of Jermantown sat a road running north-south from the Little River Turnpike to the Warrenton Pike, a portion of the Ox Road, which Lee might easily use to flank the Jermantown position and then turn west and attack Centreville. To prevent this from happening, Pope determined to send a blocking force up Ox Road as far as the Little River Turnpike and selected for the task the two small divisions of Reno's IX Corps. Calling back in the two cavalrymen who had brought the late morning news of Lee's turning move, Pope directed them to find General Reno, pass on his orders, and then personally lead the general and his IX Corps to Ox Road.[7]

Riding quickly to the IX Corps' field headquarters south of Centreville, the two troopers asked for General Reno, indicating that they had an urgent message from General Pope himself. The staff officers they met informed them, however, that General Reno was ill and indisposed but they could talk to General Isaac Stevens instead. Reno's unexpected illness made General Stevens, now the only IX Corps division commander on the field, the acting corps commander.

They found General Stevens not at his headquarters tent but rather in the bivouac of his division's artillery. Stevens had been worried all morning about the condition of his command and Lieutenant Benjamin remembered that when Stevens arrived for the inspection of his battery Benjamin "soon saw that he [Stevens] felt very blue, that he felt the effect of the defeat very keenly, and feared the effect on the men." His gloom certainly was made worse by the reports of his division's condition offered by his staff late that morning. General Stevens had directed his son and adjutant, Captain Hazard Stevens, to count the stacks of muskets remaining; Hazard reported finding only 2,012, meaning that Stevens's division had been roughly halved since arriving from the Carolinas only six weeks before.[8]

Despite his concerns, the opportunity to write a short letter to his wife presented itself around noon and must have improved Stevens's mood somewhat. Lieutenant Benjamin recalled that he had offered to get a letter through for him: "Well, general, you write, and I will send it by some Christian or Sanitary man. We have just sent some letters, and I will have a man watch the turnpike until someone will take it." Benjamin remembered, years later, that "[h]e seemed much pleased with this. I brought him the envelope, etc. And he wrote on a book, sitting on the ground."[9]

When the two cavalrymen dispatched by General Pope found him around 1:00, General Stevens was in the middle of writing his letter home. Lieutenant Benjamin recalled, "[b]efore [the general] had finished, the order came to move. He closed it hastily, after giving some orders, gave it to me, and went to his headquarters. The letter was given to a gentleman going to Washington with a wounded man."[10]

Stevens needed no time to digest the orders before deciding what to do. Upon returning to his headquarters he quickly dispatched aides to alert the IX Corps' brigade commanders to have their men ready to move immediately and directed his staff similarly to prepare for the march. Within minutes of receiving orders to move, the laughter and relaxed chatter of the IX Corps campground was replaced by the clank of tinware being secured, shouted orders to fall in, and muskets being unstacked. Despite the short notice, most men in the division probably grumbled little about having to pack up their gear, for few had had enough time there to turn their bivouac spot into the soldier's version of home. Around 2:00 General Stevens and his division were underway, moving north toward Centreville before turning east onto the Warrenton Pike. After going one mile, however, they halted to wait for artillery under the command of Lieutenant Benjamin—two guns from Battery E of the 2nd U.S. Artillery and two guns from the 8th Massachusetts Light Artillery—and Ferrero's 2nd Brigade of Reno's 2nd Division to join them.

Ferrero's brigade, consisting of the 21st Massachusetts, the 51st New York, and the 51st Pennsylvania, had already earned a reputation as seasoned fighters with a bit of a wild streak. In a little over two weeks hence Ferrero's men would earn their fame by charging through a hail of Rebel shot and shell to establish a foothold on the western side of a bridge across Antietam Creek, all for the promise of two barrels of whiskey. But for now Ferrero's brigade compliantly fell in line behind Stevens's brigade and by 2:30 the bulk of the IX Corps was on its way east to find the Rebels.

At army headquarters, John Pope was becoming increasingly worried as to whether he could continue the game he had begun to play, risking the army's safety to preserve his career. He had set in motion a defense of Jermantown but the message from Halleck he longed for was still not forthcoming. A measure of just how worried the commanding general had become is reflected in his decision to visit General Porter for advice—a man Pope considered his most troublesome corps commander and a leader of the McClellanite cabal within his ranks. After entering Porter's tent at about 2:30 P.M., General Pope began by explaining that the army's current and increasingly dangerous position was "not due to him, that he had been pushed to the front against his advice and been compelled to conduct a campaign contrary to his views—by order of Washington." He apologized that "he now held the army at Centreville by order from Washington." Following this litany of excuses, Pope meekly asked Porter what he believed to be the best course to pursue.[11]

Porter reiterated what he had told Pope that morning, flatly stating that the army should withdraw. Porter lectured his commander that "he was responsible for the safety of the army and the results of its operations." Porter continued, telling Pope "he should not permit the government to control his movements—he being on the ground and knowing what was proper & they distant & uninformed." Changing his tone somewhat, Porter advised that "he alone should not be consulted—that the other generals were entitled to his confidence and that he had a right to demand their advice." General Porter concluded by promising Pope that these other generals would offer their advice "freely & honestly." Pope, stymied in what clearly was an effort to secure approval from Porter and the McClellanites for his "defend and wait strategy," sullenly returned to his headquarters without taking any of Porter's proffered advice.[12]

After the meeting with Porter, John Pope swung back into the gloom and uncertainty in which he had started the day. He waited frantically for some word from Washington to absolve him of responsibility for whatever happened to the army in the coming hours. Making matters worse, he apparently now realized that the situation on his right flank was more serious than he had earlier believed. The waiting game he was playing simply was growing more dangerous by the minute and Lee was about to take complete control of the situation. In the meantime, Pope's waffling leadership was becoming ever more obvious to his corps commanders. General Heintzelman hinted at this indecision in his official report: "I had scarcely returned to my headquarters [from being ordered to wait until daylight to move] and given the necessary orders before I received notice from the commanding general that the enemy was about to attack us, and to get my corps under arms. I was next sent for to general headquarters, and at 3:30 P.M. ordered to fall back on the road to Fairfax Court-House 2 1/2 miles and face to the left, to aid General Reno in driving back the enemy. . . ."[13]

By ordering Heintzelman's III Corps to immediately move east from Centreville and support the IX Corps, Pope was at least providing Stevens's small command with much needed reinforcements. But Pope never bothered to send word to Generals Reno or Stevens that he had assigned Heintzelman this duty, leaving General Stevens marching east to meet the Rebels without knowing if he had support or, if he did, whom to turn to for reinforcement. Compounding the confusion, it is not clear if General Heintzelman ever notified his own division commanders why the III Corps was leaving Centreville or who they were going to support. Clearly, control of the unfolding drama that September 1 was slipping away from the Union's ranking generals.

Unfortunately, General Pope was setting the tone for his subordinates and his weak leadership was having far-reaching effects, his personal confusion extending well down into the ranks. Typical of this confusion was the experience of the 21st and 23rd New York. Late on August 31, they had been ordered to escort part of the wagon train to Fairfax Court House and remained there for the night. Early on September 1, they started for Centreville to rejoin their brigade but soon returned to Fairfax after meeting the rest of Patrick's brigade, who had instead been ordered to join the 21st and 23rd New York at Fairfax. The reunited brigade now returned to the very ground the two regiments had left a few hours before. Around 1:00 P.M. General Patrick received orders to rejoin the division and within the hour Patrick's men were once more underway, returning to Centreville. But when they had covered about half the distance to Centreville, the brigade ran into General Hooker, who had left Centreville with his staff at 1:30. Hooker stopped Patrick's brigade in their tracks and asked General Patrick where he was going and under whose authority. Citing General Pope's directive to collect troops for the Jermantown defense, Hooker countermanded Patrick's orders and diverted the brigade to follow him. Having no choice in the matter, the 21st New York and the rest of Patrick's brigade once more changed direction and headed for Jermantown.[14]

General Hooker and his staff led Patrick's brigade into Jermantown around 3:00 P.M. After a short conversation with Colonels Torbert and Hinks, Hooker set to work preparing Jermantown for the Confederate attack Pope had warned him about. The new commander of the Jermantown position first directed the 1st Rhode Island Cavalry—another of the units he had collected on the way from Centreville—to probe west up the Little River Turnpike in search of Lee's men. As the Rhode Island cavalrymen trotted out of the ruined hamlet, the first of

McDowell's III Corps units, sent in compliance with Pope's noon order, arrived from the west. Hooker quickly rushed these men of Rickett's 2nd Division, four brigades strong, into a defensive line northwest of the Jermantown intersection. At nearly the same time, the men of Patrick's brigade were filing into position alongside Rickett's men. As they did so, the weary men of Torbert's command moved to the rear of Jermantown. They would now act as the reserve for Rickett's and Patrick's fresh troops and get a well-deserved rest.[15]

As Hooker and Patrick's brigade were marching into Jermantown, the first of Jackson's skirmishers, men of the Stonewall Brigade, were reaching Ox Hill. The fighting on Stringfellow Road earlier in the morning had given Stonewall good reason to be ever more concerned about the safety of his command. The Yankees he had faced there were certainly not alone and, with General Pope apparently aware of their flanking march, there probably were even more Federal troops on the way. Adding to this concern was his worry about the whereabouts of General Longstreet and his command. Until the entire Southern army was united, Stonewall Jackson had good reason to avoid a battle. So for now he would choose a deliberate, cautious pace as they neared their objective at Jermantown. This deliberate pace was noticeable to nearly everyone, despite the reduced speed the command had adopted since leaving the Manassas field. A Georgia private remembered Jackson's Command moving at "a very slow advance with skirmishers out 200 yards to the right." Clearly their commander anticipated some sort of action.

The pace of Jackson's Command was slowed even more by the rapidly worsening weather. As the afternoon of September 1 wore on, the bright, cheerful morning yielded to a drenching, steady rain, soaking everyone in the two armies and making the already slow roads nearly impassable. And as the wind grew wilder, everyone knew a real storm was brewing to their west.

Upon reaching Ox Hill though, General Jackson must have worried less about the weather than about the Federals, who were now only one and a half miles to his east. Sending for Fitzhugh Lee, Jackson directed the cavalry general to probe east toward Jermantown with his command to find out exactly where the Federals were and how many of them were facing him. Until Lee's cavalry reconnaissance provided some idea of what was facing him, Jackson would have to be content to wait and rest his weary troops.

Riding picket at the front of Lee's column, the men of the 5th Virginia Cavalry rode for some time without great concern. They were veterans now and used to having to find the Federals for the infantry to fight. Riding beside the 5th's commander, Colonel Thomas Rosser, was Heros Von Borcke, whom General Stuart had sent to assist with the reconnaissance. "We were discussing our late fights and adventures," remembered Stuart's chief of staff, "when suddenly the few men who formed our extreme advance and were riding a few rods ahead of us, came back at full gallop, and at the same moment a rattling volley from the thick pinewoods which lined the turnpike on either side sent a shower of balls over our heads." Without knowing it, Colonel Rosser and his men had found Hooker's cavalry pickets.

The 1st Rhode Island Cavalry had nearly reached Difficult Run, not even a mile from Jermantown, when they spotted Lee's column of horsemen. The Rhode Islanders dismounted and sent one of their number racing back to General Hooker with word of their discovery. Once in position, they fired on the unsuspecting Confederates hoping to establish the battle line far from Hooker's main position and to give the infantry in their rear time to come up.[16]

Though the Yankee's fire was having little effect, Colonel Rosser knew his command was unprepared to handle this threat alone. Ordering his 5th Virginia Cavalry to wheel about, Rosser and his men rode quickly to the rear. Fitzhugh Lee, though, was unwilling to give up a fight this quickly and directed a dismounted line of battle to form on a low ridge overlooking Difficult Run. In the midst of this line Lee put two guns of Stuart's Horse Artillery, serving as an anchor to the Confederate line. Once in position, Lee's men and cannons returned the Rhode Islander's fire in spades.[17]

The Federal cavalrymen could do little in the face of this fire but hold their ground and look to the rear for the infantry fire. One Rhode Islander recalled, "[T]he enemy sharply assailed us with artillery . . . Here again the metallic shower poured down furiously upon us. It seems that we were usually the favorite command for drawing the enemy's fire, and we always drew it strong." After what seemed to the men of the 1st Rhode Island like a very long time, their infantry support finally appeared, charging up the road to their rescue, and the 1st Rhode Island Cavalry retired.

Pushing past the retreating cavalrymen was Duryee's 1st Rhode Island Brigade from Rickett's division. They rushed in a column formation up the turnpike at the double-quick until they reached a gentle rise in the ground, a perfect spot on which to set up a defense. While the brigade was busy closing up its column and restoring order from their rapid forced march, a skirmish line was sent forward to establish Duryee's battle position.

The brigade's skirmishers, men from the 97th New York under the

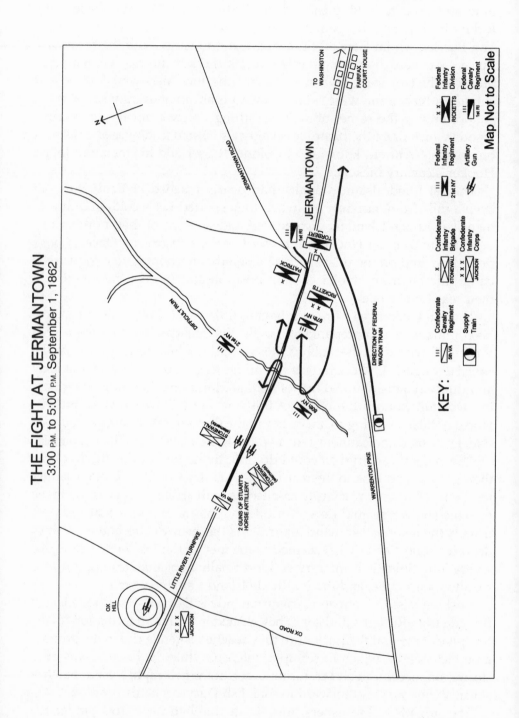

THE FIGHT AT JERMANTOWN
3:00 P.M. to 5:00 P.M. September 1, 1862

KEY:

command of Captain Eggleston, stepped out from the line and quickly deployed on the left of the turnpike into their staggered skirmish formation. At Captain Eggleston's order, they advanced as one toward the woodline in their front, beyond which they all knew the Confederate host lurked. Reaching the edge of this woods, Captain Eggleston sized up the terrain in his front—an open field that gently sloped down for 300 yards or so until it began rising again and stopping at a thick woods. Unfortunately for Captain Eggelston and his men of the 97th, the thick woods which the enemy held commanded not only the field that separated the two forces, but the ground on which they now stood as well.[18]

After a few minutes, Confederate skirmishers appeared scattered among the trees in the woodline on the opposite ridge. Had the captain known that these skirmishers were not cavalry, but infantry working ahead of the Stonewall Brigade, he certainly would have been even more concerned than he was. One veteran of the 97th remembered that soon "the enemy opened from the opposite bluffs and his shells passed over, exploding in the woods to the rear." Captain Eggleston had done his job, finding the enemy and establishing the ground of the fight. And with that task complete, the captain and his skirmishers were recalled to join the rest of the 97th New York Regiment and Duryee's brigade.[19]

General Hooker, who had ridden forward with his staff to observe the fighting himself, saw the strong Confederate position in his front and immediately sent a staff officer back to Jermantown with orders for General Patrick to send forward one of his best regiments. Patrick selected the 80th New York Infantry, telling them, "General Hooker has sent an order for one of my best regiments to report to him at once, on the Little River Turnpike, and I am going to send you." The 80th was a good choice, for they had gained a reputation as a stubborn, hardfighting lot, whose demeanor was summed up by their steadfast refusal to adopt their state-assigned designator—the 80th New York—preferring instead to use their prewar moniker, the "20th New York State Militia."[20]

The 80th, commanded by Colonel Theodore Gates, quickly formed up and marched the mile or so to General Hooker in short order. Hooker directed Colonel Gates to move his regiment into the woods just vacated by the 97th New York's skirmishers and "hold it at all cost!" The colonel did not immediately reply and instead cast a questioning glance at his battle-depleted force and then back to General Hooker. Without a word, Hooker knew what Colonel Gates was thinking and quickly shot back, "Oh, I will support you; I will support you." And with that, Colonel Gates rushed back to his command and ordered it forward.

Gates recalled, "The regiment moved as fast as possible through the woods, and approaching the farther side, found the enemy's skirmishers advancing rapidly, and within 150 yards of the woods, the cover of which they wished to gain." The colonel realized that if he did not act quickly, the oncoming Southern skirmish line would soon overrun his position. Somehow he would have to make the enemy believe they faced a larger force than the 80th. In an instant an idea came to him. He ordered his entire regiment to deploy as skirmishers along the edge of the woods, a move he probably hoped would give the Confederates either the impression that they faced the skirmish line of a much larger force or that the 80th itself was a large and formidable body of troops. As the Confederate skirmishers pushed ever closer to the 80th's tenuous position, Gates ordered his men to open fire. Gates's trick apparently worked. "[T]hey opened fire at once on the approaching enemy," he recalled, "and compelled them to fall back. But taking advantage of the inequalities of the ground, and seeking cover wherever they could, they kept up a steady fire . . ."[21]

Although his dismounted force had stalled, Fitzhugh Lee was hardly finished yet. He next ordered one of the artillery pieces deployed on the ridge to move up closer to the enemy and support the Southern skirmish line. As quickly as it could be limbered up, the gun and its cavalry escort were sent racing across the open field toward the skirmishers. Once in the left of the line, the piece was unlimbered as fast as its crew could move and began pouring forth case shot into the enemy ranks in the woodline beyond.

Colonel Gates watched the Confederate field piece appear in his front and immediately realized that his men of the 80th New York could do nothing about it in their present location. The shells were already exacting a toll on the 80th, a price he knew it could not long afford to pay. Volley fire from his infantry line might eventually kill some of the gunners but their fire would certainly do greater damage to his thinned ranks in a fraction of the time. Glancing to his right, Colonel Gates noticed a cornfield full of tall, thick stalks, which lay across the turnpike and perpendicular to the Rebel gun. In an instant he ordered a squad of his best marksmen hustling off into the corn. Their orders were simple—silence that gun by killing its crew. Only a few minutes after they had disappeared into the field, well-placed shots began to pour forth from the tall corn.

Lee's gunners and their cavalry escort lost one man after another to the Yankee sharpshooters and immediately knew they could remain in this exposed position no longer. Within minutes the gun and its crew were beating a hasty retreat to the safety of the woodline to their west.

Seeing his skirmisher's artillery support running for the rear, Fitzhugh Lee ordered his entire line of artillery on the ridge to open on the Yankees in the woods. "[T]he enemy opened upon the regiment with shot and shell from their guns on top of the hill," observed Colonel Gates, "and thoroughly shelled the woods." But the extreme range at which the gunners were required to fire and the widely scattered target they were firing at caused most of their shells to fall harmlessly around Hooker's men.[22]

Meanwhile, to the rear of Colonel Gates and the 80th New York, General Hooker was busy bolstering his main position in preparation for the Confederate attack he believed certain. Hooker ordered the 21st New York to deploy abreast Gates's line on their right. Torbert's brigade—now rested, fed, and restocked with fresh ammunition—was moved forward nearly to its former position on the turnpike to provide a second line of defense and some much needed depth to Hooker's position. To the rear of this position, Beardsley's cavalry brigade—including the 6th Ohio, 9th New York, and two companies of the 1st Connecticut Cavalry Regiment—worked to keep the Warrenton Pike open to Union wagons and units moving through Jermantown to the rear and safety. Around 4:00 P.M., six regiments of Brigadier General Darius Couch's 1st Division of the IV Corps were moved up from Fairfax Court House, as was Sedgwick's 2nd Division of the II Corps. These troops would finally give the Union a fighting chance to meet Jackson's attack on Jermantown.

But Jackson's much anticipated grand assault on Jermantown didn't come. The fighting near Difficult Run continued throughout the late afternoon at a moderate though steady pace. Colonel Gates recalled, "whenever they tried to advance . . . the fire from the woods was as vigorous as ever; and about five o'clock they fell back out of range, and their artillery ceased." Fortunately for General Hooker, the 80th New York, and the other Union regiments hastily cobbled into a defensive line at Jermantown, Stonewall Jackson found he had more pressing issues to attend to late that day than attacking Jermantown, Virginia.[23]

Knowing his command's position relative to the main Federal line must have forced Stonewall Jackson to consider how to react if his flanks were attacked. The fight at Jermantown was not going well by 4:00; clearly the Federals were well aware of his flanking move and had reinforced their hold of the Jermantown crossroads. The earlier fighting on Stringfellow Road meant that Pope was probing his right flank, and it would only be a matter of time before another such probe was launched, probably up the Ox Road. He had not stolen a march on Pope's army and his plan to carry out General Lee's directive was dashed. And yet, he had turned worse situations to victory in the Shenandoah Valley; the day may yet be his if he were skillful enough in reading the Yankees. Even so, he was in an exposed position in the enemy's rear and the only reinforcements he might have—Longstreet's Command—were still not in view. And though General Lee was now ensconced in a farmhouse on the Little River Turnpike not far from Ox Hill, he would take no direct role in the impending fight. For whatever reason, Stonewall Jackson was on his own in this one and he would have to be very careful lest the situation turn suddenly and violently against him.

Without hesitating, Stonewall issued the orders to quickly move his entire command into position to meet this new threat. His first task was to ensure that his right flank was securely protected while the rest of the command moved into place. This would require a body of troops large enough to be able to at least blunt any Union attack that might come on the right but one that could, at the same time, move quickly. To provide this holding force, General Jackson ordered A. P. Hill to send forward Branch's Brigade and Field's Brigade, commanded by Colonel James Brockenbrough.[24]

Once the men were in their battle lines and a strong skirmish line deployed across their front, the two Confederate brigades stepped from the roadway of the turnpike and swept across the open field to their front, moving southeast. They had not gone half a mile before they encountered a thick line of woods. Into the woods they plunged, pressing on ahead as quickly as they could given that each tree and fallen log challenged their ability to retain an orderly brigade battle line. Soon enough they reached the southern end of this patch of woods and found an open field to their front, half of which was planted in tall, stiff corn, seemingly standing their own small picket post, while the other half apparently was empty and fallow. Pushing skirmishers into the corn, while the main line of Branch's and Field's Brigades stopped at the woodline, here they would wait for the Yankees.[25]

7

STEVENS'S BATTLE

★————————————————★

It was just after 3:00 P.M. when the two cavalrymen leading General Stevens and the IX Corps knew they had come to one of those moments in life when a personal victory was about to become a crushing defeat. They had stumbled upon a string of good luck early in the day by finding the huge Rebel force where no one expected it to be. General Pope had been cognizant of the importance of this intelligence—and their personal roles in bringing it to him—and personally gave them the task of leading the IX Corps to the Little River Turnpike in search of Lee's army. They had found General Stevens and spent the last few hours at the center stage of this unfolding drama. But now, at the very head of the IX Corps' column and guiding its every move, they were suddenly unsure just where to turn to reach the turnpike. If they went as far as Jermantown they would have gone too far and the entire column would have to double back, in an instant undoing all the good they had done so far this otherwise dreary day.

The question of just where to turn must have troubled the two cavalrymen until they reached a small dirt road. This road veered sharply to the left just east of where the Warrenton Pike crosses Little Rocky Run and disappeared from view into the woods. Though this was certainly not the road they had followed to the Little River Turnpike that morning, they must have considered that because it traveled in the right direction they would almost certainly end up at the turnpike anyway. They led Stevens's column north here. Anticipating that trouble might not be far away, Stevens detached Ferrero's brigade, telling the colonel to remain on the Warrenton Pike until he and his men might be needed. Moments later, General Stevens and his division once more were underway behind their cavalry guides, turning left onto the dirt road.[1]

At first the small road seemed like the right choice, being a clear, wide path moving steadily northward. But after a few hundred yards—too far to turn back easily—the road narrowed, clearly becoming little more than a farmer's cart path. Stevens's regimental commanders could easily adjust to the change though, telling the column to undouble on the march. The order would move the men from a four-abreast line to only two, halving its width and neatly fitting the road's new dimensions. But soon the road began to twist and turn, passing through thick woods and nondescript fields, thoroughly confusing both General Stevens and his cavalry guides as to the nature of their direction. In the midst of this confusion no one could tell for certain whether they were moving northward toward the turnpike anymore.

Stevens's men for the most part were blissfully ignorant of the purpose of their march. Lieutenant George Parker of the 21st Massachusetts recalled that "not a man in the regiment had the remotest idea of a fight." Many of Stevens's IX Corps boys talked lightheartedly as they marched along the muddy dirt road, certain they were heading generally east, toward Washington and safety. Only a few of them instinctively felt they were headed for a fight, despite the inclement weather and the seemingly good signs their comrades talked of so certainly.[2]

While Stevens's command was wandering along the cart path in search of the Confederates, Heintzelman's III Corps was still in Centreville, forming up to begin their march east. Unlike Stevens's men, many of Heintzelman's veterans sensed their movement's true purpose. "We were ordered into line," wrote Sergeant Daniel Fletcher of the 40th New York's Company H, "[e]veryone was given the usual rounds and the cap box filled. We expected some sort of brush with the enemy, but did not expect much of a fight." When Sergeant Fletcher and his fellow III Corps veterans finally left Centreville it was nearly 4:00 P.M. Kearny's 1st Division was at the van of the column, followed by Hooker's 2nd Division. With General Hooker away commanding the Jermantown position Brigadier General Cuvier Grover, who normally headed Hooker's 1st Brigade, was temporarily in charge of the division.[3]

Heintzelman's men marched eastward at the common time and there appeared to be no sense of urgency to their redeployment, despite the initial feeling in the ranks. The pace of the march was such that Sergeant Fletcher and his comrades engaged in some sightseeing. "As we passed along the road," he recalled, "we could see nice carriages broken in pieces by the rebels, they belonged to people in Washington, who had come to see the fight and were returning." Overhead, the weather was turning sour again and many of the men took this as a sign that whatever awaited them on this march, it was unlikely to be a fight of any consequence.[4]

Two miles or so to the east of Heintzelman's troops, Isaac Stevens's men were still wandering through the thick woods. The muddy cart path was being turned into a soupy quagmire by the compressed column, so that the unfortunate men at the rear of the formation had to step carefully through the mud to avoid losing their shoes in the deepening muck. To make matters worse, when the head of the column managed to find a field, the path nearly disappeared in a dense tangle of thorny overgrowth. But still onward they marched, each man following another and all of them still following the cavalry guides.

Around 4:00 P.M. the head of the column finally emerged from the heavy woods into a series of fields where they could regain their orientation. The sight that greeted those at the head of Stevens's division was welcome indeed. "[T]he column was crossing a tract of high, open country, which sloped down gently in front to a marshy hollow covered with shrubs and partially timbered," noted the 79th New York's Private William Todd. "Beyond it open fields appeared again, and beyond them dense woods." Within moments, though, the Scotsmen's sense of relief at leaving the dense woods behind them would be shattered.[5]

General Stevens was among the first to notice them—gray and brown-clad men, the closest of whom comprised only a handful on the south side of the railroad cut. These scattered men most likely were guarding the farthest extent of a stronger Southern position. Beyond them, north of the cut, was another, more densely populated line, deployed in a standard skirmish order near the base of the opposing slope. A second look revealed even more enemy skirmishers spread out here and there over the slope. And a cursory glance at the far woodline showed nearly a solid line of them, perhaps a brigade or more in all. The IX Corps' two cavalry guides could now rest a little easier for they had successfully led General Stevens to the Rebels. For Stevens and his IX Corps boys, though, the work was only beginning.[6]

Almost instantly Stevens halted his column and surveyed the scene that lay before him. He stood on a low ridge that ran eastward for several hundred yards and ended near a farmhouse on his right, while on the left the ridge disappeared into the woods they had just come through. In front of the general the ridge dropped sharply away to a marshy patch of ground in the center of which was a small run swollen from the recent rain, full but clearly not a major obstacle to his men. Beyond the run lay the bed of an unfinished railroad line, a continuation of the very same one that so many of his fellow Union men had died trying to breach two days before. On the left-hand side of the clearing the railroad line took the form of a low ridge that sloped gradually down to the center of the open field.

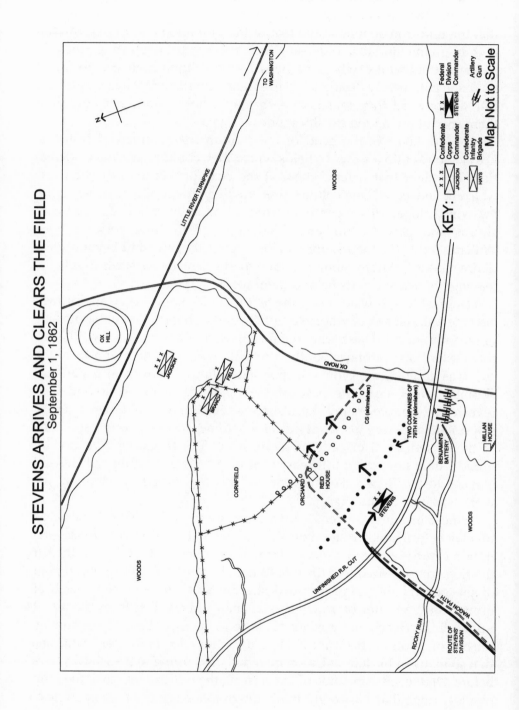

STEVENS ARRIVES AND CLEARS THE FIELD
September 1, 1862

The line continued across the flat center of the field and, on the right-hand side of the field, gradually sloped down into a shallow cut. In all, the rail line would be an obstacle, though not a major one. Beyond the railroad line was a flat, open field, beyond which another field rose along an even more gradual slope to a thick stand of trees. Gazing at these trees some sky could be seen, suggesting it was perched on another ridge. Looking at the crest of the opposite ridge—along which he already could see Confederate troops forming—the woodline ran westward and appeared to undulate before turning south along the edge of a cornfield. In short, the terrain on which he must now consider fighting was almost nearly a mirror image of itself looking north or south.

Stevens's impression of the field's symmetry was broken, however, by the presence of a small farmhouse positioned nearly in its center, behind which stood a modest orchard. The road on which the general and his men had arrived here continued northward to the house then turned and crossed the eastern half of the field until it intersected with the Ox Road. Beyond the house and running nearly due north—dividing the field almost equally in two—was a split rail "worm" fence of the type general- ly favored by farmers in Virginia. The western half of the fenced field was planted in corn, which being late summer was tall and still flush with unpicked ripe ears, and the western edge of the cornfield bordered a thick forest. The eastern half of the field was covered in grass, intended either for livestock to graze in or to remain fallow for the season. This grassy field bordered a wide, well-traveled road—certainly the Ox Road which they had originally been searching for—that followed on north to another main road, likely the Little River Turnpike.

The Rebels in his front were certainly Stonewall Jackson's men that General Pope had ordered him to find. And Stevens knew that if this was Ox Road, Jackson was already within striking distance of Jermantown. Regardless of the terrain he now surveyed, he would have to fight here if Jackson was to be diverted long enough for McDowell's III Corps to rein- force the Jermantown position. Stevens quickly decided that he would have to attack—rather than wait for reinforcements—for nothing less than a quick assault would draw the Confederates attention away from Jermantown. Waiting to act, after having been spotted by the Rebel skir- mish line, also risked letting Jackson seize the initiative and attack him in force, something his small corps was certainly unready to repel.[7]

It took only a few minutes for General Stevens to formulate his attack plan. Stevens could see across the open fields to the opposite woodline and the main body of the Confederate enemy posted there. Infantry troops, at least a brigade and maybe as much as a division, were in those woods. There certainly were more troops than these nearby, but it was clear that the best way to fight what he could see in his front was to rapidly strike their left flank. Other options for an assault were simply too costly to consider. An attack on their right flank would mean exposing his own flank to enemy fire just to reach their objective, while a frontal assault on the Rebel's left flank would mean taking his attacking division rapidly across the open ground in their front, pushing them into the woods on the enemy's left, and striking that flank before they could reinforce their position.

With only two divisions at his disposal, he would use his own 1st Division to stage the main attack and hold Reno's 2nd Division in reserve. Reaching the Confederate line would be difficult, requiring his division to advance through the open field while under fire nearly the entire time. He knew in an instant that the most suitable formation for reaching the Confederate line was something called a "column of brigades." This called for each of the three brigades to deploy in a column, the first brigade in front, followed by the second and third brigades respectively. Deployed so, the division would present the smallest possible front for the enemy to fire at and could march rapidly to the point of attack. Once there, they could very quickly swing into a division battle front, maximizing the firepower an infantry division could pour into an enemy. His impromptu personal planning session concluded, General Stevens shared his plans with his staff to prepare for the attack.[8]

The line of Federals appeared quite suddenly from the wooded ridge in the Confederates' front. The Southern soldiers on the picket line immediately snapped into their own preferred stance, either kneeling or crouching, and readied their weapons for action. Back in the main line of the two brigades the men were mentally and physically readying themselves for battle, too. Whatever these Yankees were doing there, it meant that their afternoon had just taken a turn for the worse.

At once, the Confederate skirmish line was called to attention and ordered forward. They pressed deeper into the cornfield, men largely dodging the tall, green obstacles rather than crushing them in their path. They moved gradually down the slope and out of view of most of the rest of their respective brigades in the woods to their rear. The purpose of their advance, if anyone in the line knew it, was to take and hold the ground before the Yankees did; the objective was the farm only a short distance ahead at the base of the slope.[9]

Stevens moved swiftly to prepare for his general advance. Before any of his attack plans could be realized, he would have to quickly seize the unfinished railroad line before the Rebels did and clear that skirmish line from the center of the field. While its geography here simply wouldn't afford him the luxury of using the position as a defensive work—as Jackson had last Friday—he could not let Jackson have the position again. He had seen firsthand how hard it was to break and, in any case, it would impede his movement toward the main Confederate line in the woods to the north. Failing to clear the Rebel skirmishers, likewise, could slow not only the pace but the determination of his main attack as well. Detaching two companies of the 79th New York and placing them under the command of his son and adjutant, Captain Hazard Stevens, the general turned to deploying his main column for action.[10]

Captain Stevens quickly conferred with his two company commanders, Captains W. T. Lusk and Robert Ives, and deployed his line for battle. Breaking from the rest of the regiment, the two companies—fewer than 150 men—looked small in the midst of the wide field that lay before them. But within moments after deploying as skirmishers—Captain Ives's command on the left and Captain Lusk's men on the right—the two small companies filled nearly the width of the entire field. After loading their rifles, Captain Stevens barked from his horse, "At the double-quick, forward, march!" and the two companies trotted steadily forward into action.

Down the slope and through the muddy banks of Rocky Run the two companies flew. Now well within range, Captain Stevens ordered his command to fire a volley that was the opening shot of a fight that the men would soon come to know as the battle of Chantilly. Hazard was well satisfied with the effect of his skirmishers' fire, for he would later record that "exchanging a sharp fire with the opposing line and driving it back . . . [we] pushed on after the rebel skirmishers into the farther fields." The Confederate pickets returned fire but, outnumbered and outgunned, were simply overwhelmed by the surging Federal skirmish line. Offering only a few token shots at their attackers, they quickly skedaddled over the railroad line to temporary safety. Their job, after all, was merely to provide warning to the main line of an enemy attack and the time had now come to do just that in person.[11]

Up to the railroad line Captain Stevens's skirmishers pressed. Once past the railroad embankment the Scotsmen dressed their lines momentarily and advanced once again for the Southern skirmish line. This time, though, they moved with deliberation, for the next line of Rebels facing them was stronger and would not yield so easily. Advancing at the common time, they encountered the retreating pickets once again, some of whom occasionally stopped to fire as targets appeared before them. One such target was Captain Stevens himself. "I rode up the railroad embankment to observe," recalled Hazard, "and while standing there saw a rebel soldier at some distance helping a wounded comrade off the field, with one arm around his waist. Seeing a mounted officer on the embankment, he took his arm from the comrade's support, deliberately aimed his piece, and fired." Hazard knew he was the target but could do nothing before the Rebel's gunshot rang out. ". . . [A]t that instant, the bullet passed through the rim of my hat, inflicting a sharp rap on the head, which made me tingle and ache for some time." Seeing their commander come under fire, Hazard's Highlanders responded, but to no avail, "[t]wenty muskets were fired at him in return, without effect, and with perfect deliberation he shifted his musket to his left hand, clasped his right arm again around his comrade's waist and helped him slowly back until they disappeared in a field of corn behind them."[12]

The main Rebel skirmish line, like their pickets, was overwhelmed by the sudden appearance of the Union line and began almost at once slowly falling back into the corn and toward their main position on the wooded crest behind them. Unlike their pickets, though, the Southern skirmishers planned to stay and fight. Rather than fully retreating they consolidated their position, using the thick folds of the dense cornfield for cover. As soon as the Union targets presented themselves, the Southern boys commenced pouring a lively fire into the southern end of the field.

By this time Hazard's two skirmish companies had reached the center of the flat plain, halfway between the railroad embankment and the farmhouse in their front. "[T]he enemy's skirmishers opened a brisk fire . . . but as they were well covered nothing could be seen but the puffs of smoke," recalled William Todd. The Rebel fire was not enough to stop the Federal advance but it was beginning to take a toll. Men here and there were felled to the ground, while the rest of the Union line could only fire at the hillside in frustration. Finally, Hazard had had enough of this and ordered his command forward to a stronger position. "Our line advanced steadily," Todd remembered, "firing an occasional shot as a glimpse was obtained of anything to shoot at, and when within a hundred yards of the house, our men, in order to gain the cover of the fence and trees, started on at a run."[13]

Captain Stevens's men broke into a flatout run, each man racing the other to gain what cover the house, orchard, and fence line offered from Rebel fire. As they moved forward, the Confederate skirmishers moved correspondingly toward the rear and took up a new position farther up the hill. The few Confederates who had remained in the shelter of the farmhouse—named "Fruitwood" but called the Reid house by locals—broke into a dead run for the rear, lest they find themselves guests of the Yankees. Once in place around the house Captains Lusk and Ives instinctively dressed their lines and restored order to the formation. Seeing the enemy skirmish line stop and re-form, the Scotsmen knew their work was far from over.[14]

While the men of the 79th readied themselves around the Reid house for another advance, a scene unfolded near them that later would strike many of the war-hardened veterans as a comical anecdote in the midst of war's carnage. No sooner had the Union boys arrived at the house than its occupants, an elderly couple named Heath who currently rented the Reid farm, emerged from the doorway and strode up to Captain Stevens. They were greatly concerned for the safety of themselves and their property and implored the captain to leave. "We haven't seen any Southern soldiers about here at all," pleaded the aged farmer, "and we hope there won't be any fighting about the house!" Before Captain Stevens could offer a reply the redeployed Rebel skirmish line proved the old gentleman a liar, loosing a volley into the Union ranks that dropped two more of Hazard's command. With the argument now moot, Hazard turned and strode off to attend to his command seeing no need to offer a verbal reply to the old farmer's plea.[15]

It was now time to press the Rebels more directly and Captain Stevens ordered his skirmishers to advance. The men rose into a low crouch and walked deliberately forward. As they did their opponents stepped up the fire to a nearly constant pace. But the New Yorkers pressed on. Hazard was determined to clear the field as his father had ordered and pushed his line as far as the northern edge of the orchard. But enemy fire once again halted their progress. They were now within easy view—and range—of the main Confederate line in the wooded ridge at the end of the field. For now Captain Stevens would remain here as long as he and his men could and await further orders.

While the Highlanders clung to their position on the northern edge of the orchard, some of the luckier men in the line's left found themselves with an unexpected bounty hanging over their heads. Looking up they could see the apple trees laden with nearly ripe fruit which caused many of the men to begin scheming to get some for himself. But all knew that to stand and reach the apples would risk certain death. Still, they had to have some of that rarely gotten treat hanging just beyond reach and it occurred to the more enterprising skirmishers to shake the trees and force the fruit to the ground. If they could not go to the apples, they reasoned, the apples would have to come to them. "We found, however," wrote Private Todd, "that shaking the trees brought more than the fruit; it told the enemy . . . just where we were, and their bullets rained into the orchard, severing twigs and bringing down as many apples as we cared to pick up." But their harvest carried a high price for some of the men: "Several of our men were hit while engaged in this occupation; they fell as did Mother Eve, victims of their desire for forbidden fruit."[16]

At the same time that Captain Stevens was clearing the field, his father was equally busy back by the Millan house preparing the main attack. His skirmishers having secured much of the field and the potentially important railroad line for the Union, General Stevens was free to deploy his column for battle. Ordering his column once more forward, they continued north on the muddy farm path and over the railroad bed until it turned east giving them one less obstacle to cross in their attack.

Once clear of the railroad bed, Stevens directed the column to strike from the farm path, turning to the north and into the open field. As they advanced, General Stevens barked a series of orders that would make sense only to the most senior officers in the division who understood and flawlessly moved their commands into position. But once completed, what General Stevens directed his brigade commanders to do would be clear even to the dullest private in the ranks. Officers from full colonels to the greenest of second lieutenants were soon calling out their own orders as the machine called Stevens's division of the IX Corps swung into position for battle. Thus the division deployed in a column of brigades—one brigade in front of another—with each regiment ending the movement in its familiar two-rank battle line.

Leading the formation was the 3rd Brigade, now commanded by Lieutenant Colonel David Morrison, with the 79th New York Highlanders on the right of the line and the 28th Massachusetts, an Irish regiment from Boston, on their left. While the Highlanders looked to their colors bearing the cross of St. Andrew and were instantly reminded of their Scottish heritage, so the men of the 28th looked proudly up at their green regimental flag as a constant reminder of their Irish descent. Next in line was Benjamin Christ's brigade, the 8th Michigan, holding the right with the 50th Pennsylvania on their left. The last brigade in line was Leasure's brigade, the smallest of the three with only 320 muskets present, with the 46th New York on the right of the line and the 100th Pennsylvania on their left. Once in position, the division stopped to dress their lines and await their next order.[17]

Word of the presence of a large body of Union troops confirmed

Jackson's fears about the safety of his right flank. Though Branch's and Field's brigades were firmly in place, an increasingly large portion of the command would need to quickly move right to support them and gain as much ground between the Yankees and the turnpike as possible. Jackson began a process that would have the effect of shifting his center—and his focus—rapidly to the right to face this new threat.

Starke's Division would be the first to move and would end up posted on the left of Stonewall's line. Once in place, Starke's line would have its left flank on the Little River Turnpike and its right flank near the Ox Road. To reach this position, the Stonewall Brigade—Jackson's old command—was recalled from its fight with the 80th New York at Jermantown and moved into position on the extreme left of Starke's position. In the center of Starke's line was positioned Taliaferro's 3rd Brigade, while the right of Starke's line consisted of Starke's Brigade, now under the command of Colonel Leroy Stafford.

Next in line, holding Jackson's center, was Ewell's Division. Trimble's Brigade, with Colonel William F. Brown commanding, moved into place on the left, with its left nearly touching the right flank of Starke's Brigade and its right on the eastern edge of the Ox Road. On Trimble's Brigade's right was Hays's Brigade, perpendicular to the Ox Road. Behind this two-brigade front was posted Early's Brigade and behind them Lawton's Brigade, both with their left flank resting on the Ox Road.

The right of Stonewall's forming line would be occupied by A.P. Hill's Division. Gregg's Brigade held Hill's left, and they eventually would join Field's Brigade on its right in the northern end of the cornfield and Branch's Brigade holding the extreme right of Hill's Division and the entire Confederate line. Supporting Hill's three front brigades were Thomas's and Pender's brigades, posted left to right in a second line in the woods. Well to the rear of the entire formation, at the center of this vast semicircle, was Jackson's reserve, Archer's Brigade. Once this move was complete, and it would take some time, Stonewall would be in a better position to challenge Pope's next move, whatever that would be.[18]

Jackson's line slowly began taking on a semicircular appearance. The disposition of Hill's frontline brigades, however, clearly destroyed the symmetry of this line. The fence line along which they were posted turned sharply in a series of right angles as the fence conformed to divide the cornfield from the woods to its north. This geographic feature was the result of an innocent farmer's effort to enlarge his field. But it created for a military commander posting his line there a deep salient that cut straight into the right of Jackson's overall line. And as General Hill watched his troops deploy along the fence line, he realized that there were huge gaps in the line, the result of his three front brigades trying to cover too much ground for their number. The only option available to plug these holes was to move Pender's and Thomas's brigades into the main line, and fast. This would leave Hill with no depth to his line, no unit to hold in reserve to plug a potential break, but he would have to risk it. And so General Hill rode off to make these changes to his line before the Yankees discovered just how weak his position was.

On the opposite side of the field, Isaac Stevens was moving about preparing for this fight as if it were any other. Having set in motion the formation of his infantry, the general rode off to position Benjamin's battery to support the advance. Stevens personally posted the guns on the Millan ridge, just south of the railroad cut. From there the battery's guns could soften the Rebel line for the men of Stevens's division as they advanced. The ground on which they posted was perfect for artillery, for it afforded a nearly clear field of fire all the way to the enemy line. Once in place, Benjamin's men unlimbered their guns and prepared for battle.[18]

Hazard Stevens and his skirmishers, meanwhile, were doing their best to hold on to their exposed position. The fire of the Confederate skirmishers had been enough to keep the captain from trying anything daring and he had to consider that the Rebels in his front might try a general advance, which he certainly could not resist with only two companies of men. And as he scanned the wooded crest in front of him, the thing he had feared most since taking this exposed position happened, the long, still gray line in the woods suddenly surged to life. Hazard didn't know it but the Rebel commander opposite him in the field had been emboldened by the growing number of reinforcements appearing around them and an entire regiment soon stepped forward from the tree line, probably in an effort to see if the Yankee skirmishers could perhaps be dislodged. As the Southern battle line stepped in unison forward through the corn, Hazard knew he and his men were in trouble.[19]

The Southern regiment advanced at the common time through the cornfield toward the 79th's skirmishers, cutting a wide swath through the corn, unhindered by the Highland skirmisher's meager fire. Watching the spectacle from the opposite ridge, General Stevens knew that if he didn't act quickly, his skirmishers would easily be driven from the field by this larger force and with them would go his initiative to attack. Instantly he galloped back to Benjamin's battery and directed the artillerists to fire on the advancing Rebel line. As first one and then another of Benjamin's 20-pounder Parrot guns opened fire, dropping their exploding shells ever-closer to the Confederate battle line, the Southern commander apparently rethought his tactics and hastily withdrew his men to the safety of the woods. For now, the Union would retain control of the two fields.[20]

Even before Benjamin's battery had begun its work, General Stevens returned to preparing his infantry division for the attack. Gazing once more over his command, now fully deployed in its column of brigades, the general could feel comfortable that all was now in place for the attack. Glancing across the field to the Confederate position on the opposite ridge, Stevens could see ever-growing numbers of gray- and brown-clad men appearing in the woodline. This clearly was going to be a bigger fight than his small division, or even the entire IX Corps, could handle on their own; he would need reinforcements. Pulling Lieutenant Horatio G. Belcher, the general's provost marshal from the 8th Michigan, aside, Stevens ordered him to race back to the Warrenton Pike to get some reinforcements. Since this fight was completely unplanned, and Stevens couldn't be certain if reinforcements were on their way, it might be difficult to find someone willing to take their men into battle without specific orders. But the success of Belcher's errand was vital to the Union cause, which itself now was fixed to Stevens's success. And without a word, Lieutenant Belcher dashed south in search of help.[21]

Isaac Stevens could see from across the field that the Rebel officers were ordering their men into position and he understood that he did not have much time. If his attack were to be successful he would have to move quickly before Jackson turned his entire command southward to meet it. His men were ready and now it was time to set them in motion. Calling to his bugler, General Stevens directed him to blow "recall" to the skirmishers. And at the sound of the bugle call, which each man knew instinctively now, the New Yorkers withdrew, clearing the field for the general advance.[22]

As Stevens was issuing the last of his orders to his staff, onto the field rode General Reno leading his own staff, Ferrero's brigade, and Durrell's Independent Battery D, Pennsylvania Artillery. While Ferrero's and Durrell's men halted to await their orders, Reno rode up to Isaac Stevens to find out just what his corps was about to be thrown into. Stevens must have been annoyed at this last minute appearance of his superior. Reno easily might not understand the import of the situation, having been sick since the close of the Groveton fight, and order the attack called off. At the very least, taking the time to explain the events of the last half hour or so and what his plan was would take away valuable time, time that would be traded from the Union cause and given as a gift to Stonewall Jackson.

But Stevens understood the importance of the chain of command—even if that chain sometimes weighed heavily—and Reno would have to approve the attack before it could be launched.[23]

Jesse Reno sat somberly on his horse, still feeling under the weather, and listened to Stevens's plan. William Todd of the 79th New York recalled, "General Stevens pointed out the position of the enemy; in a few strong words showed the necessity of hurling back his threatened advance, and declared his intention to attack." After listening to Stevens for a moment, General Reno expressed a measure of skepticism about the plan but did not directly countermand it. And with that, Reno turned his mount and rode back to deploy Ferrero's brigade and Durrell's battery to support Stevens's effort.[24]

Reno's actions during his first few minutes on the field would come to have enormous impact on the outcome of the impending battle. Clearly he had concerns about what Stevens was planning to do. And yet, Reno did not take any steps to personally direct the action on the field but rather accepted the plans his subordinate had already put in motion, effectively deferring command of the IX Corps to Isaac Stevens. For the remainder of the day General Reno would do little more than direct troops as they appeared on the field.

Riding back to Ferrero's and Durrell's commands, General Reno quickly apprised their commanders of the situation and ordered them to support Stevens's attack. Durrell's battery would follow Stevens's attacking division and then deploy southwest of the Reid house, between the house and Ox Road. The 51st Pennsylvania would act as their infantry support and post on the battery's left. Durrell's artillery was then to open fire on the Rebel line in the woods, weakening it for Stevens's men. They didn't need to be told that, should things go wrong, their excellent field of fire would allow them to hold off any Confederate counterattack that might come.[25]

Reno also must have understood that if Stevens's plan of drawing Jackson into a fight to forestall a larger Confederate attack was to be successful, the Union would have to present a wider attacking front, even if only a slightly wider one. To accomplish this, Reno dispatched the 51st New York from Ferrero's brigade across the Ox Road and into the thick woods on the road's eastern side. Their orders were to feel out any enemy position that might be there and then await further orders. Within moments the New Yorkers detached from the rest of the brigade, marched over the Ox Road, and disappeared into the dark woodline to their northeast. The 51st had barely passed from view when General Reno ordered the 21st Massachusetts to follow the New Yorkers into the woods and support them in whatever they may find themselves engaged. And moments later, the 21st Massachusetts, too, disappeared from view of the brigade as they sliced into the woods at the same point the New Yorkers had entered it.[26]

Until Ferrero's men found the enemy, their division comrades in Nagle's brigade would wait in the rear for further orders. While these two regiments idly waited, some men of the 48th Pennsylvania apparently decided to venture to the Reid orchard for a late afternoon snack. The men were veterans of the march and knew that when the opportunity to gather ripe fruit presented itself the wise soldier would not hesitate. So some of these men broke from the ranks and, when the order to march came, were enmeshed in the fruit-laden branches of the Reid's apple trees. Their harvest would be short-lived, though, for a "shower of Rebel bullets brought these chaps scampering out of the trees to their places in line, their pockets, shirts, and mouths filled with apples," noted Oliver Bosbyshell of the 48th. Apparently for one of these men in Company G the close call was too much. When a lieutenant demanded a share of the loot the trembling man pulled out his shirttail and let his spoils roll in heaps to the ground. "Here, take 'em all!" was his only reply.[27]

Having dodged the specter of conflict with General Reno, Stevens turned to "open the ball." It was 4:30 P.M. when Stevens called his division to attention, as he had so many afternoons before. But today was different; this would be no dress parade and, while all in the ranks had tasted the horror of battle before, never before had they been thrown up against such odds. Not only were they facing a much larger enemy force, but they were going forward without any reinforcements save their fellow IX Corps men who were then still not even formed in the field. And to make matters worse, the sky had turned dark as night, the constant drizzle growing into a steady downpour. As the wind picked up, pulling hard at the regiments unfurled flags as if it wanted to rip them from the colorbearer's hands, all knew that this would be a fight not just against the Rebels but against nature as well. General Stevens climbed down from his horse and instructed his staff to do likewise. He then dispatched them to accompany each of the leading regiments to ensure they maintained good order during the advance and that the attack was carried out as planned. This would be a difficult fight and Stevens needed all the help he could get in directing the action. Having posted Hazard to join his own Highlanders, Stevens directed a rider to order Benjamin's battery to open fire on the Confederate woodline as they advanced.[28]

Striding to the front of his division, General Stevens called to his com-

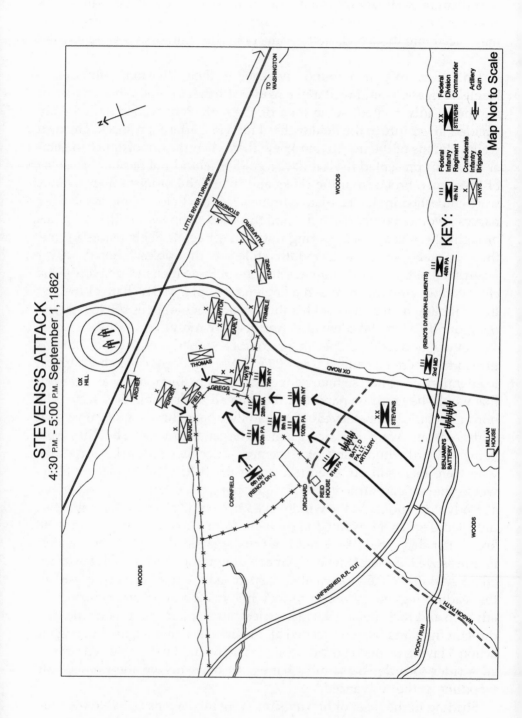

STEVENS'S ATTACK
4:30 P.M. – 5:00 P.M. September 1, 1862

TO WASHINGTON

LITTLE RIVER TURNPIKE

STONEWALL

TALIAFERRO

STARKE

WOODS

TRIMBLE

LAWTON

EARLY

OX HILL

THOMAS

ARCHER

PENDER

FIELD

GREGG

HAYS

79th NY

BRANCH

28th MA

46th NY

8th MI

50th PA

100th PA

OX ROAD

(RENO'S DIVISION-ELEMENTS)

2nd MD

STEVENS

CORNFIELD

6th NH
(RENO'S DIV.)

ORCHARD

REID
HOUSE

51st PA

BATT. D
PA LT.
ARTILLERY

BENJAMIN'S
BATTERY

MILLAN
HOUSE

46th PA

WOODS

UNFINISHED R.R. CUT

WAGON PATH

ROCKY RUN

KEY:

Federal Infantry Regiment — 4th NJ

Confederate Infantry Brigade — HAYS

Federal Division Commander — STEVENS

Artillery Gun

Map Not to Scale

mand, "Division! . . . guide center! . . . forward! . . . march!" And with that the New Yorkers and Bay Staters in the front line of Morrison's brigade stepped off as one. And for more than a few of the men their collective first step in the fight would open their last advance.

Morrison's men advanced down the long, gentle slope to the base of the hill. As they marched steadily on at the common time, the first shells from Benjamin's guns screamed overhead and slammed into the woods in their front. In the ranks of Stevens's division the men could hear the first claps of thunder intermixed with the booming guns and saw the first flashes of lightning slicing through the darkened sky. Rain that had been so annoying minutes before now grew in intensity, stinging the men's faces. The storm that had been brewing all day was about to break on them in full.[29]

Word of the advancing Federal line surged throughout the Confederate ranks on the northern end of the Reid fields. All along the line the order to load was given—if it hadn't already been done—and men steadied themselves for the impending fight. The Yankees had taken barely a dozen steps when their artillery, posted well to their rear but in plain view of the Southern line, opened fire. As the Union infantry line drew closer to their position, so did the deadly artillery shells. Their accuracy was aided by the clear view the Federal gunners had, and within moments of the first shells falling near the Confederate ranks, Southern officers ordered their men to lie down and take cover—a more needless order was never given.

Stevens's men pressed on. Within moments they crossed the marshy flats between the two slopes and started up the longer, more gradual slope toward their destination atop this rise. Passing through the marsh temporarily obscured their view of the enemy and as Morrison's men advanced to within sight of the woodline once more, they were surprised to find no sign at all of the Confederates. Throughout Morrison's ranks the men buzzed excitedly of this revelation. Hazard Stevens, on the right of the line with the 79th New York, recalled, "Not a sight nor sound betrayed the presence of the enemy. There was nothing to be seen but the open field, extending two hundred yards in front and closed by the wall of woods, with an old zigzag rail fence at its edge."

"There is no enemy there," Captain William Lusk exclaimed to Hazard, marching by his side in the rear of the 79th New York's line. "They have fallen back; we shall find nothing there," Lusk offered hopefully. The men of Morrison's brigade had now reached within a few dozen yards of the woodline and the sight of trees, shrubs, and the fence line empty of any enemy that greeted them could only fill them with hope. Perhaps there would be no fight today after all.[30]

But the words had barely slipped from Captain Lusk's mouth when suddenly a Rebel line rose from behind the rail fence and delivered a volley into the front of Morrison's line. The shock of the Confederate presence was nearly as great as the damage inflicted by the volley. Morrison's ranks shuddered as the minie balls sailed through the line, cutting down dozens of front rank men in the process. Whether they knew it or not, Stevens's men had stumbled into the very center of Stonewall Jackson's now almost fully deployed battle line, meaning that their flank attack had suddenly turned into a frontal assault. And whatever the challenge this new development presented, they would have to do the best they could.[31]

Despite the unexpected carnage, Morrison's men held fast. The Highlanders of the 79th New York and the Irish volunteers of the 28th Massachusetts were combat veterans who had seen all this before. They were not stunned into collapse, as green men might have been, but responded by tightening their lines and pressing on. And on they plodded, ignoring the individual fire that had now opened on them from the woods. And when they could go no further, they finally opened their own fire on the enemy line that now lay fewer than two dozen paces in front of them. Their volley ripped into the woods in their front, tearing holes through the thick foliage and the line of Hays's Brigade taking refuge there.

One of the first men to go down in the first Southern volley was the general's son himself. Hazard Stevens lay on the cold, wet ground, shot in the arm and hip. All around him lay the others of the brigade who had fallen at the same moment. Some were trying to get away while others hugged the ground for what little safety it offered. From his vantage point in the rear, Hazard could see not only the other wounded lying near him but the thinning ranks of his father's attacking force as well. "The enemy was smiting the column with a terrible and deadly musketry," he recalled, "[t]he men were falling fast."[32]

Well to the rear, General Stevens monitored the progress of his division's attack and the sight that greeted him through his binoculars was a terrible one. The line of men he had sent into battle was stalled directly in front of the enemy, completely exposed to their murderous fire and with no place at all to go. Making matters worse, the general could see that Rebels in the woods across the cornfield to their left—almost certainly the troops they originally had been trying to flank—had opened on the left of his line as well. The 28th Massachusetts had marched directly into a slaughter pen. But what must have terrified him most was the scene directly in his front. For as the general watched in horror the blue and white regimental colors of his own 79th New York Regiment were cut down, then raised again only to be once more cruelly dragged to the earth by the effect of yet another Confederate ball. His regiment, his Highlanders, his men, were dying.[33]

Without a word Isaac Stevens left his position in the rear and strode at nearly a run to the battlefront. His attack was failing and only he could save it and his men. The now constant, heavy rain had filled the marshy ground beyond capacity, creating a swamp that tugged at the general's boots as he splashed through it. Within moments he reached dryer ground and was soon on the upward slope of the hill, racing to meet his division. It was here that he met Hazard. His son had managed to get on his feet and was surveying the full extent of his wounds when he realized his father was at his side once more. Hazard recalled that his father "asked me if I was severely hurt and ordered a non-commissioned officer near by to help me off the field." Seeing his son on his way to the rear, Isaac Stevens returned to his duty and moved on up the hill to where his division stood. Seeing his father heading into the thick of the fight, Hazard called out imploring him to spare himself from what both knew lay atop the hill. But General Stevens, now driven to the front, never answered his son's cries.[34]

Stevens reached the rear of his division a few moments after leaving his son's side. He had known even before leaving his post at the Union rear what must be done. Since the division had failed to flank the enemy, they would have to strengthen their current position and then strike to punch a hole in the Confederate line. The first step toward this new tactic would be to extend the line as far as possible on each flank. Finding Captain Lusk in the rear of the 79th New York, Stevens selected his son's friend for this important task. Captain Lusk had spotted the general coming and shouted to him over the din of the battle, "Have you seen your son?"

"Yes!" Stevens called back, shouting to be heard over the fury of the musket fire, "I know he is wounded. Captain Lusk, I wish you would pass to the left of the line and push the men forward in that direction!" The young captain nodded affirmatively and raced left to find the 50th Pennsylvania. Within moments Stevens's orders were being carried out and the Pennsylvanians moved at the left oblique, passing into the cornfield. Facing once more to the front they posted in line to the left of the 28th Massachusetts. At once they unloaded their muskets into the Confederate line in their immediate front. The recipient of their volley was Gregg's Brigade, which until now had no one in their front on whom to fire. But with the appearance of the Pennsylvanians the fight was on and they gave as they got. "We were on one side of a cornfield, and the enemy on the other," one veteran of the 50th Pennsylvania recalled, "and the way we made the cornstalks fly between us was a caution—fired 50-60 rounds."[35]

With Stevens's battle line now extending some 40 yards farther to the left, the rest of the division adjusted to reinforce the growing front. The 8th Michigan shifted left from their position behind the Highlanders to support the 50th Pennsylvania, posting the center of their regiment on the light blue and gold left guidon of the 28th Massachusetts. At the same time, General Stevens ordered Leasure's brigade forward to reinforce the center of the division. Up to this point in the battle Leasure's men had been so many spectators, intentionally remaining a few dozen yards to the rear of Morrison's men. But now it was their turn. Up and down the lines of the 46th New York and the 100th Pennsylvania, men and officers dressed their lines in preparation for the advance. For many of the men, the driving rain that had been so annoying only moments before now seemed a mere distraction as their minds focused on far greater matters. Over in the 100th Pennsylvania the chaplain paced the rear of the line, encouraging the men and offering words of comfort. Reverend Browne's words reportedly had a calming effect on the men, who moments later were on their way forward into the cornfield to bolster Stevens's line.[36]

While General Stevens was adjusting his line, General Reno was making his own deployments to support Stevens's effort. Though he had heard nothing yet from his regiments on the east side of Ox Road, Reno decided he would wait no longer to act. Calling up Nagle's 1st Brigade, he dispatched staff officers to each of the regiments with their orders. Each of Nagle's units were to move to the right of Stevens's position and support the 51st New York and 21st Massachusetts of Ferrero's brigade, who were still feeling out the Confederate position in the woods. Apparently Reno intended to extend the entire Union line much farther to the right. Having set this plan in motion, General Reno turned back to monitoring Stevens's progress. As ordered, the 48th Pennsylvania and 2nd Maryland broke from the brigade front and marched off to the right. Once across the Ox Road, the 2nd Maryland posted on the intersection of the road and the railroad bed, while the Pennsylvanians continued on to their right and stationed themselves at the base of the railroad line facing the woods to their north.[37]

The last of Nagle's three regiments, the 6th New Hampshire, however, would never reach its intended spot on the Union right. For some reason the New Hampshire boys found themselves wandering directly ahead of their former position rather than to its right, a march that took them directly into the growing firestorm north of the Reid house. After passing cautiously to the west of the Reid farmhouse, the 6th found its new, if unintended, objective. They would join the battle in their front with or without orders. Marching purposefully forward, their battle flags unfurled and pulling at the rain-soaked wind that filled them, the Hampshiremen strode on to join the fight. Without any orders from General Stevens they posted on the left of the 50th Pennsylvania, extending the Union battle line even further to the left. Their appearance, unexpected as it was, must have heartened the general for at that moment he greatly needed more troops to bolster his line, which was already threatening to collapse. And almost immediately after arriving in Stevens's line, the 6th New Hampshire went to work swelling the Union's fire at the Rebels in the woods. Private Showell recalled that he fired 160 rounds during their time there, firing so often that he was forced to discard his fouled musket for another taken from a wounded man.[38]

Meanwhile at about 4:45 in the afternoon, just as Stevens's men were in the midst of their attack across Ox Road, in the woods the 51st New York found the Rebels they had been looking for. After leaving General Reno they had wandered to the northeast and after 20 minutes of feeling their way through the chokingly wet woods they sighted a line of skirmishers crouching ahead in the mist. "Our Regt. was ordered into a Cypress swamp on the extreme right where the trees were so thick we could hardly walk and the rain falling in torrents completely soaking us," wrote George Whitman. As they pressed forward the enemy skirmishers retreated without a shot. "We found only a few of the enemy's skirmishers," Whitman continued, "who we drove out." Having accomplished their mission—to find the enemy line—the New Yorkers halted to await further orders.[39]

The Rebels who the 51st New York had found were General Starke's men of the Stonewall Brigade, under the command of Colonel Andrew Grigsby. Starke was holding the extreme left of Jackson's line and, as the firing to his right grew in intensity, the general apparently became worried. His brigades were tired and thinned by the recent fighting and marching; if the Yankees attacked in any force at all his line would collapse and with it would go the entire Confederate left. Making matters worse, the Stonewall Brigade's depleted ranks were trying to cover too much ground. Their right reached only into the woods and a considerable gap existed between Starke's left and the road itself. When the first Federals appeared in his front Starke had to act before the fighting became general. So before the situation could turn against him, General Starke rode off to find some reinforcements.

Starke dashed west across the Ox Road and soon found Jubal Early and his brigade. At that moment Early's Brigade was posted in the rear of Hays's Brigade, serving as reinforcements for Lawton's main line in the Confederate center. Jubal Early recalled that "General Starke, then in command of Jackson's division, represented to me that a heavy force was threatening his left, between which and the pike there was a considerable interval, and requested me to cover it with my brigade to protect him from the apprehended danger." This request put General Early in a difficult position. Colonel Strong, commanding Hays's Brigade, had warned Early that his own position was "critical" and Early could hardly leave this assigned position. At the same time, he could hardly refuse General Starke's, his superior officer's, order. Early's only legitimate recourse was to ask General Lawton for permission to support Starke. But General Starke was here in front of him and clearly would not settle for such an obvious stall tactic. "After examining the position," Early noted dryly, "I reluctantly consented to yield to General Starke's entreaty, without awaiting orders . . ." Within moments of issuing the order to move, the first of Early's seven regiments began falling back to come to General Starke's aid.[40]

In the open fields opposite Jackson's protected line, Isaac Stevens was finally ready to move. Captain Lusk had the 50th Pennsylvania firmly in place and the line had been unexpectedly lengthened by the arrival of the 6th New Hampshire. But the casualties his command was taking by waiting in full view of the Confederates were severe. They could not stay there much longer without falling back or being destroyed altogether. The time to act was now.

General Stevens ordered his men to advance to the tree line. As he did so the skies erupted in a torrent, the soaking rain turning to a driving flood as if from the mouth of the great Niagara. Private Andrew Greely of the 19th Massachusetts, posted well to the rear of the action where he could afford the luxury of watching the storm, recorded of it: "The roll of musketry and the roar of cannon left all of us unmoved, but the crash of thunder and the vividness of lightning, whose blinding flashes seemed to be in our very midst, caused uneasiness and disturbance among some of the bravest men." And for a moment they hesitated, every man certainly disbelieving that they could move at all in this deluge and knowing what awaited them if they did move any closer to the deadly woods. But suddenly the line moved. Haltingly, sluggishly it moved. To the apparent disbelief of many a rain-soaked veteran, they were indeed driving forward. They had hardly taken two or three steps when a massive Rebel volley slammed into the front rank like a lightning bolt and Stevens's line once more ground to a halt.[41]

Behind the ranks of the 79th New York, Isaac Stevens's mind was whirling. The attack was stalling again and about to fail. It was obvious that if they didn't breach the Confederate line now, right now, they would all be killed or captured by the certain counterattack. Which fate would be worse he didn't have time to consider. In an instant General Stevens found himself racing through the confused, thinning ranks to the color guard at the center of the Highlander's line. In the last half hour he had watched five men of that color guard fall holding the sacred banner. It had entered this battle torn from their action at James Island and the recent fighting near Bull Run and now was soaked and stained by the mud of this field. It had been the regiment's rallying point throughout this horrible war and now would serve as the spear to drive these men—his Highlanders— through the Rebel's ranks.

Stevens grabbed the flag from the latest wounded bearer who lay crouched in the mud at his feet and stepped to the front of the line. "For God's sake General!" cried the wounded man, "don't take the colors; they'll shoot you if you do!" But the experienced man's cries fell on deaf ears, for Isaac Stevens was no longer thinking, he was acting, moving about in a world that was both surreal and, at the same time, all too real. Facing the ranks Stevens called out, "Highlanders! My Highlanders! Follow your general!" With that he turned and headed to the woods. This time the Union line did not hesitate, they instinctively followed their general to the attack.[42]

For the first time that afternoon men in Union blue reached the worm fence that had taunted them since opening this attack. And for the first time that afternoon Hays's Louisianians fell back from the fence to the safety of the thick, wet woods behind them. With the fence clear the Scotsmen and Irishmen of Morrison's brigade tore at it with wantonness suggesting they wanted to wipe the hated fence from the earth. Posts and rails flew in the air and into the woods beyond, kicked and thrown from their place. The destruction followed the line of the arrival of the troops at the fence, for the men of the 79th on the right reached it first—due to the crooked angle at which they marched—and it ceased to exist a few dozen feet at a time moving like a wave from right to left. Within moments, barely slowing down to accomplish this task, Stevens's line surged forward once more, following their gallant general into the woods after the Rebels.[43]

General Stevens stepped over the fence's remains with the Highlan-

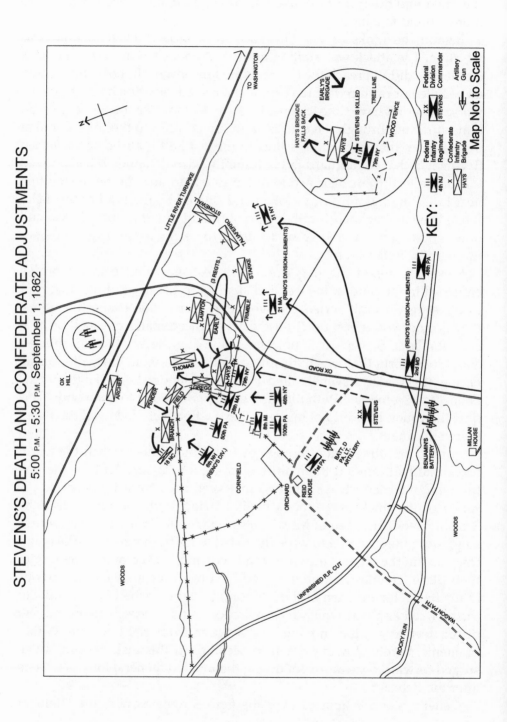

STEVENS'S DEATH AND CONFEDERATE ADJUSTMENTS

5:00 P.M. – 5:30 P.M. September 1, 1862

KEY:

Map Not to Scale

der's flag still clutched in his grip. He didn't notice the driving rain, booming thunder, or the flashes of lightning which occupied other men's attention, for he could see only the Confederate line that was racing away from them, abandoning their former line in which he was now standing. The attack was finally working, and the Rebels were not only retreating, they were running.

The Union line was still moving forward, sweeping the Rebels before them. But the sight of his Highlanders advancing victoriously forward would be the last thing Isaac Stevens would ever see, for at that very instant a Southern ball slammed though the general's brain. As the small lead ball continued on its appointed flight it took with it the life of the engineer, governor, congressman, general, husband, and father. Stevens's body, still moving forward, twisted lifelessly to the ground, wrapping itself in the Highlander's flag, his hands still clasping the staff. As his body lay on the ground, Stevens's blood poured from the wound, forever staining the Highlander's color with the last evidence of Isaac Stevens's life. For the charging men in the ranks the sight of their beloved general falling before their eyes only served to make the attack even more determined. The advancing line suddenly grew wild with fury and anger at their leader's death and they broke into a dead run for the Rebels in the woods.[44]

Hays's Brigade had been hanging on as long as they could but their Rebel line was thinning under the Yankee's fire and their ammunition was growing scarce. Colonel Strong, in charge of the brigade, paced impatiently in the rear, looking longingly for the reinforcements he had asked for when this attack had begun. Now they would have to replace his brigade, rather than simply reinforcing it, for his men were spent; holding them here alone risked losing the line under a determined Yankee attack. When Strong finally received word that he could withdraw his men, to be replaced by Thomas's Brigade, he was appropriately relieved. Without thinking how best to handle switching the two units at such a delicate time, he simply ordered the men to fall back. Colonel Strong's timing, and his choice of orders, could not have been worse.[45]

Strong's order reached the ranks just as Stevens's men were beginning their attack. Hays's Brigade needed no more urging to leave this fight and they began slowly falling back. But at that very moment, the Yankees came surging over the fence and were on them almost immediately. The weight of the Union attack and the confusion of the colonel's ill-timed orders created instant chaos in the Confederate ranks. As Strong's line disintegrated, the brigade's officers tried valiantly to re-form their lines in the woods. Shouting at the men to stop and dress their lines, they worked furiously to restore good military order. The first Federals to reach the scraggly Rebel line—the men of the 79th New York—went to work immediately with their bayonets and commenced swinging their spent muskets like so many primitive clubs. Within moments, the Irishmen of the 28th Massachusetts joined in the melee and the once safe woods erupted into the sheer brutality of hand-to-hand combat. Dennis Ford of Company H of the 28th Massachusetts would write of the fight, "When we got into the woods, we ran through what we did not shoot. We bayonetted them. One man begged and got no mercy, a yankee ran him through. Thank God it was not an Irishman did it." The Louisianians had had enough. Almost as a mass they broke and ran for the rear, charging back through the woods as maniacally as Stevens's men had charged to reach them. The center of Jackson's line was crumbling.[46]

As Strong's disorganized mob raced for safety they stumbled unexpectedly into three regiments standing almost alone in the woods. Running through the ranks of these units, the men of Hays's Brigade could do little more than shout warnings to the fresh men about what was coming at them through the woods. These three regiments were in fact the 13th, 25th, and 31st Virginia of Early's Brigade who had not yet completed the just-ordered move to the left to assist General Starke. But seeing Hays's Brigade break, their commanders acted at once to plug the gaping wound in the Confederate center. Before anyone in the ranks could comprehend that their plans had changed, they were moving forward through the woods toward the charging Yankees.

On the eastern side of the Ox Road, General Early was busy checking the progress of his brigade's movement. Upon reaching General Starke's position on the left Early found that most of his command was in place as ordered but a more careful check uncovered the fact that three of his regiments were nowhere to be found. Although he could hear reinvigorated firing from the direction of their former position, the general thought little of it: "I heard considerable musketry fire, but as the woods were very thick and it continued to rain I could see only a short distance, and took it for granted that the firing proceeded from the troops in front of where I had been." Concerned about the whereabouts of his missing regiments, the general dispatched his staff aide, Lieutenant Early, to find them and hasten their movement to the left. He could not know that at that moment, his three regiments were trying desperately to save the Confederate center.[47]

The men of Morrison's brigade pressed on through the thick woods, rolling like a rising tide across the wet, green summer leaves, gaining ground with each step. They had moved only a few dozen yards, though, when a volley rang out in the depths of the woods in front of them, accompanied by a shower of lead. The New Yorkers and Bay Staters were stopped in their tracks, the first halt in their forward movement since General Stevens had ordered the charge. Within seconds the woods parted to reveal a strong Rebel line coming straight at them. And as the Rebel line surged forward the weakened ranks of Morrison's brigade disintegrated, each man taking his own route out of the woods to safety. Within moments the tide of battle had once again turned and this time it was Stevens's line, on the right, that was disintegrating.[48]

Colonel Christ, meanwhile, had his own problems commanding the left of Stevens's line. By virtue of General Stevens's death and his position as the ranking officer on the field, Christ was suddenly in charge of this attack. But for now the colonel was blissfully unaware of his new and greater duties and was focusing on pushing forward the Union left. Christ's chief immediate problem was the geography of this field and the nearby woodline. The new center of Stevens's extended line was posted on a crest that bisected the cornfield from the grassy field, so that neither end of the line could see its opposite end. In effect, Colonel Christ was blind to what was happening on the right. Making matters worse, the woodline turned abruptly north on this ridge and when the Highlanders and the 28th Massachusetts were slogging their way through the enemy's position, Christ's men were still exposed to fire from three sides and yards away from meeting the enemy. In the face of all this, he was doing what he could to fulfill General Stevens's orders.[49]

Christ ordered his command forward through the cornfield toward the Confederates, who were already firing on them from the woodline. As the two regiments in his front line advanced he aimed them at that point by ordering them through a series of left obliques. The men of the 6th New Hampshire and the 50th Pennsylvania did the best they could, the thick corn and the driving rain slowing their advance.

On the opposite side of the cornfield, Confederate General Branch could see the Union attack shifting increasingly toward his right. He, better than anyone else, knew the approaching blue-clad men posed a great danger to his line for it was hanging in the air, with no geographic position to strengthen his flank. And even though his men were pouring as great a fire as they could into the Federal line, it still moved on. If this position were flanked, the entire Confederate right might break and roll up like a rug. Branch likewise knew that he had no time to call for reinforcements—if there were any to be had—and that he was on his own. So the general did the only thing he could under the circumstances, pulling the 18th North Carolina from the center of his line and posting them on the brigade's right flank. Once there, they would form at an angle to the main line, a position referred to in the books as "refusing the right."[50]

Seeing the Rebel's line shifting about in his front may have convinced Christ that they were either retreating or confused. In either case, they were ripe for a charge designed to exploit the disorder. At the order to charge, Christ's line broke into a dead run for the Rebels in their front. The suddenness of the attack cowed Gregg's Brigade to retreat from their exposed position in the northern end of the cornfield to the safety of the woodline. As they fell back the veterans of Branch's Brigade realized that without Gregg's troops on their left, they soon would be left alone and cut off from the rest of Jackson's Command. Instinctively Branch's men drew their line back in concert with Gregg's moving front. The retreat of Branch's men, though more intentional than Gregg's move, was disorganized and for a moment it appeared the entire Confederate right would give way. But the crumbling Southern flank was saved by the appearance of the tree line and the two brigades quickly re-formed their line on the edge of the woods. Once there, they regained their composure and order, not to mention their confidence, and returned to firing on the Yankees with abandon.[51]

The retreat and re-forming of these two Rebel units meant Christ's men were once more under fire from three sides. The murderous long-range work of the Rebels was clearly having the desired effect, for the Union line slowed and then stopped altogether as more and more men fell. They had had enough and now settled into trading shots with the Southerners for a dozen minutes or more. That half of his division had become disconnected from the rest of Stevens's line must have worried Christ and the effect that this exposed position might have if the Rebels counterattacked was obvious. For now, though, they would remain there.

As Stevens's men were in the midst of their attack, the men of the 21st Massachusetts were still wandering through the woods west of Ox Road in search of the 51st New York. As the regiment picked its way hesitantly through the woods, it became obvious to every man in the 21st Massachusetts that they were lost. "It was soon evident," wrote Private James Stone, "that each command had lost all connection with the other, and was advancing no one knew where or why." As the 21st Massachusetts continued on in search of the New Yorkers, they spied a group of Rebels crouched behind a low rail fence. "They were rebels," remembered

Captain Charles Walcott, "but we took it for granted that it was all right, for the 51st were ahead, and passed them by." As the 21st stumbled on through the woods their lines became nearly nonexistent and many of the regiment's companies were separated by several dozen or more yards. They were hardly ready for battle.[52]

After going on another half mile or so they encountered a dark line of men to their front. Advancing to within 20 yards of the men, the 21st stopped to dress its lines. The regiment's officers were unanimous in declaring these to be the 51st New York boys, even though the darkness and rain prevented them from confirming their assertion. But the men in the ranks, many of whom had a closer view, were unconvinced. "Those are rebels!" they called out, but to no avail. Finally, some men on the right of the line, convinced they were facing the enemy, opened a weak, scattered fire. "Cease firing!" came a cry from the opposing line, "We're friends!" The doubters in the ranks brought their muskets back to their shoulders and a sense of relief swept over the men—they had found the 51st New York after all.[53]

But moments after receiving reassurance from the anonymous voice, a volley—the last thing they expected—rang out. They had not found the 51st New York but had in fact found Trimble's Brigade and the right of General Starke's line. "While the poor fellows were standing with their guns at the shoulder, one of the deadliest volleys ever fired rolled upon us from our right and front," recalled Captain Walcott. The men of the 21st were stunned; the deadly volley cut the regiment to pieces and nearly every man not protected by a tree was cut down. "In the sudden anguish and despair of the moment," continued Charles Walcott, "the whole regiment seemed to be lying bleeding on the ground."[54]

Those men not hit by the first Rebel volley tried to return fire as best they could. "Some standing still in line, some from behind the trees, we opened fire on our brutal enemy," declared Captain Walcott defiantly. But at that moment the skies opened up and the most drenching rainstorm many of them had ever seen fell, choking off even their response. "My gun went all right the first time," wrote James Stone, "but it was impossible to load in such a downpour. I then got out my revolver and fired away with that."[55]

Although the men of the 21st Massachusetts didn't know it, Trimble's Brigade was having its own problems. They had been badly used up in the fighting at Manassas and seemed to be unsure of themselves here. Trimble's ranks were severely depleted, as was their officer corps, and their position in the rainsoaked woods was far from secure. Their first volley had been fine enough, but now the Yankees were returning fire. And most everyone knew that there were thousands more Yankees out there somewhere who just might appear in their front at any time. The return fire from the thick woods, meager though it was, was just enough to cause some of the men to fall back in search of a more secure location. This retreat started as a trickle but soon grew in scope, until it seemed Trimble's Brigade might break. It was that fear that impelled their acting commander, William F. Brown, originally of the 12th Georgia and serving as brigade chief for only three days, to race to the line. Wading into the thick of the wavering line, Captain Brown drew his sword—a long, arcing saber—and waved it over his head. The captain began cursing at the men to halt and re-form their lines or suffer a severe punishment, which his swinging saber seemed to confirm his ability to carry out. One man in Trimble's Brigade recalled that "with his conspicuous black plume in his hat, his long saber in hand, his face aglow with excitement and indignation, [he] looked like Goliath with his weaver's beam." But just as Captain Brown was finally rallying the brigade, a Yankee bullet struck his head, killing him instantly. His effort, though, had paid off, for the men of Trimble's Brigade returned to their line and order was once more restored.[56]

Completely broken and in no position to fight back in an organized manner, the 21st Massachusetts melted into the woods in a disorganized mess. As they withdrew, the regiment left behind their lieutenant colonel, 10 other officers, and nearly 100 men, all fallen where they had been resting only moments before. "We left a lot of poor fellows in that wood for whom nothing could be done but to bury their lifeless bodies," Private Stone wrote sadly of their retreat. Another 20 or so of their comrades wouldn't make it out of the woods either and they remained as prisoners of Trimble's Brigade. One of those left behind was Captain John Frazer, the commander of Company H, who had been hit in the leg. Frazer's wound was made worse by the fact that it apparently had been caused by an explosive ball—a minie ball filled with a small amount of powder designed to explode on contact—that may well have been among the Union ammunition stores captured by Jackson's Command at Manassas Junction only a few days before. Frazer's retreating comrades were much luckier, though. Once in the safety of the wood's depths, the decimated band of Bay Staters wandered back the way they had come and, once safely out of Confederate musket range, re-formed their column and marched for the wood's edge.[57]

It was now roughly 5:30 and the battle had been underway for about an hour. And although General Stevens had seized every advantage available to him, the situation for the Union was anything but encouraging. Stevens's attack on the center of Jackson's line had completely collapsed and General Stevens—the architect of this fight—was dead. General Reno, for his part, seemed content to remain largely a spectator and avoided taking the command that was his responsibility. And the probe that Reno had ordered of the Confederate left had been weak and therefore largely pointless, causing many Union casualties seemingly for no military gain or purpose whatsoever. Things were hardly much better for Jackson and his command, though. True enough they had halted the Union attacks and their line continued to hold. But they had come near to breaking at least twice in the hour-long battle and it had been luck as much as anything that Early's three regiments had been in the right place to stop the Federal incursion that nearly broke their center. Jackson knew as well as anyone that there were thousands of additional Union troops, some of whom were fresh, that Pope could throw into the fight at any time. Having to guard against such an eventuality had so far tied Stonewall's hands from acting to reverse the course of the fighting and put himself back on the offensive as General Lee had wanted. And even though the failure of the two Union efforts had precipitated a lull in the fighting—and the pace of the torrential downpour was slackening somewhat—Jackson could only expect that both the rain and the Yankees would most likely be back for more before the day was over.

8

Kearny Takes Command

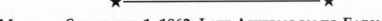

At the same time that General Stevens was issuing his final attack orders, his aide, Lieutenant Belcher, arrived on the Warrenton Turnpike to search for the general's much-needed reinforcements. By now the muddy road was utterly jammed with troops and rolling equipment moving toward the fight at Jermantown and the line of units the young lieutenant could choose from for his commander's reinforcements stretched over the horizon. Belcher wasted no time and rode against the flow of the column, asking every senior officer he came to for help, pleading that General Stevens and his men were alone in holding the Rebels on the Union's flank and badly outnumbered. Belcher and the others on the turnpike could hear the sounds of firing open up to their immediate north, a sound that should have helped his argument. But in each case, Lieutenant Belcher got back the same reply—they had orders from General Pope and would have to stick to them—until he came upon General Philip Kearny.[1]

Belcher remembered Kearny and his 1st Division of Heintzelman's III Corps from the previous day's fighting. When Lieutenant Belcher first found Kearny, he was encased in an India-rubber cloak to counter the effects of the downpour then fully underway. As the lieutenant repeated General Stevens's request once again, the crackle of musketry rang out through the woods to their north. Kearny glanced in the direction of the firing, well aware of what was at stake here. He knew of Jackson's movement around the Union right and what it might mean if it was successful. Kearny needed barely a moment to think. Now it would be his turn to offer support to Stevens, returning the favor the former governor had done by aiding his own attack two days earlier. Kearny's eyes lit up and he shot back his reply, "By God, I will support Stevens anywhere!"[2]

Springing into action, Kearny dashed from the column with his staff in tow, and raced to find General David Birney's brigade at the head of his division. General Kearny ordered Birney to take his command out of the line and turn north at the next intersection, the Ox Road. From there, he continued, they should move to join General Stevens's command and reinforce his fight. To support Birney, Kearny directed the two remaining brigades in his 1st Division, Berry's brigade, under the command of Colonel Orlando Poe, and John Robinson's brigade to post on the northern edge of the Warrenton Pike. And Graham's battery of the 1st U.S. Artillery was soon added to their line for good measure. As Birney began issuing the orders necessary to get his brigade underway, General Kearny wheeled his horse and, with his staff once again trailing behind him, rode west against the flow of the column in search of some artillery to reinforce his division. Coming upon an artillery unit, the general stopped abruptly to inquire who they were. When the battery's commander replied, "Randolph's 1st Rhode Island Artillery, Battery E," Kearny boomed back, "Just the battery I want, follow me!" And with that they sped off in pursuit of Birney's brigade and Stevens's fight.[3]

Having stopped the first wave of Union attacks on his former right, Stonewall Jackson considered what the Yankees would do next. The prospect that General Pope might hit him unexpectedly with his fresh troops probably worried Jackson most now. The most recent attack had been stopped—though not easily—but it had been so small and uncoordinated that it must only have been Pope's probing maneuver. Larger and better coordinated attacks would most certainly be coming. If this would be the case—and Jackson could prudently plan for nothing less—then he must use this lull in the fighting as time to make preparations to defend against such an attack.

The first thing Jackson did was what any officer in his tactical position would do—get the artillery to safety. Since the weather and terrain conditions had so far prevented his guns from playing any role in the fight, there would be no reason to think they would do so in the little remaining daylight. And next to the baggage train, these guns were his most vulnerable asset and military prudence dictated that they should be moved to safety. Stonewall directed his artillery to move from their position near Ox Hill to a point about a half mile west of the hill on the Little River Turnpike. From that vantage point they would not only be less vulnerable to Union attack, but could conceivably cover any retreat he might be forced to order as well.[4]

Jackson's next move was to tighten the position of his infantry brigades to meet the next wave of Federal attacks. If the first Federal attacks had been mere probes, then this next wave of attacks would likely take place in the same area they had just finished defending, the grassy field. He ordered Thomas's Brigade to complete their move—the one that had been interrupted by the first Yankee attack—and relieve Gregg's Brigade. Other brigades on the line were to re-form their lines and adjust as necessary in preparation for the next Union assault. Early's Brigade, in particular, soon could expect more action, for they now held the position that had proven weakest to the first Yankee attack.

Once the men in Early's seven regiments had settled in for their next fight, they quickly took to talking, grabbing a smoke or a chaw of tobacco, or doing one of the thousands of things veteran soldiers are wont to do during a welcome break in the fighting. Indeed, some of Early's boys even found something to laugh at in the midst of their largely humorless circumstances. The unlikely subject of their mirth was, in fact, the colonel of the 49th Virginia, William Smith. Colonel William "Extra Billy" Smith, a former governor of the Old Dominion, was well-known among those of both high and low rank for his disdain of his West Point-educated colleagues. Colonel Smith not only took every opportunity to heap opprobrium on the anointed few from "the Point," but he made it a point to dress in the polar opposite of anything resembling a military uniform. On this particular day, Smith was decked out in his uniform coat—certainly in defense of the weather—but he had decided to cap off the outfit with a high-crowned beaver hat, reportedly to remind his fellow Virginia volunteers that he was no soldier but rather a patriot. Adding to his ensemble, the colonel had brought along a blue cotton umbrella, which he would raise and lower in relation to the present storm's fury. At that particular moment, the rain picked up once more and Colonel Smith correspondingly raised his blue cotton shield. Finally, the men in the ranks could take this comical sight no more and one wag called out, "Come out of that umbrel! I see your legs; come out of that hat, want it to boil the beans in!" The resulting laughter was a welcome relief for all in hearing range of the colonel.[5]

General Jackson, however, had no time to laugh, for he needed to eliminate the deep salient that posting on the woodline had created on the right and center of his line. The Union probe attack had already discovered the existence of this weakness and he could not ignore the likelihood that they would strike him there. To remove this dangerous position Jackson ordered his line fronting the cornfield to move out of the woods and into the corn to form as straight a line as possible. The first of several moves to fix this problem saw Field's Brigade march straight out from their location on the northern end of the cornfield salient and post a few dozen yards into the corn, with their right posted on Branch's left. General Branch responded to this move by pivoting his own brigade and placing his left nearly in line with Field's right and his own right deeper into the woods. These two moves not only solidified Jackson's flank but also greatly straightened, and strengthened, Jackson's entire line. To fully reinforce this position, Pender's Brigade moved into the cornfield in the rear of Branch's and Field's position. Now the line was straight and strategic depth had been added.[6]

But no sooner had the men of Field's Brigade taken their new position in the corn, then they were ordered to fall back. As they withdrew, Pender's Brigade, which had not yet seen action this day, moved to take their spot on the front line. Pender's Brigade moved to nearly the same spot Field's line had been posted on and deployed. Pender placed the 16th and 34th North Carolina on the right of his line and in direct connection with the left of Branch's Brigade. On the left of Pender's line, the 22nd and 38th North Carolina regiments extended as far as they could, reaching toward Thomas's Brigade. But the fighting of the last week had depleted their ranks and no matter how thinly they stretched, they could come nowhere near Thomas's right flank. To fill this small but important gap the 13th and 14th South Carolina were pulled forward from Gregg's Brigade and posted between Pender's left and Thomas's right.[7]

At the same time that A. P. Hill's Division had been shifting itself in the shattered cornfield, General Jackson was busy putting the brigades on his left to better use. The dismal failure of the Union probe on his left and the thick, wooded terrain of the area probably would convince whomever was in charge of planning the next Union attack of the futility of another assault in that location. These facts must have been enough to convince Jackson that he could feel secure in pulling the Stonewall Brigade from their spot on his extreme left flank and he moved them to the center of his line. Here they would be of better use as another reinforcing brigade that could be moved quickly to wherever they might be needed. The other three brigades in Starke's Division—Trimble's, Starke's and Taliaferro's, from right to left—would pull back a few dozen yards and tighten their line in the direction of Ox Hill. While repositioning his command in this way abandoned any pretense of offensive operations Stonewall may have harbored earlier in the day, by 5:45 or so his line was ready to meet the next Yankee attack, which the Confederate warrior apparently believed would come once again at his now-strengthened center.[8]

The mood in the Union ranks as Birney's men marched through the thick woods that framed the Ox Road had noticeably darkened since leaving the road. For one thing, the skies had opened upon them once again. Lieutenant Ford of the 101st New York noted that "suddenly the sky darkened and we were deluged with one of the worst thunder storms I ever saw." And while this weather was an annoyance in the best of times, going into battle soaking wet could turn an inconvenience into a life-threatening hindrance. But more importantly, the men seemed to understand that this would be a particularly difficult fight. Perhaps it was the sudden change in the day's fortunes, from the "lighthearted" ease of marching to Washington to going into yet another battle. Perhaps it was the fact that they could hear the struggle ahead, for as Lieutenant Ford described, "Mingled with the roar of the cannon was its more than rival, Heaven's artillery, while the lightening flash seemed to convey to us in meaning words, 'What is your power compared to mine?'" But whatever the cause, as Daniel Fletcher of the 40th New York's Company H remembered, "The men seemed to dread going forward more than usual. The whole company seemed to hang back. Lieutenant Gould, seeing what was up, pulled out his sword and said to the sergeants, 'Don't you let a man leave the ranks.' He looked as though he would bite the men's heads off if they did not keep in their places." But despite their sense of dread, Birney's command moved ominously forward, and the men did what they could to keep their weapons dry.[9]

About the time that Jackson's last units were moving into place, General Birney and his brigade arrived on the field and reported to General Reno as Kearny had ordered. Listening to Reno describe the current sorry tactical situation for the Union, Birney knew he had his work cut out for him, for he could see the remains of Stevens's attack retiring before his eyes. General Reno then hastily instructed Birney to move his command into the cornfield to relieve Stevens's division and oppose any forward movement the Rebels might make. Reno apparently promised to re-form Stevens's men in the meantime to support Birney's advance. Satisfied with this plan, Birney immediately set to work deploying his brigade for battle on the Union left.[10]

Marching to the northern side of the unfinished railroad line, Birney quickly deployed his battle line. For many of the men, all of whom had seen battle already, the scene appeared unusually horrific, perhaps because the fight was so unexpected. One veteran of the 4th Maine recalled, "As we passed our batteries on the hill and descended into the valley we met scores of wounded . . . The thick smoke of battle [and] heavy mist of storm filled the valley with darkness. Our artillery opened just as we passed, throwing shot and shell directly over our heads. Their long streams of fire dazzled our eyes for the moment, and the sharp concussion almost prostrated us." Despite the shock of the field they were

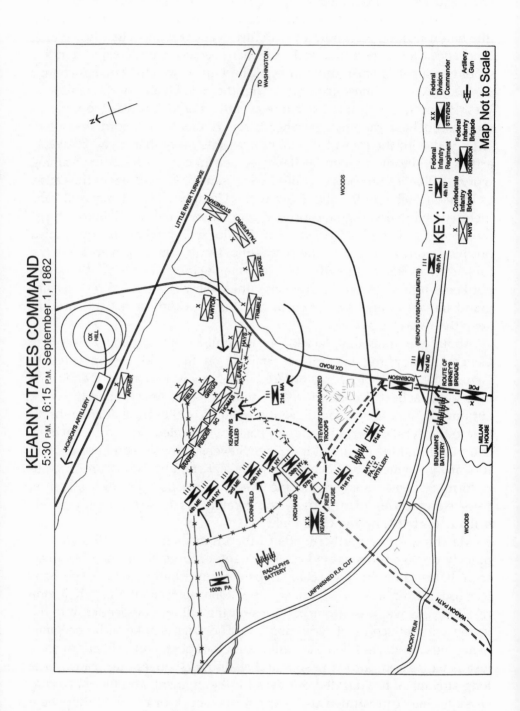

KEARNY TAKES COMMAND
5:30 P.M. – 6:15 P.M. September 1, 1862

TO WASHINGTON

LITTLE RIVER TURNPIKE

WOODS

STONEWALL

TALIAFERRO

STARKE

LAWTON

TRIMBLE

OX HILL

HAYS

ARCHER

JACKSON'S ARTILLERY

EARLY

FIELD

GREGG

S.C.

PENDER

THOMAS

BRANCH

KEARNY IS KILLED

21st MA

OX ROAD

STEVENS' DISORGANIZED TROOPS

ROBINSON

(RENO'S DIVISION ELEMENTS)

2nd MD

48th PA

ROUTE OF BIRNEY'S BRIGADE

POE

51st NY

BATT. D PA L'T. ARTILLERY

BENJAMIN'S BATTERY

MILLAN HOUSE

WOODS

38th NY

40th NY

1st NY

3rd ME

57th PA

51st PA

4th ME

101st NY

CORNFIELD

ORCHARD

REID HOUSE

KEARNY

RADOLPH'S BATTERY

100th PA

UNFINISHED R.R. CUT

WAGON PATH

ROCKY RUN

KEY:

Federal Infantry Regiment
4th NJ

X X
Federal Division Commander
STEVENS

Artillery Gun

Federal Infantry Brigade
ROBINSON

Confederate Infantry Brigade
HAYS

Map Not to Scale

entering, Birney's men moved into place with the quiet efficiency of bat-tle-hardened veterans.[11]

General Kearny and his staff, with Randolph's battery in tow, reached the field about the same time Birney's brigade was deploying for battle. After passing the unfinished railroad bed, Kearny and his retinue turned off the road into the rain-soaked field. For the first time since responding to General Stevens's plea for help, Kearny could survey the field of battle. The sight that greeted him could not have inspired confidence in the great warrior. The entire stretch of grassy field, all the way to the woods on the horizon, was littered with a disorganized mass of Union troops, most of whom were wandering pointlessly about as if they had no reason at all to be there. Here and there officers could be seen and heard trying in vain to re-form their commands. The adjacent cornfield, though, remained large-ly intact, although sizable sections of it had been laid flat by moving troops or musket fire. In fact, the only unit still firing at the Confederates was a battery situated to Kearny's left—Battery D of the Pennsylvania Light Artillery—who continued launching shells into the dense woods to their north.

It must have occurred to Kearny at that moment that something dread-ful had happened to Isaac Stevens. He had seen Stevens in action and understood that only death or capture could compel General Stevens to permit his division to lapse into such utter chaos. Across the field to his north, Kearny could see the Confederates adjusting their lines. They were not moving forward but rather only shifting and reinforcing their current positions, a sign that the general of five wars knew could be either defen-sive adjustments or preparations for an attack. The sight of Birney's men filing into place at the southern end of the cornfield must have been heart-ening, for until that moment there simply had been no Union force defending that part of the field.

Kearny, though, had no time to ponder the tactical situation he was in, for part of his division was about to go into battle and action was what was called for now. The general drove his horse forward to begin prepar-ing for his division's attack, all the while barking orders to his various staff officers. Colonel Graves of the 40th New York, then serving on Kearny's staff, recalled, "We rode along the line, and Gen. Kearny sent off one staff officer after another with orders, until I was the only one left with him." Two of the officers were sent back down the Ox Road, in the direc-tion they had just come, with orders for Colonel Poe to quickly bring up his brigade. Kearny and his remaining staffer then led Randolph's battery to a spot just north of the wagon path leading to the Reid house and ordered them to unlimber. From this point, at the base of the cornfield, they could support Birney's assault that was just then about to get underway.[12]

Birney's brigade quickly moved into position at the southern end of the cornfield preparing for their attack. The 4th Maine held the left flank of Birney's line. To their right was the 101st New York, followed by the 3rd Maine and 40th New York. General Birney ordered the 1st New York to post on the right flank of the line. Acting as a reserve for the attacking force, the 38th New York and the 57th Pennsylvania were placed in the apple orchard of the Reid house. For the next few minutes, just after 6:00 P.M., the brigade's officers moved busily along the line finalizing their formation and ensuring that every unit was ready for the impending attack.[13]

With the officers busy dressing the lines for battle, the men had time to contemplate the scene into which they were about to be thrust headlong. For many of these men, battle-hardened veterans though they were, what they observed here made them more than usually fearful. "I never saw the men backward about going into a fight before," noted Sergeant Fletcher curiously. "The officers talked to them, and called them cowards. One of the men stepped up to me and said, 'Do you call me a coward?' Very well, said I, then go along with your company. I told another man who held back: You fought well at Bull Run, you can fight now. He said he was not going in there. I told him he must go with his company or there would be trouble." After a stern talking-to by the officers and sergeants, though, the men of Birney's brigade were ready for battle, even if they remained more unsure than usual of their fate. "The men did better after the officers had given them a good talking to. I do not think a man left the ranks," Fletcher recalled.[14]

Although it seemed to the men like hours had passed, in mere minutes Birney's five regiments were soon moving into the cornfield. The brigade did not step off as one line as the men were generally used to, though, but rather each regiment moved forward one at a time starting with the 4th Maine on the left. Seconds after the Maine men had entered the corn, the 101st New York broke from the brigade front and moved off. This peeling off of regiments continued on down the line until the entire brigade was underway, forming what from the air would have looked like a living stairway, plodding and slogging its way to the north.

All along the right of Jackson's line the gray-clad veterans waited, searching the field in their front. They had seen the Yankee troops forming opposite them only moments before, but darkness was growing thicker by the minute making them now nearly impossible to see. "The exact location of the enemy's lines was uncertain," observed one Southerner bordering the cornfield, "until . . . it could be outlined by the flashes of his guns, and apart from the dangers involved, reminding one of myriads of fire flies." And adding to the difficulty in finding the enemy was the rain, which once more grew in fury and volume. "A beating shower of rain blinded and drenched those engaged," recalled one of Gregg's men, "almost drowning the line in reserve, who lay on the ground for protection from the bullets." For a time Branch's, Pender's, and Thomas's lines couldn't see the Yankees at all. They had seen them move out of their position at the base of the hill but, once they dropped from their view into a swale, they appeared to have vanished. Only the sound of the officers yelling to be heard over the rain and the sound of corn stalks breaking betrayed the presence of their foe.[15]

The veterans of the 4th Maine moved forward guiding their center on the western woodline of the cornfield. The effect of this was to place the regiment's left nearly all in the thick woods while the unit's right remained in the open part of the cornfield. While the wooded cover sheltered the men on the left of the line, those on the right almost immediately came under fire from Jackson's line directly in their front. Within moments each succeeding regiment received a similar fire. Here they halted, about one third of the way across the rain-soaked cornfield, and opened fire on the Rebel skirmishers in their front. The skirmishers, who had been so active only moments before, skedaddled to the rear, their job over for now. With their way clear, Birney's brigade pressed once more forward.

Birney's line had moved fewer than a dozen more yards when the enemy opened fire on them in earnest from the hill's crest and woods in their front. They halted once again and opened their own full fire on the dimly lit Confederates. But they didn't need light to see their enemy, for the muzzle flashes told them where to fire. The firing became general and fierce, with both sides unleashing their pent-up fury on the other. And if Jackson's line held firm to their high ground, Birney's men stayed glued to their self-defined line in the corn. In the 101st New York, their commander called out "Give it to them, boys." Another of Birney's men remembered, "If a man was killed, he was left. If wounded, a couple took hold and carried him out, and there we stood, not a man leaving unless he was obliged to until the whole regiment was gone."[16]

Over in the 40th New York, on the right of Birney's line, things were much the same. "After we reached the cornfield we commenced firing," remembered Sergeant Fletcher, "I was well to the front . . . kneeling down on my right leg, making a rest for my rifle with my left hand, my left elbow on my left knee. I was putting a cap on my rifle, to fire for the third time, when a ball struck my knee that was on the ground on the inside. It entered the crack of the joint diagonally, striking the knee . . . cracking the bone nearly to the hip. I immediately jumped for the rear as soon as I was hit. It was very painful." For Daniel Fletcher, the battle of Chantilly was over and a new and more personal battle, the fight for survival, had just begun.[17]

Things were not much better for A.P. Hill's men on the receiving end of Birney's fire. In the growing darkness the casualties were beginning to mount in the three regiments holding the far right of Jackson's line. Making matters worse, the rain had soaked their ammunition to a point that the senior commanders on the field wondered if they could continue to resist the Yankees with musket fire. This concern apparently prompted General Branch to alert A. P. Hill about the dire state of his command's ammunition supply, to which Hill ordered curtly that Branch should hold his ground at the point of the bayonet if the fighting came to that. But Hill was not unsympathetic to his subordinate's plight and, knowing very well that other units then in reserve were in better fighting trim than they were, he soon sent a courier to General Jackson bearing a message. The dispatch was straightforward in its pleading: "My compliments to General Jackson and my request to be permitted to take my command out of the line because all my ammunition is wet." Jackson's response to this query was equally direct: "My compliments [to General Hill] and tell him the enemy's ammunition is equally wet as his!"[18]

Watching his brigade advance through the corn was the unit's commander, David Birney, who stood well to the rear in order to better direct the fight. As the line crushed through the corn and drifted to the left of the field, Birney suddenly realized that their right flank was completely unsupported. This certainly had not been his intention when preparing the assault but nevertheless he knew that leaving this situation unresolved might permit the Rebels to flank and overwhelm his small command. And adding to his concern, Birney could not yet see the reinforcements General Kearny had ordered in the form of Robinson's and Poe's brigades. Something would have to be done now, and it would be up to him to do it. Scanning the field once more, David Birney spied his one-armed commander, busy discussing the situation with some officers on foot. If anyone could pull reinforcements from nowhere to shore up his flank, it would be Philip Kearny. With that, General Birney wheeled his horse to ride over to his commanding officer.[19]

Kearny, meanwhile, had been riding all about the rear of the Union position preparing for his division to enter the fray. With so few Union officers on the ground at that moment, and his own staff all off attending to similar tasks for the general, he was left with no choice but to personally place most of his troops. Not that such duty would bother Philip Kearny, for he was the kind of commander who felt that much more confident about a fight when he could personally attend to the details. He had already found the ideal ground for Randolph's men to post their guns in support of his impending assault. And once Randolph's guns were unlimbered and ready for action, the general ordered them to commence firing on the Confederate position in the opposite woods. Before riding off to attend to another such task, General Kearny ordered Lieutenant Jastram of Battery E to relay to General Grover, commanding the 1st Brigade of Hooker's 2nd Division, to bring up the right of his command and join it to Kearny's left. Clearly, Phil Kearny expected a have a full-blown fight in those remaining hours of daylight. Kearny also directed Sergeant Millan of Randolph's battery to watch for the return of Kearny's staff aides. Should any of them return, the general directed, they were to wait there with the battery—where his headquarters would remain for the time—until his return. With these tasks attended to, Kearny rode off.[20]

At the moment that General Birney reached him, Kearny was in the midst of placing the 100th Pennsylvania on the left of Randolph's battery to serve as their infantry support. Having no infantry of his own command yet available to support his artillery, Kearny had turned to the only source of such troops, the mangled remains of Stevens's division. The 100th Pennsylvania had been lucky so far today for they had been in the third line in Stevens's attack and so had suffered only a few casualties. More importantly for General Kearny, though, they had retired in good order and instantly stood out from the rest of their scattered comrades as the only one of Stevens's units available for such a task.[21]

Birney briskly saluted his commander and apprised him of the danger facing his own brigade in the corn. Following Birney's outstretched arm in the direction of the cornfield, General Kearny was shocked to find it was true—Birney's right was hanging exposed in the center of the field. Kearny knew what this meant and reassured Birney that he had sent a staff officer to bring up Poe's 3rd Brigade, who could easily plug the hole in their line. The one-armed general simply couldn't believe that General Reno, a commander of proven talent, could permit such an advance without proper support on his right flank. But looking back down the Ox Road in the direction they had come revealed no sign of Poe's brigade. In fact, no Union reinforcements at all could be seen. Kearny knew that the sight of this empty road meant that his own division would not arrive in time to avert a possible disaster. Kearny's blood must have begun to boil at the thought of Poe's delay. But he didn't have time to fume at the failings of his subordinates and staff, for this situation required action. Assuring Birney that he would personally see that his right flank was immediately supported, General Kearny instructed him to return to his brigade and the two men rode toward their respective tasks. Riding together as far as they could took the two officers to the rain-swollen ditch at the base of the field. Reaching the ditch Kearny's mount, Bayard, shied from the jump, while Birney's horse easily leaped over the obstacle. Kearny, somewhat embarrassed by the animal's failing—which he perhaps feared Birney would attribute to him—remarked sheepishly, "How disagreeable to have a horse behave that way in battle!" And with that they parted company.[22]

Riding down the slope of the hill toward the mass of men that had been Stevens's command, Kearny knew that it was up to him to cull from this mob something resembling an organized regiment to support Birney's right. What he found couldn't have been encouraging. Men were wandering about with no direction at all, while others simply sat on the soaking ground, showing no signs of moving again during the few remaining minutes of daylight.

Searching the forlorn scene, the general came upon the only thing resembling a regiment within view. Perched on a slight rise, what remained of the 79th New York huddled around their bloodstained flag. Kearny raced up to them and asked who they were. Finding himself in the company of the 79th New York, a regiment whose fighting reputation Kearny knew well, he boomed out, "Scotchmen, you must follow me!" But the sad state of the regiment told him instantly that they were in no condition to fight. So when the ranking officer in the 79th pleaded with the general that they were completely out of ammunition, Kearny unhesitatingly responded, "Well, stand where you are and it may be you will be able to assist my men with the bayonet."[23]

The other regiments from Stevens's command were in even worse shape. The men of the 28th Massachusetts clustered around their own national and green regimental colors but could muster nothing approaching a fighting form. Enduring fire from two directions in Stevens's attack had cut nearly 200 sons of Erin from their ranks. They could be of no further help to Kearny today. And the other units in this tangle of men, though they had not suffered nearly the same losses as Morrison's Celts, were likewise in no condition to fight. Kearny was searching in vain for some unit to send over to Birney and he must have felt his temper rise at the frustration of being surrounded by so many men who were of no use. But anger would not restore their order; they were beyond that now. Looking out over the field, past the mob at his feet, Kearny suddenly spied a unit he had not seen before. And this unit was in a battle line and appeared to be ready for action. This was just what he needed and without hesitation, the general spurred Bayard and bolted in the direction of these fresh troops.[24]

The men of the 21st Massachusetts had finally emerged from the thick woods around 6:00, only to find the battle seemingly fading before their eyes. Looking back from the eastern edge of the Ox Road, they could see only their own artillery lobbing shells into the woods beyond, while from the enemy woodline only the movement of troops and the shouting of officers could be heard. Within moments, though, infantry fire sounded in their front and they could see muzzle flashes coming from the Rebel line to their right. But mostly they could only hear the fight, for not only was it taking place over the hill's crest but the stormy darkness was making it hard to see anything at all let alone concealed troops hundreds of yards away. Whatever might be happening, the 21st's officers—those who remained—did what by now came naturally to them, they ordered the men into line to regain order and control of the regiment.[25]

If any of the Bay State boys believed that their day was over at that moment, the arrival of an officer on horseback quickly set them straight. "[T]he regiment was again formed and had hardly got in line before Kearny rode up," recalled George Parker, "and ordered us up on the other side of the road." Finding the officer in command, Kearny barked, "By God, they are cutting us off!" and hastily ordered the 21st across the road to reinforce General Birney's right. When the 21st's Colonel Clark protested that his weapons were fouled by the recently concluded torrent of rainwater, Kearny brushed his argument aside and repeated his orders to advance. With his task completed, Kearny dashed back to the Union rear to continue planning for the arrival of Poe's and Robinson's men.[26]

Neither Kearny nor the officers of the 21st Massachusetts knew it just yet, but the short exchange there on the side of the Ox Road had set the stage for disaster. While both the general and the 21st's officers knew what their task was, they unknowingly had arrived at very different ideas about where the regiment should go to accomplish that task. Apparently Kearny, in his haste, had given the 21st Massachusetts directions to cross the field but had been no more specific in offering a clue as to exactly where Birney's right flank was located relative to their then-current position. If the 21st's officers felt their directions were unclear, they apparently never asked for clarification. Perhaps Kearny's temper cowed them into submission or maybe they thought they knew where he wanted them to go. Regardless, within moments of crossing the Ox Road the 21st Massachusetts was headed right for the center of Jackson's line.

The darkness that had made it annoyingly difficult to sort out the battle only moments before now became a cruel enemy, hindering their progress and very likely concealing Rebels in their very front. "The rain had now ceased," remembered Captain Walcott, "but the sky was still heavily overcast, and it was so dark that at a few yards' distance it was impossible to tell friend from foe. . . ." The 21st moved ahead at as slow a pace as they could manage, General Kearny's famous temper notwithstanding, for they had already suffered the effects of overconfidence and haste in these fields and had no intention of making the same mistake twice this day. "We moved to the edge of the corn-field, with our right still close to the woods, and halted to advance a line of skirmishers, not proposing to be caught again, as we had been an hour before, if we could help it." So while the regiment waited, Company G was pulled from the line and deployed as skirmishers on the regiment's front and right.[27]

Sitting astride his horse, watching the 21st's progress through his field glasses, Phil Kearny couldn't believe his eyes. The regiment he had ordered to Birney's aid, to save possibly the entire Union right, was stopped dead in its tracks. If Kearny wondered what they were doing, it would not have taken long to figure out that they were deploying skirmishers to cover their move. They were given a simple order—to post on the right of Birney's line—for which they would need no skirmish line. After all, in the direction they were advancing the 21st Massachusetts was moving toward their own men, not the enemy. Kearny's temper was running out with these men. From his vantage they appeared to be either cowards or incompetents. But whatever the case, they were all he had now and like it or not, they would fight. Kearny turned to one of his recently returned staff aides and directed him to ride with all haste to the Massachusetts men and tell them to advance as ordered. Before the rider could depart, though, Kearny told his aide to warn the reluctant regiment that if his orders were not complied with, and fast, they would face a barrage from their own artillery. Armed with General Kearny's none-so-idle threat, the mounted aide dashed off.[28]

The 21st Massachusett's skirmish line had barely begun its careful probe of the enemy front when the rider came thundering across the grassy field. Upon hearing the news that he had better comply with the general's orders or face being shelled by their own guns, the 21st's commander was dumbfounded. Certainly the general didn't understand their current situation or he would never order such an advance without skirmishers. But whatever was the case, Colonel Clark knew that Kearny's threat was not idle and within moments he recalled Company G's skirmish line to rejoin the regiment. Moments after that, the 21st was moving once more forward.[29]

The Bay Staters moved cautiously forward, despite Kearny's warning, for they still had no desire to repeat their earlier experience on the other side of the road. The darkness of the storm and battle smoke had now become so oppressive that no one in the regiment could see beyond the dozen or so yards that revealed the rail fence and tall corn beyond. "Up we went again—more cautious—crept across a field and laid down behind a fence," recalled Lieutenant Parker, when without warning Rebels opened on them from the dark cornfield in their front. And while the fire seemed to the Massachusetts men to be galling—"a dropping fire," as Captain Walcott described it—in reality they were only facing the skirmishers of Thomas's Brigade. This fire, though, was enough to stop them in their tracks once more. For while Colonel Clark understood the threat from General Kearny, at that moment the more immediate threat was issuing forth from the corn not 20 feet away.[30]

Once more Company G was deployed in skirmish formation across the 21st's front, while the company holding the right of their regimental front "refused the right," by pivoting backward and stopping at an angle to the main line. What ensued for the next few minutes was a confused, small firefight between the 21st's skirmishers and the 49th Georgia, acting as the skirmish line for Thomas's Brigade. The firing became general between the two bodies of skirmishers, with anyone capable firing at anything they could see. The 49th Georgia, though, having accomplished their mission to stop the Yankee advance, retired to their main line. But as they moved back they did so without two of their number who now stood captives of the 21st Massachusetts. One of these two, an officer, had been caught confused and unaware in the darkness and was overwhelmed by the Union skirmish line. The other, a private in the same Georgia regiment, had been literally hauled into captivity by Sergeant Gardner of Company E. Apparently the sergeant had watched the lone Rebel load and fire and, seeing his piece empty, charged him and brought the Georgian back to his line at the point of his bayonet. The mere presence of these two prisoners gave Colonel Clark ample reason to believe General Kearny would be convinced of the wisdom of his recent actions, should he bother them again today.[31]

When the 49th Georgia came racing back to join the rest of Thomas's Brigade, every man understood that the ball was about to start again. Up to that moment all they could see from their vantage had been the fire fight between Pender's and Branch's men and the Yankees, and that had been only in the form of light bursts of fire that spewed forth from the competing guns. That they had been standing in the pouring rain doing nothing so far had only served to make them more skittish, for everyone expected a large Union attack. The return of their skirmishers confirmed that their turn was about to come. All along the line the soaking, dirty veterans checked their weapons, some craning their necks and peering fixedly into the dark in hopes of catching a glimpse of the enemy advancing through the corn. Whispered news from the 49th filtered its way into the ranks but the lack of concrete information about their advancing foe only heightened their apprehension. Yankees were coming, that much was clear, but no one could tell just how many there might be.[32]

It was incomprehensible to Kearny but was nonetheless true; the Massachusetts regiment had once more stopped dead in its tracks. Kearny couldn't believe it even though his eyes beheld it plainly enough. There they sat, like a damned bump on a log apparently doing nothing. They had been ordered to simply march across the open field and join Birney's right flank, a task so simple a private could have led the way. Perhaps this Massachusetts colonel was so incompetent that the task was beyond him. Or maybe he was a coward who simply wanted to avoid battle as best he could. As he mulled the situation in his mind, Kearny's temper began to flare. No longer able to control his boiling rage at the sheer insubordination and incompetence of this officer, Kearny spurred his jet-black horse and headed for the reluctant regiment.

Colonel Clark had the situation under control once again and the 21st Massachusetts was ready to hold off the Rebels at least for a time if they chose to advance. But the sudden pounding of hoof beats racing toward them from the regiment's rear told the colonel that a new threat—physically less deadly but nonetheless potent—was descending on them. Within moments Colonel Clark was facing the full brunt of General Kearny's considerable fury. Explaining that they had halted to drive in the Rebel pickets did no good. Kearny would have none of these excuses and ordered the regiment forward. And since the regiment's commanders had proven themselves unable or unwilling to lead them he would personally take the 21st Massachusetts to its appointed spot on Birney's right flank.[33]

With no choice whatsoever in the matter, Colonel Clark reluctantly ordered the regiment to move forward once more. Under Kearny's watchful and critical eye, the 21st re-formed and dressed their line and stepped as one toward the dark, forbidding cornfield. Slowing only to tear apart the rail fence, they pressed on into the corn, slicing a wide swath through the stalks. Even so, Colonel Clark and the other officers of the regiment knew they were walking into sure disaster for they had seen the Confederates waiting on their right and front just moments before. Talking among themselves they determined to try once more to dissuade General Kearny from his course. Captain Walcott pushed the two prisoners from the 49th Georgia to the rear and led them over to the mounted general, so he might see for himself that they were being truthful about the enemy presence so near their own lines. "If you don't believe there are rebels in the corn," pleaded Captain Walcott pointing to the two captives, "here are two prisoners of the 49th Georgia, just taken in our front!"[34]

Perhaps it was the impertinence of the young captain that did it, but whatever the cause, Philip Kearny exploded with rage. "God damn you and your prisoners!" he shouted. And spurring Bayard with a vigor that must have given his tired mount more than a start, the one-armed warrior raced around the regiment's left and plunged headlong through the corn. That it would be up to him, a general officer, to reconnoiter the way for these timid "soldiers" explained much about the Union's current sagging fortunes. But if that's what it would take to get Birney his support, than that's what Kearny would do.[35]

On Bayard, Kearny tore through the corn, riding up over a ridge and out of the view of the Massachusetts men, now several dozen yards to the rear. Kearny had barely crested the ridge when he rode out of the corn and into a dark clearing. He pulled back on Bayard's reins and the horse almost instinctively slowed to a walk. The clearing was in hazy darkness and the rainy mist only made it that much harder to see. He searched for any sign of the troops the 21st Massachusett's officers had so feared. At first he could see nothing, but then he heard movement in front of him and to the right and realized that it was a line of troops. It must suddenly have dawned on him that the cowardly colonel might have been right after all. But there was only one way to check that.

Calling out softly to the almost unseen men Kearny asked, "What troops are these?" Without hesitation a dozen or so of the men in the opposite line replied matter-of-factly, "The 49th Georgia." Kearny replied in an equally matter-of-fact tone, "All right," a statement that he certainly hoped wouldn't betray the fear that flashed through his mind at the utterance of the word "Georgia." But Kearny had been here before, face-to-face with the enemy where every second and every move counted. He had barely comprehended the existence of these enemy troops when he pulled his mount's reins hard over and dug his spurs in for all he was worth. At the same time, he dropped to grasp Bayard's huge neck and back with his right arm, now riding in the manner called "Indian style" in hopes of avoiding any lead that might be coming his way. It was now a race with the comprehension of these Rebels for the safety of the cornfield.[36]

In the ranks of the 49th Georgia they had heard the rider coming before they could see him. Even when he was no more than a few yards from them, many of the men couldn't make out just who it might be on that dark horse. At nearly the same instant that they responded to his query, someone in the 49th's ranks called out what was now obvious to nearly everyone, "That's a Yankee officer!" while another handful of the men ordered him to halt. But the mounted rider was already turning away from them and racing for the corn. Major Pate, standing close to the scene behind the regiment's line, called out, "Shoot him, fire on him!" Within seconds a few dozen rifles were up and aimed at the receding rider. As they fired, very few of the men must have been at all sure they could hit him in the haze.[37]

Kearny was nearly to the edge of the cornfield when he felt a ball strike him. It would be the last thing he would feel on this earth. Only one of the dozen or more balls fired hit him but it slashed through his body in such a way that no one could have survived it. The ball entered the seat of his trousers and tore a path through nearly the entire length of his body, stopping to lodge in his chest. The impact and shock of the ball hitting his body knocked Kearny from Bayard and he hit the ground hard, staining his still-clean uniform with wet mud. His rider violently twisting from his back nearly turned Bayard around and in his own sense of panic the horse bolted away toward and then through the Confederate line in his front. Lying within reach of the corn, Kearny was gone. The brave soldier of five wars luck had finally run its course.

Seeing the fleeing Union officer fall, Colonel Thomas ordered his brigade forward into the cornfield. Whether this move was one of fear, hoping to seize the initiative before the Yankees could flank their position, or whether it was an effort to exploit a perceived weakness that might come from losing their senior commander is not known. They pressed through the dark, misty night in search of an as-yet unseen foe. The Georgians had barely moved two dozen paces when a body of troops appeared instantly through the haze. The right of their line was easily recognizable, so close was it to Thomas's left-most regiment, the 49th Georgia. The rest of the Yankee formation, however, disappeared in the darkness and over a ridge in the ground, making it impossible for Colonel Thomas or the other brigade officers to size up the enemy or figure out just what they were facing. Making matters worse for the Confederates, they were marching nearly parallel to the Union battlefront and the proximity of his left to the Union right gave Thomas virtually no room to maneuver. For an instant Colonel Thomas didn't know what to do but he knew that if his brigade were going to maneuver at all they would have to clear the Yankees from their front.[38]

In the ranks of the 21st Massachusetts, the men had been loaded for some time now and were fully ready for this moment. In particular, Companies D and G had not been engaged earlier in the woods and were ready to fight. They could see the Rebels moving at them through the corn as only a dark mass, bobbing in unison as they advanced. Each of the company commanders ordered their men to the ready, and tension flew through the ranks as every man awaited the order to fire. The dark enemy line moved ever closer to the 21st's position and then, when they were close enough to make out the Rebel's faces, the entire line halted. For some reason no one, Yankee or Rebel, would fire. Suddenly someone called out of the darkness, "Surrender!" until nearly every man in both lines was demanding the same thing of his foe. For several seconds the two enemies stood in the hazy darkness firing verbal bullets at one another. Then the inevitable happened; Captain Ira Kelton shouted above the din, "Fire!" and the 21st loosed a deadly volley into Thomas's ranks. Though they couldn't see the effect of their fire for the blinding muzzle flashes, they could hear the sound of the balls tearing through the corn and the sound of men falling. But when the men of the 21st regained their sight, the enemy was still there and readying their own firing line. The Bay Staters knew that now it would be their turn to act as the amorphous target.[39]

Colonel Thomas readied his entire brigade to return the Yankees' fire. Every man in the four regiments knew that their impending volley was intended to get the Yankees out of their front and, just maybe, get them to break in a panic. As soon as they fired, the tired Southerners knew their deadly work had had effect. None of the Bay Staters would consent to defeat quite so easily, though. The moment Colonel Thomas had issued the command to fire some of the companies of the 21st Massachusetts were so close that they could swat the Southern guns out of the way with their arms or muskets. Captain Kelton of Company D swung his sword at a musket aimed directly at his chest and managed to put off death for a few more days. The rest of the regiment, however, had no such option. "[T]he moment the command 'Fire!' passed the rebel colonels lips, I fell flat on my face. Every man around me, but one, fell dead or wounded," George Parker later lamented.[40]

Peering through the dark as the smoke cleared revealed great gaps in the Yankee line. But no sooner had these gaps appeared then they closed up with men shifting about or rising from the ground. The volley, even at this range, had not been enough to break them. This Yankee regiment was going to be a tough nut to crack.

Colonel Thomas, too, could see that the volley had not had the desired effect and knew instantly what would have to be done. Yelling at the top of his lungs, the colonel bellowed the command men on both sides of the issue had come to fear and loathe: "Battalion, at the double-quick, Charge!" And with that short command the entire fury of Thomas's Brigade was loosed on the 21st Massachusetts. "Then followed the direst confusion I ever saw," wrote Lieutenant Parker. Within seconds the entire mass of Rebels was on top of them, pouring in, through, and around the ends of their line. The 21st's position in the field had erupted into that little slice of hell that appeared each time a bayonet charge occurred. Men thrust their bayonet-armed muskets like so many primitive spears at nearly anyone who appeared to threaten them, with little regard for which side they might really be on. Others turned their guns into clubs and began swinging wildly around themselves, lest they be pierced by a bayonet. "[A]s the rebels charged our line in overpowering mass, men snatched the guns from each other's hands, and for the first, and so far as I know the last, time in our experience wounds in fight were given with the bayonet," recalled Captain Walcott. The scene was one of madness and abandon and seemed to the veterans on both sides as even more violent and severe than usual.[41]

For some in the 21st Massachusetts, the scene was too much to bear and they reflexively exercised the better part of valor. James Stone, like many of his comrades, reacted in just as natural a way to the horror as his comrades who lit into the fight with renewed vigor. "When the Johnnies saw we were unable to return their fire they . . . came to capture prisoners, and before I knew it one of them was quite near me shouting: 'Halt, throw down your gun,' etc. but I did not halt, nor throw down my gun, but I did run and he ran after me." Private Stone raced instinctively back in the direction the regiment had come with General Kearny, running for all he was worth. "I soon decided in my mind that he was not gaining on me, then I thought I was increasing the distance between us; directly I discovered a ditch in front of me. It looked very wide [and m]y shoes were loaded with Virginia mud; could I jump it? I realized that everything depended on that jump and I made a great effort. Glancing back, I saw the Johnny who had chased me ordering some of our boys out of the ditch; they had made the fatal error of trying to secrete themselves in that ditch." Despite his comrades' misfortune, James Stone had escaped the Rebels clutches. "I kept on going to the rear, until I reached the part of the field from which we had started on that advance with General Kearny; then I began to hunt around for the boys."[42]

Just when it seemed that no one would emerge from the bitter fight, the two lines inexplicably stopped their carnage. "[I]t seemed as if the fight must go on till ended by death or surrender, with mortal enemies mingled together; but, strange to say, the fighting almost ceased entirely," recalled Captain Walcott. "It was so dark that one could not tell whether the man next to him was friend or foe, and nobody was willing to say who or what he was." Then something even more remarkable happened; Thomas's and Clark's men fell back, driven perhaps by the hand of God Himself— tired of the human waste—or perhaps by the collective return of their humanity, checked so recently by the utter fear of the struggle. "[B]oth parties, scarcely knowing how it happened, found themselves drawing apart again, and falling back towards their original position, leaving the cornfield neutral ground."[43]

The men of Thomas's Brigade fell back only to find themselves suddenly alone and alarmingly disorganized. Their officers scrambled to regain control as their units continued drifting rearward. By the time they reached their starting point they had regained order and were once more ready for a Union attack, should it come. Upon reaching the left flank of Pender's Brigade, they halted their line and breathed a collective sigh of relief. In fending off the Union "assault" their casualties had been mercifully light and they had taken some prisoners for the effort. Now most of the men knew, or at least hoped, that the darkness they faced would mean their work for today was done.

The 21st Massachusetts pulled back from the fight in the cornfield in less military order than Thomas's men but with no less a sense of relief. They clearly had borne the brunt of the fight but given the size of their foe, most considered that they had emerged well enough off. And as the men moved in bunches and clumps southward toward the Reid house, slowly the regiment restored order to their ranks. "As we reached the fence at our end of the corn-field we were delighted to find our colors with their plucky guard," reported Captain Walcott proudly, "and what there was left of the 21st was soon formed upon them." September 1, 1862, had been a very hard day for the 21st Massachusetts but now, at long last, it was over.[44]

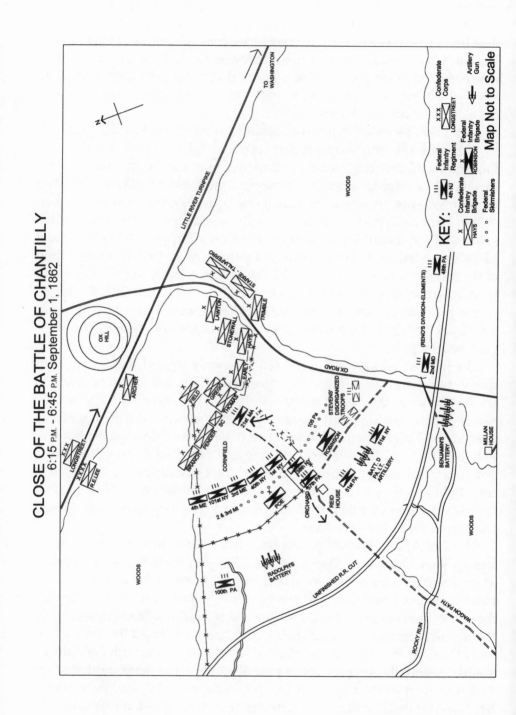

CLOSE OF THE BATTLE OF CHANTILLY
6:15 P.M. - 6:45 P.M. September 1, 1862

TO WASHINGTON

LITTLE RIVER TURNPIKE

WOODS

OX HILL

ARCHER

R. LEE

XXX
LONGSTREET

XXXX
LONGSTREET

TALIAFERRO

STARKE

TRIMBLE

LAWTON

STONEWALL

HAYS

EARLY

FIELD

GREGG

THOMAS

BRANCH
PENDER
SC

CORNFIELD

OX ROAD

(RENO'S DIVISION-ELEMENTS)

2nd MD

48th PA

STEVENS'
DISORGANIZED
TROOPS

79th NY

70th PA

ROBINSON

51st NY

BATT. D
PA. L't.
ARTILLERY

51st PA

BENJAMIN'S
BATTERY

MILLAN
HOUSE

79th NY
1st NY

4th ME
101st NY
3rd ME
40th NY

2 & 3rd MI

ORCHARD
57th PA

POE

REID
HOUSE

WOODS

RADOLPH'S
BATTERY

100th PA

UNFINISHED R.R. CUT

ROCKY RUN

WAGON PATH

WOODS

KEY:
Federal Infantry
Regiment
4th NJ
Confederate Infantry
Brigade
HAYS

Federal Skirmishers

Confederate
Corps
LONGSTREET

Federal Infantry
Brigade
ROBINSON

Artillery
Gun

Map Not to Scale

190

It was now after 6:15 P.M. and General Birney had been searching in vain for his division commander for nearly 20 minutes. Poe's and Robinson's brigades had arrived in the rear of the field awaiting only orders to advance into the fray. But General Kearny was nowhere to be seen. That General Kearny had not returned greatly worried David Birney, for if his commander was anything it was a man of his word. Since the promised reinforcements for his right flank had not appeared and, at the same time, he had received no word that providing these reinforcements was impossible, Birney assumed the worst had happened to Kearny. He knew that only death or capture could keep Philip Kearny from his duty.[45]

Calling his aides, Lieutenants Lee and Phillips over, General Birney informed them of his fears for General Kearny's safety and that on those grounds he was assuming command of the division. One of the young lieutenants was dispatched to Colonel Poe to pass along Birney's decision and order him to deploy his command in the rear of Birney's men on the southern end of the cornfield. Birney's remaining aide was dispatched to General Robinson with orders to advance to the southern end of the grassy field east of the Reid house. Within minutes of receiving their orders the two brigades were underway. Colonel Poe threw the 2nd and 3rd Michigan out in front of his brigade to act as skirmishers, while Brigadier General John Robinson deployed the 105th Pennsylvania for the same task in advance of his command. As the two units advanced nearly in unison past the Reid house they pressed only as far as the Reid orchard and halted to await further orders or action.[46]

As David Birney scanned the growing darkness for any sign of a Confederate advance he must have been struck by the sheer impossibility of launching an attack now. The field was cloaked entirely in a thick, black shroud and he could see his own brigade only by the occasional flash of a musket firing blindly in the dark. Birney wasn't fool enough to try an attack in these conditions and most certainly Jackson would avoid launching an attack now, too. Still, the possibility of Jackson renewing the fight, however slim, called for constant vigilance. And although the fight would almost certainly be renewed with the morning's light, Poe's and Robinson's positions were the most solid footing the Union had on this field. As the division's other two brigades completed their move only a few dozen yards behind him, Birney knew his next move. Calling over an aide, Birney sent word to his tired brigade that they had been relieved and should move to the rear of the 1st and 3rd Brigade's new position.[47]

General Birney was unaware of it at the time but even more help was on its way. At the same time that he had been assuming command of

Kearny's division, some two and a half miles to his east at Jermantown, Hooker's 2nd Division of Heintzelman's III Corps arrived in the rear of the defenses there. Commanded now by Brigadier General Cuvier Grover of the division's 1st Brigade, they reported to General Hooker, who now had a firm command of the hastily prepared Jermantown defenses. General Hooker directed Grover to post his division on the northern edge of the Warrenton Pike, with his left stretching as far toward the Ox Road as possible with a view to connecting to Kearny's right near there. It must have become clear to Cuvier Grover that whatever might have threatened Jermantown earlier in the day, the only real threat to the Union's route of retreat now lay to their immediate left. Knowing he could move to Kearny's aid and still hold Hooker's left flank, Grover ordered his division, with skirmishers out front, forward into place in the thick, wet woods, where most of them would remain for the night.

For Martin Haynes of the 2nd New Hampshire's Company I, their new deployment was a test of endurance: "Cold and shivering, the men stood in line in the dense jungle of dripping bushes," he wrote. Meanwhile, only a few yards to their rear, the seemingly unending line of the Union army's wagons continued to stream eastward to safety. Even in the midst of this torment, the men of the 2nd New Hampshire found some source of amusement. "There was some comfort to be got out of the situation," glowed Haynes, "in nagging the demoralized stragglers who always form the fringe of a fight, and urging the nervous teamsters to hurry on out of the way before the fight commenced right there." Though they didn't know it yet, their only real solace would be that they would completely avoid combat during the night.[48]

Meanwhile, Stonewall Jackson had been out on his horse, Little Sorrell, riding the rear of his command's position. What he found did not make him happy. The Federals had launched another wave of small attacks, which his men had managed to fend off, and they were now engaged in a firefight in the cornfield on the right of his position. The ease with which his men quashed these assaults brought little comfort, though, for Stonewall could only expect a wider attack to come, if not tonight then certainly in the morning.

Jackson already knew Longstreet's Command had finally arrived on the right of his position, ensuring that the entire strength of Lee's force would confront anything John Pope might throw at him. The first of Longstreet's units to arrive—in the midst of the lull between Stevens's and Kearny's assaults—heard nothing of the fighting Jackson's men had experienced all afternoon. ". . . [we] filed out of the road to camp. After we stacked arms, the rain came down in torrents," recorded First Sergeant W. Andrews of the 1st Georgia's Company M. Soon enough, though, the sergeant's illusions of a quiet camp were shattered by the sound of fighting starting up again in the woods to their right front. "Gen. Anderson gave the order to fall in, take arms, double-quick march, and we were off down the road like a flash, leaving our baggage behind." Moving about one mile farther east toward the sounds of gunfire, Longstreet's lead units were quickly deployed in line of battle on the southern edge of the Little River Turnpike, which they had just marched along. "We were ordered by the right flank, jumping a fence by the roadside," remembered Sergeant Andrews, "marched down through a field some 400 yards to a piece of woods. It was then dark, but the enemy's batteries were still shelling, crashing through the tree tops over our heads." But fortunately for the 1st Georgia and Longstreet's other units moving to Jackson's aid, they were to be spared battle that evening.[49]

Around 6:45, as Jackson continued to ride his lines, General Longstreet and his staff appeared through the hazy darkness. After their usual greetings, General Longstreet observed that an unusually large number of his men were moving to the rear and commented, "General, your men don't appear to work well today." Jackson, aware that this was a simple statement of fact with which he couldn't argue, responded hopefully, "No, but I hope it will prove a victory in the morning." Longstreet offered to send up Toombs's Brigade as support but Jackson refused. He still had two fresh brigades of his own in Archer's and Lawton's units, he observed, and in any case the darkness made it unlikely that Pope would try anything more tonight. No, for now his command could handle things. Wishing Jackson luck, Longstreet rode back to his own command.[50]

The firing in the corn, which had been intermittent now for some 15 minutes, slowed and then stopped altogether. As word spread through Birney's ranks of their withdrawal, the weary men turned and filed slowly—more out of exhaustion than a desire to stay—back through the corn in the direction they had come from earlier. In the darkness on the opposite end of the cornfield, Branch's and Pender's brigades, too, ceased their firing and adjusted their lines. And as the last muffled gunshot sounded across the shattered cornfield, it unknowingly signaled the end of the battle of Chantilly.

Major General Philip Kearny
U.S. Army Military History Institute

Brigadier General Isaac I. Stevens at Beaufort, South Carolina, in March 1862. *U.S. Army Military History Institute*

Brigadier General Isaac I. Stevens and his staff at Beaufort, South Carolina. From left to right: Capt. Benjamin Porter (8th Michigan), Capt. William T. Lusk (79th New York), Capt. Hazard Stevens (79th New York), Lt. Abraham Cottrell (3rd Michigan), General Stevens, the general's surgeon, George Kemble, Lt. Benjamin Lyons (50th Pennsylvania).
U.S. Army Military History Institute

Major General John Pope, photographed in spring 1862 before his promotion.

Centreville on Sunday morning, August 31, 1862, looking east along the Warrenton Turnpike. Pope's Army of Virginia is re-forming and reorganizing in the wake of the previous day's retreat from defeat at the Second Battle of Bull Run. A wartime sketch by Edwin Forbes. *The Library of Congress*

Centreville, Virginia, looking southwest along Braddock Rd. toward its intersection with the Warrenton Turnpike. To the right of the stone Centreville Methodist Church is the main Confederate-built fort on the heights of Centreville. *U.S. Army Military History Institute*

A 1907 view of the grassy field, looking south from the Confederate position on the wood line. Stevens's Union IX Corps emerged from the woods on the opposite end of the field to open the battle. The Reid house is visible on the far right edge of the photo, and the fence leading to the house stands on the same spot as the wartime fence dividing the grassy field from the cornfield. The undulating nature of the field's terrain is clearly visible in this picture. *The Fairfax County Public Library, Virginia Room*

The cornfield at Chantilly, looking north toward the Confederate position on the wood line. The imagined location of Kearny's death is probably accurate, and the downward slope into the grassy field—off the right edge of the drawing—is implied. The side vignettes depict graves on the battlefield and souvenir hunters cutting bullets from trees. A wartime sketch by Charles Reed. *The Library of Congress*

Col. A. T. A. Torbert. His quick action secured the Union's hold on Jermantown and blocked Jackson's advance. *U.S. Army Military History Institute*

Officers of the 21st Massachusetts Infantry Regiment

Colonel William S. Clark

Lieutenant George C. Parker

Captain Charles Walcott

(All three photos—*U.S. Army Military History Institute*)

Brigadier General Alexander Lawton. He commanded Ewell's Division of Jackson's Command during the fight at Ox Hill.
U.S. Army Military History Institute

Lieutenant General Thomas J. "Stonewall" Jackson. *U.S. Army Military History Institute*

A postwar engraving depicting General Isaac Stevens's death at Chantilly. Stevens probably died wrapped in the 79th New York's regimental flag, bearing the Scottish cross of St. Andrew, rather than the U.S. national colors. *U.S. Army Military History Institute*

A postwar inaccurate engraving depicting the heroic death of General Philip Kearny. In reality, Kearny rode alone in the dark into Thomas's Brigade and was killed while racing away, clinging to his horse's back. *U.S. Army Military History Institute*

9

The Aftermath

★───────────────★

Birney's command moved quite willingly out of the cornfield and past the Reid house to regroup. "[A]s we fell back from that corn field to the open," Lieutenant Ford of the 101st New York remembered, "we noticed that hardly a stalk was left standing on that whole field, except now and then a solitary one which apparently escaped the storm of lead and was left a lonely sentinel to watch the remains of its companions. We fell back a short distance and encamped for the night in the wet grass without fire or shelter." Once their move was complete, Poe's and Robinson's brigades posted on either side of the Reid house formed the Union front for the night. Opposite their position, across the grassy field and what remained of the cornfield, lay the Confederate front. As at the start of the fight, they held the woodline on the northern end of the two fields. The Southerners of Jackson's Command had much the same expectation for the night as New Yorker Lieutenant Ford: "A cold, wet night that would be spent in the open with no fire to cheer the comfortless scene."[1]

In front of both armies' lines lay a loose string of skirmishers who knew they would spend an even more trying night than their comrades in the rear, for they were the first line of defense against enemy trickery. Making their situation even worse, the thick, misty darkness that covered the field made each man in this line eerily alone, trapped in a void by the duty each knew he could not dare shirk, no matter how he was pressed by human instinct. Confusion had reigned in the Reid fields for the first few dozen minutes after the battle, until the skirmishers moved hesitantly forward to restore some order. But even their presence was not enough to overcome the dark void. Some men were posted and simply lost any sense of where their lines were and each approaching footstep held danger in their anonymity.

One Confederate officer, moving about his picket line to check on his men, lost his way completely. Finding the next post in line, his unease grew until he stopped dead, unsure of himself or his direction. When challenged by the man in his front, the officer regained his composure and replied confidently, "3rd Louisiana," only to find this post manned by Pennsylvanians and himself a prisoner. Over on the eastern side of the Ox Road, Sergeant Plunkett of the 21st Massachusetts cautiously searched the dark woods for his friend Moultie, who had disappeared after the earlier fight there. Plunkett had gone back into the woods without his musket, apparently thinking he might need both arms to carry out his presumably wounded friend, and so was taken aback when he suddenly found himself in the presence of a Rebel picket. But without a thought the sergeant wrenched the gun out his enemy's hands and led the man back as a prisoner.[2]

Nearly an hour after the battle ended in earnest, the dark sky suddenly cleared as the trailing end of the once-fierce storm passed overhead. As the clouds raced away, the bright half moon and stars made a welcome appearance on the Reid fields, illuminating the entire scene. For the pickets this sudden lightening meant order in the form of a comrade nearby. It also meant that targets once covered by darkness were now visible to the emboldened pickets and an intermittent but regular round of firing resumed. For some of these men it was the first time that day that they could size up the field with any clarity.

The cornfield had been nearly mowed to the ground in many places and in its place had sprung a bounty of death. Dead men were spread over the field in appalling density for such a small area. The grassy field, too, was littered with the remains of the dead. Mostly they lay where they had fallen during the battle. The former positions of both Union and Confederate regiments could be denoted by the lines of intermittent dead they had left behind after moving. These lines were particularly noticeable in front of the woodline where Stevens's division had charged into the woods. The remains of the Highlanders of the 79th New York and the Irishmen of the 28th Massachusetts still hugged their once vital lines, as if they expected their comrades to return. A Confederate officer recalled of that night, "We camped on the field, sleeping side by side with the dead of both armies. It was very dark; occasionally the moon would come from under a cloud and show the upturned faces of the dead, eyes wide open, seeming to look you in the face."[3]

One Confederate recalled a particularly grisly scene—probably featuring one of Stevens's fallen Celts—that was all too common in this war. "Do you believe a hog would eat a dead Yankee?" asked the man in Jackson's ranks sometime during the evening. "No, I don't," replied his comrade. "Well, look there," rejoined the first Rebel, pointing to the remains of a Federal soldier who had had his chest torn open so that his liver fell from the open wound nearly to the ground. Beside the corpse stood two or three hogs "tearing it to pieces and eating away with great satisfaction." But what made this scene so uncommon was not the wound but the actions of the hogs, for such wounds and worse were commonplace on the Chantilly field that evening.[4]

The moonlit night that came as so welcome a relief for the pickets of both sides was anything but welcome for the men wandering the open fields. Between the picket lines were hundreds of men moving about, each seemingly with his own agenda. Some needed only a few brief moments of moonlight to reorient themselves and find their unit. Others searched about singly or in small groups, looking desperately for family or friends who had disappeared in the chaos of battle an hour earlier. For the 21st Massachusetts's Dennis Fogerty, who had been shot in both legs and was unable to move at all, the moonlight nearly brought an end to his life. A wandering Rebel came upon the helpless man and immediately drew up his bayonet-armed musket to exact revenge, crying out, "Take that, you damned Yankee!" But before the Rebel could finish his thrust Fogerty shot back, "I'm not a Yankee, but an Irishman." The now-disarmed enemy dropped his weapon and walked away cursing.[5]

James Stone, who had fled in terror from the 21st Massachusetts's fight in the cornfield, had by now regained his composure and gone in search of his unit. In his search Private Stone stumbled on a close friend, Billy Morrow, and the two quickly found the 21st's color guard. Satisfied that they had resumed their role as soldiers, the two friends determined to return to the field and search for a friend of theirs named Bradish, of Company E, who had been hit in the leg during the slaughter in the woods east of the Ox Road and was still missing. "Billy had seen him at about the same time I did as we came out of the wood," recalled James Stone, "and believing we were near the place we started out to see if we could find him. We thought he was badly wounded and wondered if we could not find him and do something for him. Bradish had been one of the nine who had played ball at Newport News and we were both very fond of him." The two privates moved back across the open grassy field to the spot where they had emerged from the woods and began to scour the area. "There were a number of dead men laying about but we were unprepared to believe our comrade was dead, but when we examined the dead men we found Bradish was one of them. The expression on his face I shall never forget, it was so changed and painful. Had we not been searching for him and turned him over, for as he lay his face was partially concealed,

I should not have recognized him." Saddened and shocked as the two men were to discover their friend's painful death, they were consoled at least that they could offer him a descent, Christian burial, something they knew was all too rare in this war. "We found a place under a great pine tree; we dug a shallow grave and buried him near the place where he fell. We put a stone at each end of the grave, carved his initials on the trunk of the tree and left one of our beloved comrades and one of the best soldiers in the regiment."[6]

In many respects, though, Private Stone and his dead friend were lucky, for one had escaped the fight unscathed and the other would suffer no more of the agony of battle. Others who remained strewn over the moon-lit fields at that moment were just beginning to wage their own battles with the wounds they had received. One New York soldier recalled that the wounded who littered the field "groaned and cried with agony, begged for water—pleaded to be killed to end their misery—wet and shivering in the cold." Charles Cuffel of Durell's battery remarked that "the sound of the groans of the wounded and dying, add[ed] horror to the discomfort and gloom of the situation." The cries of the wounded left much the same impression on the Confederates, who similarly could not escape the constant wail of suffering men—wearing both gray and blue—in their immediate front.[7]

For those remaining on the field in the midst of this horror the scene was especially painful. Lieutenant George Parker of the 21st Massachusetts had refused to leave his captain and a fellow lieutenant of Company D and remained behind in the cornfield. The firing between the Bay Staters and Thomas's Brigade had barely ceased when the firing was replaced by the lamentations of the wounded. "May I never hear such a cry as went up from that field again," pleaded Lieutenant Parker. "As soon as they all knew I was with them, so many called to me I knew not what to do. 'Oh, for God's sake, Lieutenant Parker, some water!'; 'Oh, don't leave me!'; Oh, I'm shot, I shall die!'; 'Some water! Quick, Quick!'" But the weary officer did what he could for the suffering men and soon organized others who had remained behind into stretcher details to move the 21st Massachusetts's wounded to the rear for medical help. "First Lieutenant Beckwith was shot in the bowels. I thought I must get him some help and so with some help from 2 or three who had come cautiously back I got him into a rubber blanket and 4 of us carried him out of the deep mud of the corn field and laid him with his head resting on a rail on the wet grass." Leaving two of the detail with the wounded lieutenant, Parker returned to the open field to fetch Captain Ira Kelton, who had begged them to return. "When I got back to him the whole spot was under Rebel guard and . . . after stating to them that I wished to see my captain safely to some place where his leg could be amputated, they furnished me with a stretcher and four men. [W]e passed on through their lines and halted just in the rear and laid the captain down on the grass. He was suffering intensely for the knee pan was blown to slivers and they stuck out like a bunch of asparagus from a tumbler." Lieutenant Parker's kindness had gotten him out of the desperation of the cornfield but at the price of his own freedom.[8]

The wounded of both sides formed a nearly constant stream of human suffering moving apart from each other in search of medical help all hoped would await them in the rear of their armies. Some of these men, like Lieutenant Parker's captain, were simply unable to move off the field under their own power and were at the mercy of friends or, for the less fortunate, army stretcherbearers, some of whom too often were all but indifferent to the pain of their charges. Others moved rearward as quickly as they could manage under their own limited power. Alfred Bellard of the 5th New Jersey, one of Hooker's troops that had reinforced Birney's line on the rear of the Chantilly battlefield, recalled, "In the woods close to our line was a large fire, toward which the wounded who could walk came expecting to find the surgeon and get their wounds dressed. No surgeon was there, and no one knew where to find them. One man came along while I was standing there to warm myself who was shot in the head, and the blood was still running down his face. Finding no one to attend to him, he traveled off. . . ." The sad truth was that for many of the men who lay wounded that night, there was no help at all awaiting them in the rear. Typical was the experience of the 28th Massachusetts, whose regimental surgeon and assistant surgeon had remained behind to care for the wounded on August 30 and were not with the regiment this day. The only medical help awaiting these poor men was John Barrington, a lone hospital steward.[9]

One of the walking wounded was Sergeant Daniel Fletcher of the 40th New York. Having "jumped for the rear" as soon as he was hit, the sergeant hobbled southward for some 50 yards by using his rifle as a crutch. Soon the strain of this effort and the blood flowing from his wound made him woozy and faint. But the strenuous effort paid off for he was now within view of the Reid house, where he saw two men from his own regiment and called them over for help. The two comrades grabbed his waist and he their shoulders and the team moved once more for the rear. Moving closer to the house, Fletcher found himself near collapse once again from the effort and soon begged to be placed on a stretcher. His two friends found a pair of stretcherbearers who agreed to take Fletcher to the Millan house, which was now serving as the main Union field hospital. Seeing blood pouring from the wound, the two ambulance corpsmen decided they would have to stop the bleeding or it would certainly be useless to make the trip. "They cut my trousers open," Fletcher remembered, "and tied a bandage tightly around the wounded knee. This lessened the pain." With his bleeding under control, the corpsmen picked up the stretcher and moved on. Now, for the first time since leaving the battle, Sergeant Fletcher took notice of something beside his own pain. "I saw a great many of our wounded going to the rear," he observed, "some had help; others hobbled along as best they could."[10]

Reaching the Millan farm, Sergeant Fletcher realized the full extent of the casualties. The house itself was full of wounded men awaiting medical treatment. The main room was used as a sort of waiting room for the officers—"[i]t was the rule to take care of the commissioned officers first," Fletcher noted dryly—and the most desperate cases among the lower ranks. Each of the adjoining rooms had been hastily turned into operating rooms, from which emanated the most hideous screams of pain and suffering. From the window periodically shot forth a severed arm or leg that fell onto a growing pile, the view of which was mercifully covered by darkness. Making the scene of suffering even more hellish was the fact that the few surgeons laboring on the wounded that night did so mainly with only the supplies they had on hand. "[S]ad to say," recalled a veteran of the 21st Massachusetts, "except a mere trifle in our hospital knapsack, there was no chloroform, and the amputations had to be performed without it."[11]

Daniel Fletcher and his knee wound, perhaps thankfully, did not warrant entry to the main house and so he was taken to a log mule shed near the barn. Then, just as fortune had favored him when he needed it most near the Reid house, so luck treated him to one more favor. "The mule house was full of wounded men. Our orderly sergeant was outside when I came up, and said to those inside, 'Lie along. Sergeant Fletcher wants to get in there.'" And so, though he would have to wait his turn for the doctor's attention, Fletcher was at least under cover should the rain return. It would be sometime well into the night before the surgeons would attend to Fletcher's wound. But eventually they crouched beside him and by the light of a lantern removed the ball from his knee. Knowing that this particular patient would live to tell the tale of Chantilly, they asked him if he wanted to keep the ball taken from his leg, which he did. His souvenir in hand, Daniel Fletcher fell asleep to prepare for whatever the dawn might hold.[12]

While the Union surgeons labored in the Millan house, their Confederate counterparts were engaged in similar efforts less than a mile to the north. Shortly after the fighting had started Confederate medical officers had set up shop in nearly every building, stable, and barn that could be found, for they all knew the flood of wounded would come soon enough. Dr. Spencer Welch, surgeon of the 13th South Carolina, set up his hospital at nearly the same moment the owners were fleeing the battle. "I went into a horse lot and established a field infirmary [as] an old lady and her daughter were fleeing from a cottage and crossing the lot in the rain," he remembered. To the doctor's dismay, the wounded began to arrive well before he was really prepared to care for them. "Lieutenant Leopard from Lexington was brought back to me with both his legs torn off below the knees by a shell, and another man with part of his arm torn off [. B]ut neither Dr. Kenedy, Dr. Kilgore, nor our medical wagon was with us, and so I had nothing with me to give them but morphine. They both died during the night." The parade of ghastly wounds intensified and Welch struggled on through the evening to do what he could for his patients with the materials at hand. "We filled the carriage house, barn, and stable with our wounded, but I could do little for them. Colonel Edwards was furious, and he told me to tell the other doctors 'for God's sake to keep up with their command.'"[13]

Lieutenant Parker of the 21st Massachusetts was led with his gravely wounded captain to the rear of the Confederate lines in search of medical help. The scene that greeted him was anything but heartening. "It was quite an hour before I could get the Capt. moved back to a hospital, and when I finally got him there, the whole house was full and even the piazza crowded; the barn, too; and at last we had to put him in a little corn barn on a bare floor, among potatoes and corn and barrels. [A]nd all the litter of such a place, with 3 sick Rebs and all thick with dirt. How I worked that night. [G]ot another Yankee prisoner some ground coffee and made him some hot drink, heated some stones and kept them to his [the captain's] feet, shifted his shattered leg and tried in vain to get a Reb doctor to dress it." Though the Union lieutenant and his wounded commander would have to wait their turn behind similarly suffering Confederates, eventually they got the medical attention they needed. Captain Ira Kelton would celebrate September 1, his 25th birthday, by having a leg removed with no chloroform to ease the pain.[14]

While the suffering of the wounded on both sides was equally intense, one key difference between the Union and Confederate lines after the battle was the availability of food. For while the Union boys complained about having to eat their crackers cold, the Southern boys resting only a few hundred yards away would gladly have taken the Yankees' cold fare. Nothing had alleviated the shortage of food that had hindered Jackson's Command during their march to Chantilly earlier in the day. When it was clear that the fighting was over for the night some of the more desperate and adventurous Southerners moved cautiously from their lines and into the open field in search of food. One such man was Private George Cornwell of the 40th Virginia, who loaded his musket and went in search of food. "Unexpectedly meeting a Federal lieutenant and four men bearing a stretcher and searching for their captain," a comrade remembered, "he was asked what regiment he belonged to. With ready wit he named a New York regiment, and then learned their business and finding that they were unarmed, he leveled his musket, demanded their surrender, and brought them back to our lines." Private Cornwell didn't find the food he sought but did get a Yankee officer's sword for his effort. Another man in the 40th Virginia, Wayland Dunaway of Company I, ventured out in search of food and came away luckier than Cornwell. "I myself did a littel searching until I found a haversack strapped to a man who would never use his teeth again. I found in the haversack crackers and ground coffee mixed with sugar; and bringing into requisition my matches, tincup, and canteen of water (three things I was always careful to have about me), I soon had a pint of steaming beverage. I ate my supper and then laid down to sleep." But Dunaway was far luckier than most of Jackson's men—or Longstreet's for that matter—who would have nothing at all to fill their aching stomachs during the cold and wet night.[15]

While the men were trying to find food—or forget about their lack of it—Stonewall Jackson was busy preparing for the next phase of the fight. Though the Union's attack had caught him off guard and kept him from reaching Jermantown, once the fight was underway and the lines properly formed, his command had shrugged it off rather easily. Certainly John Pope would be back in the morning with more men to throw at his line. And though Pope had hardly proven himself worthy of his command, there was still the issue of those fresh troops J. E. B. Stuart had seen two days earlier. He could not afford to be caught off guard, so during the rest of the evening Jackson initiated the moves that would prepare for the morning's fight. Leaving Branch's and Pender's brigades posted in the woodline as a picket force, Jackson ordered the rest of his command to fall back to a position just south of the Little River Turnpike, near the base of

Ox Hill, to camp for the night. From this more consolidated position they would be better prepared to meet anything Pope might try at dawn, either by moving up the turnpike or across the field of September 1. At the same time, Longstreet's Command moved south on the road to camp for the night on Jackson's immediate right. Lee's entire Army of Northern Virginia was now in place along the base of Ox Hill and as ready for a fight as its tired and hungry men could be.[16]

Neither Jackson, Longstreet, Lee, nor the lowest private in the Southern army knew it then, but there would be no Federal attack in the morning. In fact, if any Southerner had known how little the man in charge of the Union army was involved in the fighting at Chantilly he wouldn't have worried about their fate at all. Pope apparently had little idea what was happening only a few miles to his east. While he knew of the firing—and feared a larger battle was already underway—he seemed to have no idea what was actually occurring or how to go about gaining control of it. At 4 P.M., while Stevens's skirmishers were fully engaged with their counterparts in Hays's Louisiana Brigade, General Pope was directing General McDowell to soon expect a battle and to maintain his communication with Reno. While a laudable preparatory order from a general about to enter battle, this would in fact be the commanding general's last dispatch during the battle of Chantilly. He would make no further effort to personally direct the defense of his army only miles from his nation's capital.

John Pope had no more fight left in him, it seemed, and the very best he felt he could do now was to protect the army by moving it safely in the Washington defenses. Sometime after 4:00 P.M., General Pope and his headquarters staff left their house on the heights of Centreville and moved east to Fairfax Court House. Given the time that they left for Fairfax, Pope and his staff must have ridden right past the fighting near Ox Hill. Indeed, they must certainly have personally heard the firing, for both routes to Fairfax took them within earshot of the battlefield. That John Pope took no interest in directing the fight is a measure of his broken spirit late on September 1.[17]

Once safely in Fairfax Court House, Pope set to the task of moving his army to the safety of the Washington defenses. As the order reached the troops in Centreville, they picked up their things, formed their regiments, and moved out as they had dozens of times before. This movement had become routine. But the routine of retreating, running from the Rebels instead of attacking them, was welling up in the men as they marched east in a way that it never had before. "Who will forget the straggling, the mud, the rain, the terrible panic and loss of life from random firing, and the hopeless feeling—almost despair—of that dreadful night march!" wrote General Howard. His description perfectly captures the sense of brokenness and defeat the Union men felt as they slogged through the mud out of Centreville that night. For while they had stung after losing the fight at Manassas, they had merely repositioned themselves—not run. Most in the ranks knew they were ready to try hitting Robert E. Lee again and expected Pope to use the strong Centreville works to launch such an attack. But now it was clear that Pope had them running to their last line of defense, the Washington works, and they were doing so without a major fight. "The headquarters in the saddle sought refuge under the shadow of the dome of the Capitol," mocked a man in the 19th Massachusetts. Pope, like all those before him who dared call themselves a Union army commander, had let them down. Most would blame him— and some hate him—forever for this failure.[18]

Few of the men who marched from Centreville that night would ever recall a more depressing or disorganized movement during their service for the Union. Their ponderous sense of defeat now became manifest in sloppy movement and unkempt formations. Units that normally prided themselves on their sense of organization and order on the march now slogged uncaringly eastward. For every regiment that moved in reasonably good order, another moved like a mere mob of men stumbling their way to the same place. For most, this march was far more disorganized and depressing than the retreat from Manassas and worse than any retreat since the first run from Manassas, which few of them had experienced. The colonel of the 55th New York remembered, "Disorder began to affect the ranks. The orders of officers, the cries of the teamsters, the oaths of the soldiers, were mingled with peals of thunder. All this produced a deafening tumult, in the midst of which it was difficult to recognize each other, and from the confusion of which we could not free ourselves without leaving behind us a large number of stragglers."[19]

Some of the veterans would later conclude that the march to Washington in the dark of September 1 and 2 compared "favorably" with the "mud march" they would endure only a few months hence as one of the worst movements in the army's history. That comparison was based not only on the men's moods but on the insufferable weather that plagued both armies. It only magnified the sense of defeat in the Union ranks and made their short march even more difficult. The rain, which had abated for some time during the evening returned near midnight and, though it came in the form of intermittent showers and not the unrelenting downpour of the late afternoon, it was as unwelcome as an Old Testament plague. "We started in the rain for Fairfax," commiserated Edward Schweitzer of the 30th Ohio in his diary, "[w]e was all wet and muddy and had to lay out in the mud." And with the renewed rain came a cold front that chilled the wet, suffering men to the limits of their endurance. For Charles Haydon of the 2nd Michigan, the weather was the defining aspect of this comfortless march: ". . . we quietly left our position . . .& [in] a high wind withdrew from the triangle which the enemy were enclosing us. The night was quiet and very cold."[20]

Adding to the soldiers' hardship, the rain of the last two days had turned the Warrenton Pike and Braddock Road into two long stretches of quagmire, which the men had no choice but to slog through. While the Federal wagon train had moved quickly over still compact if slippery roads during the afternoon, by the time the bulk of the army reached the intersection with the Ox Road these wagon tracks were deep ruts of mud. And while the first few divisions to pass over the road could largely march around the wagon wheel ruts, their methodically pounding feet turned the remaining part of the road into one long river of ankle-deep mud that pulled at the men's feet and tested their resolve. The struggle with the mud was worst for the men of the IX Corps, who would be the last to take to the road. "In the march, the Mud was very deep, owing to the rain & the army trains & troops passing over it . . .," wrote Captain James Wren of the 48th Pennsylvania in his diary. "Sergeant Nelson Major of our Compny lost one of his shoos, [it] having stuck in the mud & thear was no such thing as to stop and look for it. The orders war 'go ahead'. . ."[21]

The first of the retreating Union regiments arrived in Fairfax Court House even before midnight and those that were posted there quickly sought out the best driest ground on which to bivouac for the night. Many of these units would get a much needed night's rest and begin to restore order for the day ahead. Even so, for the remainder of the night Fairfax Court House was bedlam itself. "By the light of the fires kindled all around in the streets, in the yards, in the fields," recalled one Union veteran, "one could see a confused mass of wagons, ambulances, caissons, around which [were] thousands of men." Other units had farther to go before they could rest, if indeed they would rest at all that dreary night, and continued the march on through Fairfax to Alexandria or toward the Chain Bridge. As they continued on so too continued the disorder and confusion.[22]

Though there remained confusion among the men of the III and IX Corps, who waited shivering on the slopes of the Reid farm, they all now knew one thing—their army was leaving them behind. They could see the retreating army from their elevated position on the battlefield and their own growing sense of immobility—trapped on this wet, cold, and dreary spot—only added to their suffering. Captain Thomas Parker of the 51st Pennsylvania recalled that "[th]e regiment suffered this night from cold more than any time since it had been in the army. Cold chilling rain fell during the whole night, the men being without a gum or even a painted blanket, and many without any shirt at all, only their blouse and pants on, and lying all night in wet grass that could not be less than two feet and a half high. Their condition can safely be compared to that of a man being compelled to stand in cold water up to his chin for eight hours in succession." There was some comfort for the Chantilly veterans, though. As fires began to appear in ever increasing numbers along the Confederate-held woodline—a sign there would be no attack tonight—Generals Reno and Birney rescinded their earlier order and permitted the cold weary men to build fires to dry themselves and cook what food they could. This small comfort wasn't much, but on this night it was a most welcome gift.[23]

Near midnight General Reno ordered the IX Corps and III Corps men under his command on the battlefield to slowly and quietly pull back toward the Warrenton Pike. The pickets and others who were posted there fairly snuck to the rear, drawing with them those men who had stayed on the field by default. For although they were in sorry spirits that evening, no one wished the fate that they all knew awaited anyone who stayed behind. They stopped upon reaching the Reid house and soon the number of fires in the valley and along the adjacent ridge grew in number as the cold, wet men tried to dry their clothes and catch what warmth they could. Sometime near 2 A.M. officers came through the bivouac near the Reid house telling the men to build up their fires and prepare to move. When the men questioned the wisdom of wasting effort in gathering wood for soon-to-be-abandoned fires, they were told that General Reno meant for the enemy to believe they remained on the field after leaving for Fairfax Court House. The men, who would have acted without such explanations, did as directed and built "rousing big fires," as one Highlander recalled. Within the hour they were moving toward the Warrenton Pike, past the Millan house, through the woods, and south along the Ox Road generally following the route they had used the previous day to reach the Chantilly field. By 3:00 A.M., those who could move were gone.[24]

At the same time that most of the army was moving eastward to safety, hundreds of their wounded comrades remaining on the field and in the hospitals and were simply unable to join the retreat. Those lucky enough to secure a place in an ambulance or in a supply wagon were soon on their way to the rear and safety. But most, too weak to march on their own or too grievously wounded to move, would have to remain behind in the hands of the Confederates. "Some time in the night, one of our officers came and said that everyone who could possibly get away, must leave," Daniel Fletcher sorrowfully remembered. "We knew then that we were to be left to the tender mercies of the Rebels." Sergeant Fletcher tried to crawl out of the mule house hospital he had been in for the last few hours but found that his leg wound was so painful that he couldn't even reach the brush near the house and wearily pulled himself back to the shed, resigned to his fate. The only consolation the sergeant had was that he was not alone. "We were a sober set of men that night, for we all knew we should be prisoners in the morning. I myself was wet, for there had been a heavy shower before the fight. There was a fire outside the cabin, but I did not feel able to drag myself to it. A pretty fix for a man to be in; dangerously wounded, soaking wet, a prisoner in the enemy's hands, and almost out of food."[25]

While wounded men like Sergeant Fletcher had no option but to stay, there was another, smaller group of men who chose to stay on the field that night. These men could easily have fled with the army to safety but instead remained behind with the wounded to await certain capture. Chief among this group were the surgeons and hospital stewards, many of whom were simply too busy tending to the wounded to worry about their fate. Nearly every Union regiment that had been engaged in the fight at Chantilly left its surgeon behind that night and, like the historian of the 21st Massachusetts who would lament that ". . . our kind and skillful Assistant Surgeon [Dr.] Joseph Hastings fell into the hands of the enemy," all would miss their only direct medical help in the days ahead. For even though most knew the Confederates eventually would let the surgeons return to their units, those men who fell sick in the interim would have to make do on their own.

Along with the surgeons remaining at Chantilly, most of the chaplains in Stevens's, Reno's, and Kearny's divisions also stayed behind to care for the wounded. The poor 21st Massachusetts, in addition to losing its doctor, lost its regimental chaplain, Reverend George Ball, that night. The chaplains not only provided comfort and attended to the spiritual needs of the wounded and dying men left behind, but they also doubled as hospital stewards. Reverend Ball worked tirelessly loading men from the 21st and other regiments onto ambulances until there were no wagons left to put the wounded in. Chaplains of other regiments worked equally hard to get the wounded to the safety and better medical care that awaited them in the Washington defenses. But for many who remained on the field, especially those men from regiments with no surgeon, the chaplain who stayed behind would be their only familiar face to whom they could turn for help in the most trying hours of their short lives. Chaplain Robert Audley Browne of the 100th Pennsylvania wrote of that night, "To attend to those dying and wounded was a sad duty. I had chosen to remain, being the only member of the 100th Penn. that remained, except the wounded."[26]

There were also a few men who remained behind with the wounded even as their duty should have called them from the field. Many of these men stayed to watch over and nurse a brother or friend who lay around the Reid or Millan houses. Some, though, stayed out of a sense of Christian devotion to the suffering, feeling that at such a time their orders came from a higher authority than General Pope or President Lincoln. One such man was Corporal Flynn of the 40th New York. While Daniel Fletcher lay wounded, watching his own army desert him, Flynn came to check on his comrades before himself leaving. Sergeant Fletcher begged the young corporal to remain behind and care for him and the other wounded in the Reid mule shed. At first Flynn objected and reminded his friend that he would be captured by the Rebels but after a moment of reflection agreed to stay. Tying a strip of white cloth around his arm to mark himself as a "hospital steward," Flynn lectured Fletcher that if he had read the Bible before the battle, as he himself had done, he would not have been wounded. Despite his lecture, Flynn remained throughout the dark night—and the coming days of hardship—to care for his comrades, some of whom he barely knew. After leaving the Chantilly field a few days later, Flynn and Daniel Fletcher parted company forever. Corporal Flynn's sacrifice so touched Daniel Fletcher that in 1884, he would remark, "I wish I knew where he was now. I would give more to see him than any other man I ever knew."[27]

10

The Honor of Two Lives

★——————————————★

Isaac Stevens's corpse was moved eastward along with the army that evening, bouncing along on the floor of an ambulance. The general's body was there only because of the love the Highlanders had for their fallen commander, and the men who had placed him in the ambulance risked certain punishment should General Reno discover their actions. His body had lain on the ground where he fell during the worst of his division's fighting, still wrapped in the flag he had been carrying at the time of his death. But when they withdrew from the woodline, several men of the 79th New York stopped to collect the general's broken remains and, as if carrying a mortally wounded comrade, took it back to the rear. When they reached the Reid house the men gently placed Stevens's body on the ground as if he were still alive. It was then that they received word from Lieutenant Colonel Morrison of General Reno's orders. In response to Morrison's earlier message that Stevens was dead, Reno ordered them to bury the body on the field and join in the retreat. The men of Stevens's division simply refused to accept this order. William Todd recalled that the men were "indignant at Reno's orders to bury the body of our beloved General on the field." Risking a strong rebuking from his commander, but earning the respect and admiration of all of Stevens's division, Lieutenant Colonel Morrison personally ordered Stevens's body into the ambulance and had it quickly moving on its way toward Washington. General Reno might not care, but his men were determined that their fallen commander would not suffer such an ignoble fate.[1]

Once in Washington the next day, Stevens's body was delivered to the house of a long-time friend, John L. Hayes. After embalming, the body was placed on a railroad car and made its last journey home to Newport, Rhode Island. Isaac Stevens's remains were finally laid to rest in Island Cemetery in Newport. His funeral service was attended by hundreds of mourners, including Rhode Island's Governor Sprague and Governor Andrews of Massachusetts. Beside his grave they erected a large granite obelisk bearing an inscription written by his brother-in-law, Reverend Brooks, extolling Stevens's patriotism and his best qualities. Isaac Stevens subsequently was promoted to the rank of major general, with an effective date posted to July 4, 1862. In death General Stevens had finally overcome the stumbling block—his "political failings"—that had so frustrated his last months on earth and attained a rank that was commensurate with his experience as an army officer. When word of his death reached Washington Territory, the legislature there passed several resolutions in Stevens's honor and ordered black crepe posted on all government offices and workers' clothing as a sign of their deep mourning. The final tribute to Isaac Stevens came on September 22, 1864, when the 79th New York, then mustered out of Federal service, presented his widow the flag he had borne when he fell at Chantilly. Isaac Stevens received funeral honors befitting the finest of 19th-century military heroes.[2]

About the same time in the night that Isaac Stevens's body was being carefully if surreptitiously loaded on an ambulance for the journey to Washington, General Philip Kearny's earthly remains were being picked over by his enemies. The Confederates of the 49th Georgia and Thomas's Brigade had known for some time that the officer they had killed in the waning hours of September 1 had been an important Yankee, perhaps even a Union general. As darkness suppressed the fighting for the night, Thomas's men dragged the unknown officer's twisted remains behind their lines. Laying the body out on the ground, everyone present recognized the single star on his shoulder strap; they had, as they had hoped, killed a Union general. But no one viewing the remains in the flickering candlelight recognized him; he had a distinctive face and only one arm but still no one recognized him. His body was placed on a stretcher—he was a general, after all—and set to the side; for the time being still-living wounded Southerners would take precedence over a dead Yankee, even a formerly high-ranking one. Sitting unattended, though, the body attracted the attention of several men from the ranks who thought they might need some of the fine accoutrements the dead man had but would no longer need. Kearny's high cavalry boots, his cloak, pistol, fine-bladed presentation sword, watch, flask, and other personal items were all stripped from the corpse and slid quietly into their new owner's pockets and onto their shoulders and feet.[3]

Lieutenant Parker of the 21st Massachusetts, now a Confederate prisoner, had been tending to the wounded of his regiment when he was pulled aside by a senior officer, possibly Colonel Thomas. The officer led him to a stretcher and asked Parker if he could identify the dead officer. Lieutenant Parker now knew the fate of General Kearny, perhaps the first Union officer to know conclusively what had happened after his encounter with the 21st Massachusetts. Parker told the officer that it was General Philip Kearny they had killed. He immediately observed aloud that Kearny's body had been stripped of his boots and coat, to which the Southern officer replied, "They shall be put on again. Our boys didn't know who it was and thought it a nice thing to get hold of his clothes." With that said, Kearny's belongings were quickly returned to his body, although most of the men returning things must have questioned the point of redressing a cold corpse when they—living, breathing soldiers— would have to shiver uncovered throughout the cold, wet night ahead.[4]

After some time, the stretcher bearing Philip Kearny's body was taken to Jackson's headquarters for the night, set up in the Stewart family's house known locally by the name "Linden Lee." On the way there the lieutenant leading the detail ordered his four-man team to stop near a fire built by several men of Longstreet's Command on the shoulder of the Little River Turnpike. Three Federal prisoners being marched by identified the body to those gathered round the fire, pointing to a cut in Kearny's coatsleeve which had been made by a shell fragment on Saturday near Manassas. These men knew Kearny's reputation and were awed by his presence, even if in the form of a corpse. Once the stretcher arrived at the Stewart house it was placed on the house's porch amid the suffering wounded of Jackson's Command. The men surrounding the stretcher knew only that it bore a dead Yankee general; they had more pressing matters occupying them at that moment. But when General Jackson returned to his headquarters and saw the body for the first time he was aghast. "My God, boys, you know who you have killed?" Stonewall reportedly exclaimed, "You have shot the most gallant officer in the United States Army. This is Phil Kearny, who lost his arm in the Mexican War!" A.P. Hill arrived at Jackson's headquarters later that night and upon seeing Kearny's wound remarked sadly, "Poor Kearny, he deserved a better death than that!" General Kearny's remains stayed at Jackson's headquarters throughout the rest of the night, under a guard to protect against more looting.[5]

The first glowing rays of sunlight that signaled the dawn of September 2, 1862, must have come as a very welcome sight to Robert E. Lee, who remained ensconced in the stone house on the Little River Turnpike one mile or so west of Ox Hill. While his wrists certainly still bothered him, he was finally out of the ambulance and in a position to actively command his army once again. During the early morning hours, the Army of Northern Virginia's commander busied himself with the task of understanding what had happened the day before and figuring out just where his army stood and, more importantly, where Pope's army stood. Sometime midmorning a messenger arrived from Jackson's headquarters bearing a number of messages and dispatches for the commanding general. Among those was one with word that Philip Kearny was dead.[6]

General Lee never recorded his feelings at this moment but his actions over the next few hours and days suggest he must have felt some sadness at the passing of a former countryman who was one of the most gallant soldiers on the continent. Lee inquired of Jackson's messenger if Kearny's remains and personal effects were intact. Informed that they were and in the same condition they arrived from the field and now under a guard, General Lee immediately directed Henry Taylor of his personal staff to make the necessary arrangements for passing Kearny's body through the lines. He sent Jackson's rider back with orders that Kearny's remains were to be returned to General Pope and that all his personal effects should be collected and returned as well. Lee also instructed General Jackson to check for any papers Kearny might have on his person and to send them back to his headquarters for inspection. Sometime later that morning the "papers found in the pocket of his coat were brought to me," as he would later write to Agnes Kearny, "but presuming them to be of a private nature I ordered them burned without being read." Other facts known about Robert E. Lee's character suggest this was most certainly the case, though Lee's actions undoubtedly would have been different had these papers appeared to contain useful military intelligence. Lee's respect for Philip Kearny and his sympathy for Agnes's mourning must have been great, though. He would later take the time to ensure that those items of Kearny's still useful to the Confederate cause and that therefore would have to remain behind that day—his horse, saddle, and sword—would eventually be returned to Agnes's care. Such was the respect of one warrior for a fallen comrade, even an "enemy."[7]

Later that day Henry Taylor had Kearny's body loaded onto Jackson's personal ambulance and driven toward Fairfax Court House, where it was delivered to Federal pickets. Riding at the head of the ambulance and its cavalry escort, Major Taylor recalled thinking, "There is no place for exultation in the contemplation of the death of so gallant a man, and as I accompanied his remains I was conscious of a feeling of deep respect and great admiration for the brave soldier." Taylor's thoughts on Kearny's passing seem to be typical of the feelings of many in the Southern ranks, who regarded Philip Kearny as one the worthiest adversaries they had faced in the war. Once they reached the line of Federal pickets, they displayed their white flag of truce, explained their purpose, left the ambulance bearing Kearny's body, and quickly rode away.[8]

Jackson's ambulance was driven to St. Mary's Church, near Fairfax Station, where it was received by a body of high-ranking Union officers, including General Birney. Once over the "unsuitable" way in which the Confederates had returned the body—apparently they felt snubbed that the Rebels had given the body to mere infantry skirmishers and had not waited for a suitably senior officer to appear—General Birney selected an honor guard, consisting of Companies A, B, C, D, and E, and the color guard of the 57th Pennsylvania from Kearny's division, to protect the general's body from curious soldiers and civilians alike. The 57th Pennsylvania honor guard marched for Alexandria, along with the general's body, and then headed for Washington.[9]

When word of the gallant Kearny's death reached Northern newspapers, the public outpouring of grief and affection for the fallen general was widespread. "The death of General Kearny is a national loss!" wailed *The Tribune* on September 4, and *Harper's Weekly* asked, "Who can replace Phil Kearny?" Even *The Times* of London wrote of Kearny's death on September 20, "At Chantilly fell one of the more gallant officers of the Federal Army, General Kearny." Nearly every newspaper in the nation carried similar sentiments, heaping praise on the dead warrior, a man who in life these publications would have considered an immoral embarrassment to polite society.[10]

Four days after he fell in battle, Kearny's remains were autopsied in Alexandria by the firm of "Drs. Brown and Alexander, Embalmers of the Dead," who determined that Kearny had died from the results of a minie ball that entered his body "through the gluteus muscles" and had lodged in his chest. The ball that killed him was given by the doctor first to Captain Monford, quartermaster of Kearny's staff, and then to the Kearny family to "keep it as the most valuable relic bequeathed to them by the 'bravest of the brave.'" From Alexandria, the general's body was returned to New Jersey and was then interred in the John Watts family vault in the yard of Trinity Church in New York City. There it would rest for the next 50 years.[11]

In 1912, Philip Kearny's earthly remains were disinterred, placed aboard a train and, like the new general of New Jersey volunteers had so many years before, moved south once more. The journey was the result of years of effort by the "Commission for the Removal of the Remains of Philip Kearny to the National Cemetery." What the group lacked in a catchy name, it made up for in zeal and highly placed connections. So on April 12, 1912, Major General Philip Kearny's body was on its way to be reburied in the National Cemetery at Arlington. Before it left, at Trinity Church a group of family and friends opened the wooden coffin to identify the general's remains—which they noted were perfectly preserved, a credit to Drs. Brown and Alexander—and placed the body in a new bronze casket. From there it was marched with great ceremony past Kearny's birthplace at No. 3 Broadway in New York City where General Dan Sickles paid his respects. The procession was the talk of New York for days; the city that had considered him unfit to command their troops had finally accepted Philip Kearny. Once in Virginia, it was moved to Arlington Cemetery and reburied with all the honor and pomp befitting a fallen hero of the United States, in a ceremony attended by President Taft, the chiefs of the armed services, members of Congress, and Supreme Court justices. When Philip Kearny's body came to rest, it lay within the grounds of the estate that once had belonged to his fellow soldier and former adversary, Robert E. Lee, who had taken such care to see that Kearny received a proper military burial.[12]

The legacy that Philip Kearny left was—and is—a sizable one. Kearny's Patch, that red diamond that distinguished his men from all the others, lived on and became the inspiration for Joe Hooker's creation of similar symbols for each of the army's corps. Fittingly, when the III Corps was assigned their new "corps badge" it was a diamond, a tribute to their former division head. On November 29, 1862, only a few days before the disastrous Union attack at Fredericksburg, General Birney and several other III Corps/1st Division officers gathered. Their purpose was to charter the creation of a private medal to recognize bravery on the field of battle and they named it fittingly enough "the Kearny Cross." This medal, which was awarded to only 335 men of the 1st Division, was a treasured mark of valor throughout the lifetimes of those few who received it. In December 1880, the first statue in the nation to a volunteer officer was erected in Newark, New Jersey's Military Park bearing the likeness of Philip Kearny in full military splendor. But Kearny's legacy extended beyond his adopted home state to the very center of American democracy; when a subject was selected for a statue to represent the state of New Jersey to stand in the corridors of the United States Capitol building, state leaders chose Major General Philip Kearny. His likeness remains there today, reminding modern Americans of his sacrifice and his heroism.

11

A RETREAT ON ALL FRONTS

★————————————————★

TUESDAY, SEPTEMBER 2 TO WEDNESDAY, SEPTEMBER 3, 1862

Around noon on September 2, John Pope finally received what he had wanted for days—political cover for retreating to Washington. "You will bring your forces as best you can within or near the line of fortifications," General Halleck instructed. While in many respects it was a needless order—the army already was well on its way to the Washington defenses—it nonetheless absolved Pope of sole responsibility for the move and reassured him that he had done the right thing by ordering the retreat. But then Halleck continued with words that must have erased any joy General Pope felt in reading the message: "General McClellan has charge of all the defenses, and you will consider any direction . . . given by him as coming from me." This phrase all but directly relieved Pope of command of the army, for it meant that as the men crossed into the first line of works they passed from Pope's to McClellan's control. In a few hours the army would walk out from under him and into George McClellan's grasp, just as McClellan's army had been slowly transferred to Pope's command only weeks ago.[1]

Still Pope realized the orders did not formally relieve him of command and there was some chance yet that he might retain his post. Perhaps the president and General Halleck did not intend him to relinquish command, but only temporarily bow to McClellan's territorial control, and when the army left on campaign once again it would revert to his control. At least until Pope was formally relieved of command there was a glimmer of hope. But the general would have to bring all his considerable political skills to bear in outmaneuvering McClellan if he was to retain his army command.

In the meantime, an order was an order and Pope would first have to attend to the movement of the army into the Washington defenses. During the afternoon of September 2, he drafted a circular instructing the commanders of his army to retreat from the Fairfax Court House-Flint Hill-Chain Bridge line to Arlington and Alexandria. But even as he attended to duty, the general returned to laying the political groundwork by blaming the retreat on Washington. "The following movement of troops will be made in accordance with the instructions of the War Department," started the retreat orders, lest anyone believe that their gallant commander himself would issue such a sign of defeat.[2]

Pope's circular ordering the retreat was in fact a no-nonsense order for a calm, purposeful withdrawal of the army. Banks's II Corps would follow Braddock Road through Annandale and post near Fort Worth, while Heintzelman's III Corps would follow the same route to Fort Lyon. Franklin's corps would march east on the Little River Turnpike to Alexandria to form the Union left. McDowell's corps was to move through Falls Church to Forts Craig and Tillinghast, in what would become the Union center. Porter's V Corps, Sumner's II Corps, and Sigel's Reserve Corps would move through Vienna to the Chain Bridge and form the Union right, where they would be joined by General Buford's cavalry. Once all this was done, Reno's IX Corps could withdraw to Alexandria. Pope even provided for the orderly disposition of the massive wagon train once the army reached safety, telling each corps' commander to detach a staff officer for the task of rounding up each respective command's wagons. And he moved the army's supply depot from Sangster's Station to Alexandria, entrusting General Banks with that task. It seemed that those qualities John Pope lacked in leading men on the battlefield were made up for in administrative acumen.[3]

In the early morning of September 2, 1862, the situation facing his army was uppermost in Robert E. Lee's mind. Having only recently arrived in the Ox Hill area, Lee had to depend on Jackson's reports and observations to form his own view of the situation that morning. Lee probably heard the argument that the Federals would renew the fight because the previous day's encounter had used so few of the thousands of fresh men Pope had at hand. Lee apparently agreed with this opinion for his army remained in a defensive posture throughout the night of September 1 and into the morning of the 2nd. The chances of John Pope throwing a larger, better-prepared attack at him—and one staged in better weather, too—still was very high. For now, until he had a clear picture of what Pope was doing and where his troops were, the Army of Northern Virginia would remain where it was.

With Longstreet's Command finally ready to join a fight, though, Lee must have felt better about his prospects for the day. The arrival of Hampton's Brigade—which had until now been detached from Stuart's Cavalry to guard the James, Chickahominy, and Pamunkey rivers—late in the morning added even more fresh power to the Southern army. Perhaps the Army of Northern Virginia might even find an opportunity to regain the offensive and attack Pope's retreating force. But before Lee could determine his army's course for the day he needed to know where Pope's men were and what they were doing.

At the first hint of daylight, Jackson's skirmishers searched the field in their front for warning of any impending attack. After some time passed they realized that no organized Union force of any size appeared to be in their front or in the woods beyond. Plenty of men were moving about near the farmhouse in their front and the fields and slopes beyond, but no lines of armed men appeared anywhere nearby who might be ready for action. In fact, only the wounded and those caring for them could be seen in any number, and the painful screams still emanating from the farmhouse and barns served as a testimonial that it was the domain of the surgeons. There also were no bugle calls or drums sounding in the opposite woods that might signal the movement of military troops. As the early morning wore on it became clear that no Union attack would come across the previous day's battlefield and word soon was sent back to General Jackson of this fact.[4]

Most of the Confederates situated around Ox Hill and the Little River Turnpike, though, simply enjoyed the hours of rest that were created by the wait for Pope to act. Marion Fitzpatrick of the 45th Georgia wrote a letter home to his wife, the first such letter in many days for it was the first day in nearly a week that they truly had for rest. The highlight of the day, though, was the issuing of rations late in the afternoon, an occurrence that occupied the diary entries of those Confederates who bothered to mention the day at all in their journals. By now the men of Lee's army had grown so used to being hungry that the seeming abundance of food caused more than one soldier an unusual problem. "Late that afternoon we drew rations again, and I ate everything without satisfying my hunger," wrote Spencer Welch to his wife in South Carolina. "A soldier came from another command and said he heard I had some salt, and he offered me a shoulder of fresh pork for some. Wilson cooked it and I ate it without crackers, but was still hungry. During the night I became sick from overeating, and the next morning when the regiment left I was too sick to march. Billie, Mose Cappock, Billy Caldwell and myself all got sick from the same cause."[5]

As the sun rose higher in the morning sky, and no Union attack appeared, Lee's mind turned to considering his options for the days ahead. These thoughts, and probably a desire for more tactical intelligence, took Lee on several rides to both Longstreet's and Jackson's head-quarters late in the morning. By now it was clear that the location of Pope's army would determine if he should launch another attack or if he should put into action a plan he and Jackson had been considering and discussing for some months, an invasion of the North through Maryland.[6]

It originally had been Jackson's idea to invade Maryland or southern Pennsylvania, though it had needed work and Lee had taken the rough plan and polished it into a solid military campaign. When proposed to President Davis in early June, the president had endorsed it, despite some initial concerns about the move. Chief among these was that a move north would leave Richmond open to attack and Davis cautioned that the move could be taken only after the threat to the Confederate capital had been removed or greatly diminished. In any case, the president left it up to General Lee to decide when the time would be right to launch this invasion. In the months since then, Lee had been planning in his own mind how such a campaign might be carried out in detail and, once that had been satisfactorily worked out, he had been waiting and watching for the right moment to carry it out. He had considered launching the invasion after the victory on August 30 but had opted to try sending Jackson on the flank march. But now was the perfect time to march north into Maryland.[7]

Lee, years after the war, explained to an interlocutor his thinking in choosing this course: "After Chantilly," the friend wrote, "he found he could do nothing more against the Yankees, unless he attacked them in their fortifications around Washington, which he did not want to do. He therefore determined to cross the river into Maryland . . ." For the first time since President Davis had approved the Northern invasion plan in June, the Confederate capital was free from the threat of attack by a siz-able Union force. At the same time, the Union army—for the time being, at least—was broken and emasculated, certainly in no shape to offer immediate chase or quickly turn south and strike Richmond in the Army of Northern Virginia's absence. All of the president's conditions, and more, were now met.[8]

One thing must have troubled Lee, though, and that was that he still did not know the exact location of the new Union position. Perhaps more importantly, he did not know the whereabouts of the thousands of fresh troops still at General Pope's disposal. If they were safely within the Washington defenses, they would certainly not come out to attack the Southern army. At the same time, though, they would be beyond Lee's reach and all hope of launching an attack today would be gone. He would have to find the location of these troops before he could decide which course to follow.

Sometime in the late afternoon Lee ordered up a reconnaissance-in-force using Stuart's cavalry to seek out the location of the Union lines. Stuart directed Fitzhugh Lee to take his brigade in the direction of Fairfax Court House to see if the Yankees remained there and, if they did, in what force. Wade Hampton's Brigade, with the Stuart Horse Artillery in tow, would march northeast in the direction of Chain Bridge for a similar purpose. At the same time that these two cavalry brigades were probing Pope's lines, Lee directed that some body of cavalry should proceed to Leesburg and confront a Unionist body of Maryland cavalry—"marauders" from the Southern perspective—who had been operating in the area of Northern Loudon County for some time. Stuart personally selected the 2nd Virginia Cavalry, under the command of Colonel T. T. Munford, for this dangerous and seemingly thankless, if not apparently unimportant, task. Though it probably was not clear to Munford and his cavalrymen that afternoon, their task would come to be the more important of the two assigned to Stuart's Command late on September 2. Early in the afternoon, Stuart's two cavalry brigades and the 2nd Virginia Cavalry were underway to find the Yankees once again.[9]

By the time that Stuart's troopers were moving out, much of the Union army had already passed through the outermost set of Washington fortifications. Most of these "forts" consisted of low earthen walls shielding one or more—but rarely more than a battery's worth—of guns, connected to one another by long strings of even lower-built trenches and works designed to provide a firing line for infantry. As they moved increasingly nearer the capital, the size and nature of the forts grew ever more sophisticated and formidable. By the time they reached the banks of the Potomac, for those who marched that far, the increasingly complex earthen forts yielded to masonry structures that held large siege guns of great caliber. It was these structures and weapons that convinced Lee that it would be useless to attack Washington itself. The retreating soldiers who passed these works must have taken comfort in their presence, though few of the men recorded such gratitude. Certainly they were weary after such a long, demoralizing march and few would have felt enough strength to record their thoughts of that moment.

Although the men in the Union ranks who walked eastward on September 2 had regained some sense of order and composure, there remained no small measure of confusion as they continued their march. The same problems that had plagued the army in its last rearward movement—that from Manassas—were reappearing with some regularity. Some units took the wrong direction and wasted the men's scarce energy in countermarching or taking longer-than-necessary routes. Others found that, once again, the omnipresent, slow-moving wagon train jammed many of the best roads and the long lines of infantry columns had to crawl behind them or break from the road to get around them. And if the straggling that had occurred the night before did not appear to be as great in the day, it was in all likelihood only because daylight kept the more discreet men in the ranks while their bolder—or more weary—comrades sank to rest on the roadside. Still, although the march was a troubled, discouraging one for most men making it, at least there was no significant fighting this day and no new casualties with which to contend. Sadly, this was not the case for a few Union regiments.[10]

The 19th Massachusetts had arrived at Fairfax Court House early on the morning of September 2, much to the relief of its weary men. But scarcely had they flopped down to rest when a bugle sounded "the general," drawing them back into ranks, "without time even to make coffee," grumbled one Bay Stater. They soon learned that, along with the 1st Minnesota and Tompkin's Battery A of the 1st Rhode Island Light Artillery, they were to deploy on a ridge that commanded the road running from Fairfax Court House through Flint Hill and Vienna, to the Chain Bridge and Georgetown. Their task while there was to guard this route of march for their own II Corps, the V Corps, and the Reserve Corps, against Rebel cavalry that could attack the retreating Union troops from the direction of Ox Hill. Leading them in the task was General Howard, who only the day before had fought Jackson's men along Stringfellow Road. While the Massachusetts men, Minnesotans, and Rhode Islanders remained at their post on the ridge, the rest of their comrades in Dana's brigade acted as the rearguard for Sumner's column and marched off for Washington late in the day.

Around 5 P.M., after the last of the column they were to guard had passed from view, the two regiments formed in a column of fours and started off to follow. As the column moved haltingly toward Vienna— caught behind ambulances and wagons—they noticed some of Stuart's cavalry and a battery of horse artillery pull into their former position on the ridge. The men watched closely as the battery unlimbered a piece and prepared for action. Howard's command did not stop to fight but, as Andrew Greely of the 19th recalled, "We took very long steps and walked fast, with bended knees, so as to keep as near the ground as possible." But escape was not to be and within moments the first shell exploded harmlessly beyond the two regiments and their battery, which had now reached some cover in a woods. The second shell, however, found its mark and exploded directly overhead of the men, wounding several in the ranks. This General Howard could not ignore, and a skirmish line was soon pushed forward to repel the enemy. Behind this Howard placed his main line—Tompkin's battery on the road with the 1st Minnesota on its right and the 19th Massachusetts on the left. Despite a fairly regular stream of shells and musketry from the Confederate position, Howard's men held their fire. After an uneasy hour enduring this, Stuart's cavalrymen made a cautious probe of the line, apparently thinking it had been abandoned. As they neared the Union line, Tompkin's guns fired twice on the enemy horsemen, "emptying many a saddle," as one 19th Massachusetts man recalled. Ordinarily the men of Howard's two regiments would have considered this fight an annoyance but tonight they were unnerved by the experience, perhaps because they knew just how weak the Union army really was at that moment.[11]

General Howard now ordered his two regiments to rejoin the rest of the II Corps. Once underway, the 1st Minnesota took the lead followed by Tompkin's battery, and the 19th Massachusetts brought up the rear. Their march to the main column of the II Corps proved to be uneventful and a welcome relief from their earlier encounter. But all that was about to change.

Reaching the rear of the main column, the 1st Minnesota marched past Dana's brigade, who were guarding the rear of the main column and, as they passed, it was surmised by the officers in charge that the 1st Minnesota constituted Howard's entire force. "What occurred [next] has never been fully explained and probably never will be," lamented one of the 19th Massachusetts's veterans. As the 19th Massachusetts approached the rear of the II Corps column, someone—either in the 19th or in Dana's brigade—called out "Guerrillas!" and the 19th moved off the road to the right, forming in line of battle. Dana's men now panicked and opened fire on the unidentified "foe" that had just fled the road in their front. The ensuing exchange of gunfire was short but sharp. "In the road there was a perfect pandemonium, sounds of musketry, shouts of men, groans of wounded and stampede of horses." It would not be until morning that enough order was restored to the Union ranks for anyone to sort out that 12 men of the 19th Massachusetts had been killed and others wounded that night and that they had been slain by their own brigade comrades.[12]

While the men of the 19th Massachusetts and the rest of the Union ranks moved eastward, General Pope focused his attention eastward as well. But the commanding general's focus was no longer on how to move his army from Lee's grasp, but rather on how to safely maneuver his army career through the clutches of his detractors in Washington. For what had started as a small but dedicated band of Pope's opponents had, by September 2, grown into a small army led by George McClellan. The disastrous retreat to Washington had indeed brought John Pope's personal fortunes to a low and it would take all his considerable political skill to reverse that trend. At the same time, George McClellan had been doing all he could since hearing news of the result of the latest battle to boost his own political fortunes.

Now that Washington had finally ordered the retreat Pope had been looking for, he might well have believed he stood on firmer ground with Halleck and the president than he had the day before. Not only had he made the right choice in withdrawing to Washington, but also the movement was going well, all things considered, and Lee was cooperating by staying away. With all these positive developments, Pope had some ammunition to throw toward Washington in his dispatches that just might save his army career. Indeed, the dispatches sent to the capital by the Army of Virginia's commander late on September 2 have an almost upbeat quality to them. The first of these was sent from Fairfax Court House probably sometime in the late afternoon: "The whole army is returning in good order, without confusion, or the slightest loss of property. The enemy has made no advances this morning, owing, no doubt, to his severe loss last evening." Pope followed this with another, even rosier dispatch issued that same evening at 7:10, after moving his headquarters from Fairfax Court House to Ball's Crossroads: "I arrived here safely. Command coming in on the road without much molestation. Some artillery firing on the roads toward Vienna and Chain Bridge, but nothing of a serious character so far as I can learn." Then the general's written demeanor took an even brighter turn: "I await your orders. The enemy continues to beat around to the north, I do not my self believe that any attack is here contemplated. The troops are very weary, but otherwise in good condition." This time Pope's characterization of the army was not an outright lie, but was at least a great exaggeration. The army was in fact weary and overall the retreat had gone well but they were hardly in any condition that could be called "good." If Henry Halleck was at all taken aback by John Pope's lightning-like flip-flop—for only the day before he had told Halleck that his demoralized army was on the verge of collapse—he never recorded it. Missing from either of these dispatches, however, is any hint that Pope knew he already had been relieved of command of his army.[13]

But President Lincoln and General Halleck had made their decision to remove Pope and restore McClellan to command the army in the early morning of September 2. It had been one of the hardest decisions of Lincoln's presidency and one that must have torn at his sense of pride. But although the president had nothing resembling respect for McClellan, he had to admit there was no one else to turn to in this hour of crisis. The decision made, Lincoln and Halleck went, hat in hand, in the early morning light of September 2 to McClellan's house on H Street to ask George McClellan if he would resume command of a reorganized Union army. As McClellan gleefully wrote of the meeting to his wife that afternoon: "I was surprised this morning when at bkft by a visit from the President & Halleck—in which the former expressed the opinion that the troubles now impending could be overcome better by me than anyone else. Pope is ordered to fall back upon Washn & as he reenters everything is to come under my command again!"[14]

Lincoln's cabinet was disturbed when informed that McClellan was to resume command of the army. Secretary of War Stanton and Treasury Secretary Salmon P. Chase—two of Pope's most vocal supporters and vociferous McClellan-haters—were especially troubled by the decision, which the president felt so unsure of that he felt compelled to justify to the assembled cabinet. "McClellan knows the ground," Secretary of the Navy Gideon Welles recalled Lincoln saying, "his specialty is to defend; he is a good engineer, all admit; there is no better organizer; he can be trusted to act on the defensive; . . . he had beyond any officer the confidence of the army. Though deficient in the positive qualities which are necessary for an energetic commander, his organizing powers could be made temporarily available till the troops were rallied." Such language suggests that Lincoln was selling himself on the change, as much as any of his cabinet that day.[15]

McClellan set to work immediately to prepare for his new command. At 12:30, the same time that he posted the good news of his restored position to Mary Ellen, the general sent a message to the president informing the commander in chief of his latest preparations to receive the army and defend the capital. While the disposition of the army's wagon train and the location of Couch's division could not have been of real interest to the president, it may have been intended to demonstrate that McClellan was already at the helm of the army, even if most of it had not yet appeared in his immediate vicinity. The message's closing, "You may rest certain that nothing I can think of shall be left undone," seems designed to inform the president that he need not bother the busy general anymore.[16]

During the rest of the early afternoon George McClellan drafted a series of messages—one more each to Mary Ellen and President Lincoln, as well as one to General Halleck, among others. But none of these could have given him the satisfaction that writing to General Pope must have. This particular message is cloaked in the justification of directing the placement of various Union corps as they arrived in the Washington defenses but appears to really have as its purpose making sure that Pope moved his army as quickly as possible into the Washington defenses—and under McClellan's command. "General Halleck instructed me to repeat to you the order he sent this morning to withdraw your army to Washington without unnecessary delay. He feared his message might miss you, and desired to take this double precaution." This certainly rubbed salt in John Pope's wound. It must have given George McClellan great satisfaction at the very thought of Pope reading it somewhere between Washington and Fairfax Court House.[17]

His correspondence done, George McClellan gathered his staff and rode out from Washington to "pick up the Army of the Potomac." The general had adorned himself for the occasion in his full dress uniform, complete with his buff general officer's sash and dress sword. Sometime late in the afternoon, near the outer ring of fortifications, McClellan and his entourage met General Jacob D. Cox, commander of the Kanawha Division, and McClellan heartily called out "Well, General, I am in command again!" Cox joined the group as they rode westward and before long they came across General Pope and his staff, who were riding along with General McDowell toward Alexandria. After exchanging the expected military courtesies, McClellan informed Pope that he, not Pope, would command the army as it fell back to Washington. Though neither man recorded Pope's reaction to the unpleasant news, it must have been a controlled one for a heated exchange most certainly would have merited note by McClellan. The only mention McClellan would later make of this meeting was to claim that, on pointing out the artillery fire all could hear in the distance—probably Stuart's Horse Artillery shelling Howard's rear guard—Pope seemed unconcerned and asked to go to Washington, to which McClellan claimed he assented and replied that he "was going to that artillery firing." Of this claim, however, General Cox later retorted when reviewing *McClellan's Own Story*, "certainly not true." But it was not what happened during the meeting that makes the incident worth noting, but what occurred afterward.[18]

Brigadier General John Hatch had been listening to the exchange between the two leaders with anticipation. Hatch had a particular hatred for John Pope, who had against his wishes transferred him from the cavalry to the infantry, and he had been chewing this bitter pill for many weeks. Now, thrilled with McClellan's return to command, Hatch saw his chance to exact some measure of personal satisfaction in Pope's defeat. As Pope's party rode away toward Washington, Hatch turned to his men and called out the news, "Boys, General McClellan is in command again! Three Cheers!" The spontaneous joy that burst forth from Hatch's command was as widespread as it was boisterous. "Such cheers I never heard before, and were never heard in Pope's army," wrote Stephen Weld of the scene. The joy expressed by Hatch's men was shared by seemingly everyone in Pope's now-former command, so glad were they to be rid of this general whom defeat seemed to stalk. And Pope could not have chosen a worse riding partner at that moment than McDowell, whom most in the army, if not the nation, blamed for the first Union failure at Bull Run. As McClellan rode westward, this scene of exuberance was repeated until one man suggested that one could track the general's progress by the volume of the cheers. Certainly John Pope could hear the cheering and understood the men's thirst for victory—a thirst he had failed to quench—even as it crushed him personally.[19]

An army-less General Pope and his staff rode on toward Washington in a sullen mood and set up headquarters at Ball's Crossroads late on the 2nd. Almost immediately Pope gathered a portion of his staff and rode into Washington to renew the fight for his position on the political battlefield he was perhaps most familiar with.

While John Pope and George McClellan were at war with each other, Lee's army was once again on the move. The cavalry reconnaissance had proven that Pope's army was well along in its move into the Washington defenses and was finally out of Lee's grasp. Lee's next move was now certain. Throughout the day on September 3, Jackson's Command and its leader were leaving their bivouac near Ox Hill and moving north. Their objective, as most in the Southern army had already surmised from rumor, was Maryland. That evening the bulk of Lee's army camped around Leesburg and the next day crossed the Potomac River to enter Northern territory for the first time. They were determined to take the war to the Yankees on their own ground—as Lincoln's army had been doing to them for too long now in Virginia—while living off prosperous Northern farmers untouched by the suffering of war. And maybe they could convince Maryland politicians to hitch their wagon to the Confederacy, though how bringing the sting of war to their land would do that was never explained to the men in the ranks. As they moved north over the following days Lee's columns would find little or no resistance, for General McClellan was busy reorganizing and rebuilding his army. But if Lee's troops moved north unfettered, it was a situation that would not last long. George McClellan's rebuilding and reorganizing was creating a more flexible and capable fighting force that would, indeed, be hot on Lee's tail and much sooner than anyone believed possible. The two armies would meet once again on the banks of Antietam Creek, near Sharpsburg, Maryland, on September 17. And by that day's end many of those on both sides of the firing line who had considered themselves lucky to have survived the Virginia Campaign would find that their luck had run out.

For the thousands of men in the Union army who arrived safely near Washington, the battle of Chantilly would quickly fade into mere memory. Most would find that the first few days of September 1862 held a large measure of rest, which they were uniformly glad to have, as well as a growing share of work. They quickly resumed the now-familiar routine of military life—drill, eat, work, sleep. Their officers were preoccupied with rebuilding their commands into a larger though more flexible Army of the Potomac than the one McClellan had taken to the Virginia peninsula. This reorganization meant that the Army of Virginia simply ceased to be and few mourned its passing into history. The army that would start off toward Maryland in pursuit of Lee's army would be a new fighting force, confident in its restored leader and ready to finish off the rebellion once and for all.[20]

Few of these same Union soldiers even bothered to mention the battle of Chantilly to their loved ones at home. But for those who had endured the fight at Chantilly there was a more personal task at hand. In the days following the battle more than one letter home carried news not just to the writer's family but to relatives, neighbors, and friends of the fate of other local boys. A letter of September 6 from Dennis Ford of the 28th Massachusetts certainly stands as typical of letters written by survivors of the battle: "I am living still, thank God. The last fight, my clothes were riddled with balls. I was grazed in the right arm. It knocked my arm dead, though thank God I have not seen one drop of blood as yet. The rubber blanket I had on my back was riddled. A ball stuck me on the shoe. They fell around me like hail. James Philips is shot dead. The rest of the boys are safe. John Maher was wounded. Peter King got something like a wound, it is nothing. John Fenning was wounded. Con Roach came out safe. Maurice and the Donnellys are safe. We lost in the last fight 130 men out of our regiment."

Thus for those who fought it, the battle of Chantilly had been more than an oddity or the latest news from the front. For while most veterans would recall only that the battle had been fought in a thunderous downpour or had cost the Union the brave Philip Kearny, those men who fought at Ox Hill would remember the battle as one of their fiercest struggles of the war. Many, like the 28th Massachusetts, would emblazon it upon their flags later in the war, standing alongside Antietam and Gettysburg in their personal experience. For those brave men, on both sides of the Reid farm fields, it had been a short, sharp, hard-fought brush with death that no one who experienced it would ever forget.[21]

12

AN AFTERWORD:
WHO WON THE BATTLE OF CHANTILLY?

★─────────────────────────────★

Soldiers on both sides of the field watched dawn rise on September 2, 1862, honestly believing that their side had won the previous day's fight. And no matter if they referred to the fight as Chantilly or Ox Hill, throughout the remaining years of their lives, the veterans for whom this was an important fight would stick fast to the belief that they had won the day. But like the never-ending arguments about the causes of the Civil War itself, the issue of who actually won the battle of Chantilly remains a contest of perspectives. All of which begs the modern observer to ask just who did win the battle of Chantilly?[1]

A strictly numerical assessment of casualties might suggest that the Confederacy won. When the smoke cleared south of the Little River Turnpike, Jackson had lost 83 men killed, 418 wounded, and 15 missing— a total of 516 casualties for September 1. Pope's forces suffered substantially greater losses, with 136 men killed, 450 wounded, and 69 missing— a total of 655 casualties on the Chantilly battlefield itself. When the Union losses in front of Jermantown are added—2 killed and 22 wounded—the Union's aggregate losses climb to 679 casualties for September 1. The South's numerical victory becomes even more apparent when treating both sides' casualties as a percentage of the total Confederate or Union force engaged at Chantilly. By this computation, Jackson certainly won the day, losing only 3.4 percent of his total force engaged versus Pope's 11.3 percent loss figure for the Union.

These casualty figures for Chantilly, however, tell only part of the story. Comparing casualty figures in a strictly numerical way is only useful for determining a victor if the forces being compared are roughly equal in size and composition (i.e. the ratio of infantry, artillery, cavalry, and other service arms engaged). Although both Union and Confederate forces that fought at Chantilly were composed mainly of infantry regiments, they were far from equal in size. The Union force engaged there under Generals Stevens and Kearny consisted of approximately 6,000 men comprising 19 regiments. Jackson's Command—nearly half of Lee's army in northern Virginia—consisted of 15,000 men in 51 regiments. That a 6,000-man Union force could fight a 15,000-man Confederate command for several hours without suffering a crushing defeat, suggests that perhaps the Union emerged the victor. Instead, I argue this suggests that we must look beyond the casualty numbers and force loss percentages to determine who won and lost at Chantilly.

In such cases where comparing casualty figures and hard data is insufficient to determine the outcome of a battle, most military analysts turn to examining other factors that can be viewed in a comparative manner for drawing analytic conclusions. Although drawing primarily on such "soft" factors for analytic conclusions is necessarily an inexact process—leaving open the possibility of nearly endless debate about the "accuracy" of an analyst's judgments—such an effort can still advance the understanding of a battle's outcome and impact on the course of the larger war in which it occurs.

Considering how closely the senior commanders involved in the battle came to reaching their tactical and strategic objectives on September 1, 1862, is one way to determine victory. For the purpose of simplicity, we will examine the actions only of those senior commanders who had a key role in determining tactical or strategic objectives and who then acted to influence their army's efforts to meet those objectives. Thus, for the Union, we will look only at the action of Generals Pope, Stevens, and Kearny, and for the Confederacy, Generals Lee, Jackson, and Stuart. Although other senior officers on the field that day, such as General A. P. Hill or Generals Reno and Birney, played key roles in the battle, they did not personally determine tactical or strategic objectives for the overall battle and were largely acting only at the direction of their superiors (or acting superiors). For the sake of convenience, we will look at both the tactical course of the battle and the strategic context within which the battle was fought—what, in the larger scheme of the war or a campaign, the army commanders wanted to achieve by fighting the battle—to fully analyze Chantilly. Following this analysis, we will conclude by considering if, in the greater context of the course of the Civil War, the battle of Chantilly really mattered at all.

The tactics used by Stevens, Kearny, and Jackson in conducting the battle of Chantilly appear to have been adopted on the spot with little advance thought or preplanning. Although both Stevens and Jackson appear to have had clear ideas about what they wanted to achieve at Chantilly, neither had extensive time to prepare for the fight and, consequently, left little or no written record of their tactical planning or thinking to inform the modern historian. This problem is compounded by the fact that all three senior commanders directing the fight at Chantilly were killed within a year after the battle. Stevens's and Kearny's deaths at Chantilly obviously prevented them from ever writing official reports of the fight, and Jackson—although he survived for nearly another year until his death after the battle of Chancellorsville in May, 1863—never wrote more than a one-page official report of the action. Jackson's report lacked a general sense of what he intended to achieve at Chantilly, concentrating more on the flow of action itself rather than indicating what tactics he selected and why. Nonetheless, by observing how these commanders deployed their troops for battle and how they acted as the battle progressed we can draw valid conclusions about their tactics and what each wanted to achieve there.

Isaac Stevens was in many respects responsible for launching the fight at Chantilly and was likewise responsible for choosing the tactics that the Union forces used there. Although General Pope may have ordered Stevens only to conduct a reconnaissance north toward the Little River Turnpike, General Pope must have understood that Stevens might very likely find himself in action before the day's end. The very fact that Pope apparently gave General Stevens no written orders regarding how to act once he found the Confederates suggests that Pope either trusted Stevens to act in concert with his strategic intentions or that perhaps he did pass along verbal orders through the two cavalry guides. If such direction ever existed, however, it was never recorded.

Stevens's primary tactical objective clearly was to immediately stop Jackson from continuing his advance on Jermantown. After quickly sizing up the Confederate position in his front and examining the terrain he would be fighting on, Stevens chose to immediately stage a small attack—using only his own troops on hand—rather than waiting for significant reinforcement to assault Jackson. That Stevens attacked quickly with his small force against a much larger foe suggests that he did not expect to gain a traditional tactical victory—driving the enemy from the field—but rather hoped only to distract the enemy from reaching its objective. Indeed, were Stevens planning to actually defeat Jackson at Chantilly, attacking as he did—greatly outnumbered and with no reinforcements—would have been foolish, if not outright criminal. But in this case, Stevens had good reason to believe that these tactics would work and were actually warranted by the situation at hand. While rapidly assaulting a numerically superior enemy risked the lives of the men in his IX Corps, Stevens must have considered that failing to act could require the entire Union army to pay an even greater price. Waiting would certainly have permitted Jackson to both continue his movement on Jermantown and to prepare more fully for Stevens's attack, virtually guaranteeing Union failure on both counts. Given these circumstances, Stevens chose a risky but potentially successful tactical approach.

General Kearny appears to have initially adopted both Stevens's tactical approach and his tactical objective. Kearny arrived on the battlefield at a point in the fight when he could do little but pick up where General Stevens had left off. Stevens's shattered troops were in such complete disarray that Kearny apparently believed he first would have to restore order to the field—if for no other reason than to get these troops out of the way—before he could begin to impose his own approach on the fight. Kearny initially launched a direct assault at the Confederate line in the woods, albeit to the left of Stevens's point of attack. In doing so, Kearny also either knowingly or unknowingly adopted Stevens's tactical objective of halting Jackson's further movement toward Jermantown. Since Philip Kearny was killed before he could fully make his mark on this fight, we can only guess how he might have directed the course of battle in the remaining hour or so of daylight had he lived. But during the time after Stevens's death when he controlled the course of the fight, Kearny hewed closely to Stevens's original tactical plans.

The course of events on September 1 suggests that Generals Stevens and, by default, Kearny clearly achieved their tactical objective at Chantilly. Stevens's attacks on the Confederate right forced Jackson to stop and fight for over three hours and ultimately kept him from reaching the goal Lee had assigned for his command early on August 31. Stevens's tactics were well-suited to the situation presented him, accentuating his advantages on the field while simultaneously taking advantage of Jackson's weaknesses. Stevens probably knew that with his small force he could distract Jackson but could not beat him. He also certainly knew that initially, at least, he had the initiative over Jackson and that Stonewall, deep in enemy territory and probably worried about the safety of his flanks, could not ignore an attack, however small. Stevens's willingness to forego a chance for decisive victory in favor of stalemate to achieve his ultimate tactical objective ensured Union success on the field at Chantilly.

General Stevens and, to a lesser extent, General Reno deserve much of the credit for ensuring that these tactical plans were successfully enacted on the field. As has already been demonstrated, Stevens made the most of his advantages of initiative and surprise. Isaac Stevens also deserves credit for selecting a flanking attack—which was called for in attacking the two brigade force he initially found—and then quickly shifting the attack into a direct assault on Jackson's line when Confederate movements changed the situation he faced. Such a formation made the most of his limited number of men, presenting Jackson with a threat he could not ignore while at the same time preserving enough of his small command to create a reserve force. Stevens also made good use of the terrain he was given, launching his attack over open ground that would permit him maximum freedom in directing his point of attack and using terrain to screen his movements. He likewise used terrain to good advantage in placing his artillery on the high ground of Millan Ridge where it could alternatively support infantry attacks and shell Confederate positions in the opposing woods. These same guns also controlled the field in front of them so that if a Confederate counterattack came, it would be unlikely to completely break a Union defensive line on the hill. General Reno, in his only real contribution to the Union's tactical plans at Chantilly, ordered a flanking probe in the woods east of Ox Road that, regardless of Reno's actual intent, was a clever way of fooling Jackson into believing he faced a much larger Union force than actually existed south of the turnpike, one that he would have to stop before he could continue his march to Jermantown.

Stevens's chief failing during the battle of Chantilly was that he did not grasp the importance of his own role, an error that ultimately cost him his life and nearly cost the Union tactical success. Throughout the early part of the battle Stevens fully lived up to his title of acting commander of the IX Corps—establishing tactical objectives, crafting plans and deployments to begin enacting that plan, and personally seeing to other tasks assigned to senior field commanders. Even once the "ball had been opened," General Stevens remained well to the rear of the action to assess his forces' progress and alter Union tactics and deployments accordingly as the battle progressed. But in the middle of the attack he abandoned that role and moved into the thick of the fight. Probably it was the sight of Morrison's attack, with his beloved 79th New York Highlanders at the center of the action, faltering and then being crushed before his very eyes that prompted this lapse. Whatever the cause, at the very same moment Isaac Stevens abandoned his temporary field headquarters post on Millan Ridge and rode forward to personally lead the attack, the general also abandoned his role of IX Corps commander and adopted instead the role of a regimental colonel. Although Reno was by then on the field, Stevens well knew that

Reno had expressed doubts about the plan and had told Stevens to retain temporary command of the IX Corps and the fight. Reno clearly wanted as little to do with this engagement as possible. And with Stevens's death, for a time no one at all was directing the fight, leaving a command void that could have proved deadly had Hill or Jackson chosen that moment to launch a counterattack. The sheer chaos within the Union lines would have played right into Confederate hands and spun forth a situation that even the well-emplaced Union artillery might not have been able to stop. Fate that day, though, was with the Union army on two counts. First, Jackson did not counterattack, but rather used the enemy's confusion to readjust his troops, and second, at just the moment that things were falling apart, onto the field rode Major General Philip Kearny.

General Kearny clearly was key to restoring life to Stevens's tactical plan at a point when it was in grave danger of completely faltering. First, Kearny deserves credit for being the only one to respond to Lieutenant Belcher's plea for assistance for the then-engaged IX Corps. Although Belcher never recorded how many other senior commanders refused to come to General Stevens's aid, Kearny's initiative reflects the bold leadership that had already earned his well-deserved reputation as a model warrior. Once on the field, Kearny seemed to understand what Stevens's tactical plan had been and quickly moved to revive it. He understood that, even with his fresh division, the Union troops were greatly outnumbered and thus Stevens's force would have to be reconstituted into a viable fighting force. After directing General Birney to launch a new attack to keep the Confederates from exploiting the Union's disorganization, Kearny turned to personally reorganizing Stevens's force. Though Kearny certainly knew that he should remain at the rear to direct the action, he may have believed General Reno would take on this role which would free him to personally take on the daunting task of reordering Stevens's command. And given the confusion among Stevens's shattered force, Kearny was probably correct in thinking that it might require a major general to accomplish this task with the speed the situation required.

General Kearny, like Isaac Stevens, still ultimately failed to understand how important a senior field commander is and unnecessarily risked his life filling a role that should have been assigned to someone of lower rank. Although Kearny's presence in the midst of the field probably was justified by the disorder of the Union position at that point in the battle, he had no reason to personally reconnoiter the Confederate line as he did after his angry encounter with the 21st Massachusetts. And despite the fact that he had successfully risked his life in such a way time and again in this and many of the earlier wars in which he had fought, Philip Kearny should have understood from the chaos created by General Stevens's death how fragile this particular fight really was. Kearny's death, like Stevens's, threatened to undo the Union's chances of tactical success at Chantilly and risked total defeat. In the end, fate would smile on the Union, for the growing darkness, rather than the intervention of another Federal officer, stalled Thomas's Confederate counterattack and ended the fighting.

Unlike Stevens's ambitious plan, Jackson's tactical objective during the battle of Chantilly appears to have simply been to maintain his command's position in the face of Federal attacks. Indeed, Jackson had adopted a very defensive posture during most of September 1, despite the fact that his command was conducting an offensive flanking march around the Union right aimed at cutting off the enemy's retreat to the rear. Early in the day and while still on the march, for example, he deployed his column as if anticipating an attack from either side of the turnpike. While this was certainly a prudent move given his location and the size of his enemy's force, Jackson early on sacrificed his column's speed—and offensive potential—for defensive preparedness. Moreover, once he neared his directed objective of Jermantown, Jackson appeared to abandon all pretense of offensive action by shifting to a completely defensive stance, deploying his command in an arc-shaped formation facing south to deal with the impending Federal infantry attacks. Moreover, Fitzhugh Lee's cavalry force, which originally had been sent to probe Jermantown prior to Jackson's advance there, ultimately functioned as a defensive blocking force to prevent Union attacks on Jackson's new left flank that was established when he reoriented his command to the south. Jackson's order to send the bulk of his artillery to the rear, rather than put it into the battle, is more evidence that Stonewall had adopted a wholly defensive stance once Stevens's attack was launched. Indeed, that Jackson would remove his artillery to the rear so early in the fight suggests not only that he was shifting to the defense but also that, very early on in the battle of Chantilly, Jackson may have been considering a retreat would ultimately be necessary.

That Jackson's Command "survived to fight another day" suggests that Stonewall successfully achieved his tactical objective at the battle of Chantilly. Because Jackson's only goal was survival, he needed only to fend off any of the attacks that General Pope threw at him to leave the field with a victory of sorts. And despite Stonewall's reputation for daring military exploits, his direction of the Confederate half of the action at Chantilly is a textbook example of a senior officer playing it safe in combat. Throughout the fight at Chantilly, Jackson showed no interest in launching a general counterattack or even in exploiting weaknesses in the Federal line. For example, after Stevens's death, when the Union right in the grassy field was disordered and on the verge of chaos, Jackson failed to push his own line forward to pour a flanking fire on the left of the Union line. Had he done so, the entire Federal position would likely have been rendered untenable. But Jackson, apparently intent on taking a defensive stand only, refused to move forward and attack, instead holding his ground to wait for the next Federal attack.

Stonewall's actions during the battle are directly responsible for the South achieving its tactical goals at Chantilly. Jackson very quickly sensed that the situation in his front and flanks had changed—forcing him to shift from the offensive to adopting a defensive posture—and he responded proactively to the changed tactical realities. Once he appeared to believe battle was certain, Jackson moved to select the terrain on which the fight would occur, terrain that lent itself well to the defensive tactics he had adopted. By placing his line simultaneously on the edge of a woods and on the crest of a long, gently sloping ridge, he ensured his troops would have maximum cover and a longer field of fire at the enemy, who would be faced with the daunting prospect of attacking uphill against a largely concealed foe. Jackson also deserves credit for the manner in which he deployed his troops for battle because it, too, was designed to maximize chances of success for the Confederacy. The arc-shaped position of his line gave Stonewall interior lines during the battle, enhancing his ability to quickly shift troops to stop an attack at nearly any point on his line and allowing him to quickly reinforce any position he chose. Indeed, these interior lines were used to great effect in halting Stevens's attack and in quickly preparing to halt whatever subsequent assault Kearny was preparing before his death.

The battle of Chantilly, however, was hardly Jackson's finest hour as a tactical commander. Even by this point in the war, Stonewall Jackson had gained a reputation as one of the finest tactical leaders on either side of the war and a general who could routinely pull victory from defeat or turn an ordinary situation into an opening for success. Marching down the Little River Turnpike on September 1, Jackson held nearly all the military cards, having the advantages of initiative, position, and morale over his Union counterparts. With less than that Stonewall had pulled out victories in the Shenendoah. But as the day wore on, Jackson's intentionally slow marching pace and seeming lack of enthusiasm for carrying out his assigned task tossed away all of these advantages save morale. At the end of the march, with the objective in sight, Jackson surrendered the last ounce of offensive intent he had left by permitting General Stevens to take offensive initiative away from him and settling down to a purely defensive fight. For whatever reason, either due to sheer weariness or lack of personal support for Lee's strategic plan, Stonewall stumbled his way through the battle of Chantilly in the safest possible course.

That both Union and Confederate commanders on the field appear to have achieved their tactical objectives suggests that the battle of Chantilly was a tactical stalemate. While the casualty numbers may be deceptive, an analysis of the commander's objectives and actions at Chantilly suggest this to be the case. Such an ending to a battle during the Civil War is hardly unique to Chantilly and many of the war's larger, more notable fights—including Antietam and the Wilderness—are considered by many military historians to have ended similarly. But simply because a conflict ends in tactical stalemate does not imply that it was fought needlessly or that the men who died there did so for no gain. Nearly all the battles of the Civil War—or any war, for that matter—were fought to achieve a larger, strategic goal. And while winning a tactical advantage on the field is often important to achieving a strategic goal, it is not necessarily a sine qua non for reaching military strategic ends.

The strategic objectives of both Generals Lee and Pope are much easier to discern than the tactical goals of their subordinates. Both senior army commanders indicated what they wanted to achieve during the two days immediately following the Second Battle of Bull Run; Lee during his meeting in the field with Jackson and Stuart, and Pope, after much wavering, through his dispatches to Washington, conversations with his corps commanders, and orders on September 1. Likewise, the resulting actions of the armies on August 31 and September 1, 1862, permit us to draw more definitive conclusions about how closely each general successfully came to reaching his strategic objectives.

General Lee's chief strategic objective in ordering General Jackson's flanking march around the Union right was—as reported by several firsthand sources—to quickly place his army between Pope's beaten Union army and its capital. Doing so would simultaneously have cut off Pope's route of retreat and threatened the Union capital with Confederate attack. However, we know only where Lee wanted to place his army and nothing at all about what he intended to do with it once Jermantown was in Confederate hands. We can speculate that Lee may have hoped either to cripple or destroy Pope's army in the Centreville works, to threaten Washington, or do both in turn. In either case General

Lee certainly knew he would have to fight Pope's army after seizing Jermantown and probably hoped to do so on ground of his choosing.

Lee's ultimate decision to try the flanking maneuver probably was not reached as simply as it appears in hindsight. Looking over the rolling fields west of Centreville on the morning of August 31, General Lee must have felt himself in a quandary over choosing the army's next move. Certainly he knew the broken and bleeding Union army was trying to repair itself on the heights of Centreville and knew that they were a ripe target, weak and vulnerable to attack. But his own army was tired and weak too, hardly in a position to spring up and assault the strong Centreville works they had built the winter before. Adding to his concerns were the fresh Union troops rushing to join Pope, troops that were not beaten and demoralized from the recent fighting. The conditions also were certainly right to launch the invasion of the north that he had proposed— and President Davis had approved—earlier that year. Lee's plan to invade the north would have had a variety of immediate benefits. Chief among these were that in the near-term moving north would give his weary force time to recuperate from the recent campaign and, in the long-term his entire army might well spend the winter living off the Maryland farmers, rather than using up more scarce Southern rations. Union troops probably would have been pulled from the Shenandoah Valley to pursue the Confederates, leaving farmers in the Confederacy's "bread basket" free to harvest their crops that fall. At the same time, Southern politicians, reporters, and the public might not have understood why he had walked away from a chance—however slim—to destroy a weakened Union army and potentially end the war, if not with a Confederate victory then at least on terms favorable to the South. At the very least Lee could have been accused of wasting the victory so recently gained at Manassas. In the end General Lee may have believed that Richmond and the Southern public would never understand how he would choose invading the North—and prolonging the war—over exploiting the gains of Second Manassas and trying to destroy Pope's army, no matter how poor a chance he might have of victory.

Knowing that Lee had been searching for a chance to launch his invasion of the North for several months and was presented with the ideal conditions for such a move immediately after Second Manassas raises a question: Did Lee really intend for Jackson to succeed in cutting off and interposing his force between the Union army and Washington? Or, asking the same question another way: Was the entire flanking move really a Potemkin march, whose only real objective was to convince Southern politicians and the public that Lee had tried to follow up Second Manassas and end the war quickly and, having failed at that, was free to adopt a fall-back plan and invade Maryland? Lee himself wrote in his official report of the action at Ox Hill that "the next morning [after the battle] it was found that the enemy had conducted his retreat so rapidly that the attempt to intercept him was abandoned." So Lee's own words would imply that his pursuit of the Union army was genuine. But reports can be, and often are, biased to serve the author's views. Unfortunately for modern historians, absent discovery of some previously unknown firsthand evidence, we are left to ponder this question with the unsettling knowledge that it may never be conclusively answered.[2]

Certain of the facts known about the Confederate senior command's actions on August 31 and September 1, however, lend credence to this "conspiratorial" view of Lee's motives for Jackson's flanking march. Jackson's languid pace for his command's march is perhaps the best evidence that Lee and Jackson may not have intended to rapidly move between Pope and his army. Jackson had marched his men some 45 miles from the Shenandoah Valley in two days before opening the battle on August 28. Yet four days later they could make no greater headway than three miles in half a day's march. Additional evidence can be found in Stonewall's chiding directive to A. P. Hill to slow the pace of his division then leading Jackson's march. Longstreet's leisurely pace in moving to support Jackson also might be viewed as evidence that Lee was in no hurry to cut off the retreating Union army. Although General Longstreet's force remained on the field on August 31 to deceive the Yankees, he certainly knew that once they left the field late that day it would be obvious to the watching Federals that the bulk of Lee's army was moving north and perhaps around their right flank. Thus, once in motion, Longstreet should have rushed his force to join Jackson and reunite the Confederate army; why he did not do so—and did not reach Jackson's Command until nearly dark on the 1st—remains unexplained. Perhaps like Jackson's Command, Longstreet's men were too tired and hungry for a forced march, despite having had a full day to rest on the 31st. Perhaps, though, General Longstreet, too, was holding back his force to prevent it from quickly joining Jackson in his forward position.

To argue that General Lee would place his weakened army in such a precarious tactical position for purely political reasons, however, flies in the face of Lee's own statements and general conduct during the rest of the war. An interviewer talking to Lee three years after the war about the decision to invade Maryland recalled that Lee told him that "after

Chantilly, he found he could do nothing more against the Yankees, unless he attacked them in their fortifications around Washington, which he did not want to do." These comments suggest that Lee genuinely wanted to hit Pope's army on September 1, while they languished in their exposed position at Centreville, but that the results of the battle of Chantilly and Pope's subsequent withdrawal to the Washington defenses convinced him that the opportunity to do so had been lost. The interviewer further noted that "he therefore determined to cross the river into Maryland . . .," clearly indicating that Lee had decided to act on his invasion plans only after the opportunity to fight Pope outside the Washington defenses—and after the fight at Chantilly—had passed. Moreover, at no other time during the Civil War did General Lee direct his army to undertake a move that placed them at great risk mainly to provide political cover with Richmond or the Southern public. Nevertheless, lacking clear historical evidence to the contrary, we can never completely dismiss the notion that Lee might have been sending Jackson on primarily a political mission when he ordered the flanking march on August 31.[3]

If we accept the bulk of firsthand accounts suggesting that Lee actually had a military-strategic goal for Jackson's march, it is clear that by nightfall on September 1, General Lee had failed to achieve any of the strategic goals set the previous day. His army was still a mile from the important Jermantown intersection and, with the Union position there growing stronger by the hour, had no prospect of taking it without a costly and uncertain fight. The Union army also was moving rapidly to the rear toward Washington, virtually ensuring that Lee would be unable to place his force between Pope's army and its capital. Moreover, the Union forces had already largely abandoned the Centreville position in which Lee had hoped to trap them; if battle had come on September 2 it would more likely have been on ground of Pope's choosing.

General Lee himself deserves some of the blame for failing to achieve these strategic goals. Although Lee's strategic plan was militarily sound, in the end it may simply have been too ambitious for Lee's battered force to execute. Not only was the Army of Northern Virginia probably not up to carrying out Lee's plan, but going ahead with the effort anyway placed the entire army at risk of seeing victory turn to defeat. After all, General Lee was gambling that Pope would be slow to respond and would not risk launching an attack; Lee needed to look no further than Pope's fresh reinforcements to understand the consequences if he were wrong about this. Lee also virtually disappeared from the command structure after the accident that injured his wrists. For whatever reason, following this accident

General Lee largely became a spectator in a drama of his own creating and the army's movements and actions flowed without his masterful grip on command. This command gap played a key role in dimming what little chance Lee had of reaching strategic success.

Stonewall Jackson, too, is responsible for the Confederacy failing to reach its strategic objectives after Second Bull Run. The pace of his march gave the Union time to discover his presence and allow Pope to reinforce his line of communication with Washington before Jackson could sever it. That Jackson's Command was forced into a slow pace might be explained by the worn condition of the men, but why Stonewall himself ordered such a slow pace, as indicated earlier, remains a mystery. He had ordered his men to endure forced marches several times before in the pursuit of an important tactical or strategic goal and, despite their poor condition, he certainly could have asked so of his men once again. Particularly if he believed the end of such a march might be the destruction of the Union army and a victorious end of the war for the Confederacy. Maybe Jackson was genuinely worried that the condition of his men not only would prevent them from achieving General Lee's strategic goal for the march but, more ominously, also placed his men at risk of being attacked by a reinforced, numerically superior enemy. Also, Jackson was in many respects the "chief architect" of Lee's plan to invade the North and had been advocating such a move since late 1861. Perhaps he intentionally held his command back to hasten failure of the flanking move and open the opportunity for an invasion of Maryland. In the end, Stonewall simply may have lacked confidence in his ability to fully carry out the task General Lee had assigned to him but felt compelled to try it anyway. But whatever the case, Jackson's slow marching pace played a major role in preventing Lee from gaining a strategic victory in the days following the Second Battle of Bull Run.

But the Confederate commander who bears the greatest responsibility for Lee's failure to achieve his strategic goals at this time is J. E. B. Stuart, Lee's cavalry commander. Indeed, Stuart's reckless behavior on August 31 and September 1 is such a gross breach of military duty that, had the action at Chantilly not been "lost" in the ensuing focus on the larger and more important battles of Second Bull Run and Antietam, he probably should have been brought up on charges of dereliction of duty. Stuart initially had followed through on Jackson's orders of August 31, reconnoitering the route to Jermantown and discovering the strength of the Union presence there. But before nightfall General Stuart committed a series of acts that in many respects doomed Lee's efforts to insert his army between

Pope and Washington on September 1. Stuart's first failure came shortly after discovering that Jackson's route was clear and that the Union position at Jermantown was extremely weak. Stuart was the only senior Confederate commander who knew that Pope and the Union army remained completely unaware of their flanking march, a development to which he should have responded by maintaining a low profile—to preserve the secrecy of Jackson's march—and by quickly reporting his important findings to General Jackson. But rather than hiding his presence in the Union rear, Stuart ordered his horse artillery to lob several shells into the Federal wagon train, a pointless gesture of military bravado that drove Pope to begin reinforcing the Jermantown position and ultimately prevented Jackson from taking the intersection the next day. Stuart's second failure came only minutes later when, after rejoining his command, he failed to inform General Jackson of the findings of his reconnaissance. Rather then racing to tell Stonewall his important news, Stuart had his men encamp for the night and then went off with his staff to initiate a party with local friends. Stuart would not bother to pass on the intelligence to Jackson until nearly noon the next day, by which time the information, rather than helping Stonewall make informed tactical decisions, actually misinformed him into thinking his route to lightly defended Jermantown was clear. In reality, Jackson was marching into an increasingly strong Union position that threatened to turn itself on his command. In the final analysis, Stuart's twin failures were key both in alerting Pope to Lee's intended flanking march and in buying Pope enough time to adequately respond to Jackson's movement.

In stark contrast to Lee's ambitious flanking move, General Pope's chief strategic objective for September 1 was simple and straightforward—to get his army safely out of Lee's trap and maintain its open line of communication to Washington. To do this Pope knew he would have to first defend his shifting right flank and prepare to fend off the impending Confederate assault there. That Pope chose these as his two objectives on September 1 is suggested by his response to intelligence warning of Jackson's movement. His first act was beefing up the defenses at Jermantown and sending infantry probes to find Jackson's Command. Once these efforts were well in place, and despite that it took Pope most of the day to finally act on his second strategic goal, he increasingly focused on moving his entire army to the rear.

The events of late September 1 and the following day clearly demonstrate that General Pope, unlike his Confederate counterpart, achieved both of his strategic goals. Pope's infantry deployments, both at

Jermantown and on the roads leading to the Little River Turnpike, successfully located and blocked Jackson's advance on the Union right flank. The second of Pope's objectives, maintaining his communication with Washington, was achieved within a few hours of his decision to retreat, a movement that on the whole proceeded largely without incident. By sunrise on September 2, 1862, Pope's army was once again safely between Lee's army and the capital, fully realizing Pope's chief strategic objective for the previous day.

General Pope, for all his myriad faults as an army commander, deserves credit for the Union's achieving its strategic goals on September 1. Indeed, in many respects Pope's actions late on September 1 are his finest moments as commander of most of the Union's eastern forces. His first commendable act was in ordering the army's huge and cumbersome wagon train to move to the rear, a move taken long before the commanding general himself became convinced that the army must retreat. This important first step was a sensible military precaution that would later prove key in permitting the army to quickly slip out of Lee's trap. Once Pope finally became convinced that his army was in danger of being flanked, and with that conviction realized the threat to the army's very existence, he acted swiftly and decisively to respond. He acted correctly in first seeing to the defense of the army's route of retreat by quickly increasing the number of troops defending Jermantown, appointing a senior officer to oversee the defense of the strategically important Jermantown line, and ordering sizable defensive probes up key roads toward the suspected Confederate route of advance—such as those led by General Stevens— which had the added benefit of guarding the army's flank as it retreated. General Pope followed up this by ordering the army to begin an orderly retreat designed to move it to safety without turning the move into a disorganized rout. But Pope's focus on achieving his strategic goal is perhaps most evident in the continued movement of the army throughout the battle. Rather than stop the army's retreat to reinforce and expand the fight at Chantilly—a move which might have improved Pope's personal career prospects but which certainly would not have yielded anything of military value—Pope continued to direct his troops to move eastward in pursuit of his strategic goal of reaching safety.

Although General Pope deserves credit for his actions on September 1, it is important to remember that he spent much of the time following the Second Battle of Bull Run laying the groundwork for what could just as easily have become a military disaster. Indeed, that the Union escaped safely and Pope reached his strategic objective may be due as much to luck as to any action Pope took. Perhaps Pope's greatest failing during these two days lay in his indecision about the army's ultimate direction. His wavering stand about whether the army should attack or retreat thoroughly undermined what little respect his corps commanders still had in their superior's ability to lead. Had events unfolded differently—resulting in a major attack by either side—this lack of confidence almost certainly would have hurt the Northern army's chances of success. Pope also can be criticized for risking the very existence of the army to preserve his own career. His risky game of keeping his army in a position he knew to be obsolete—if not outright dangerous—while trying to cajole Washington into ordering a retreat was, in even the most generous assessment, selfish and foolish. And had events transpired differently late on September 1, General Pope may well have found himself facing charges of dereliction of duty rather than simply wondering if he would retain command of his army the next day. President Lincoln, too, must have understood this, for although General Pope had succeeded in moving the army to safety, it was clearly too little too late.

Perhaps the most important task remaining for modern historians and analysts is to determine if the battle of Chantilly had any impact at all on the greater strategic scheme of the war. Writers of the late 19th century—particularly biographers of Generals Stevens and Kearny—tended to consider Chantilly a small but important battle that stopped Jackson's attack and thereby saved the Union army from collapse and complete defeat. More recently, historians, when they have bothered to consider Chantilly at all, have taken nearly a polar-opposite view. In this outlook Chantilly was a largely pointless battle, fought mainly because the two forces stumbled into a fight neither could stop until darkness gave them an excuse to disengage. These historians argue that Lee had already decided to open his Maryland campaign and was perhaps simply unable to stop Jackson soon enough to avoid an unnecessary fight. Although both of these earlier assessments of the battle of Chantilly have some legitimacy, they are only partly accurate. Somewhere between these extremes lies the truth about the battle's strategic role in the greater Civil War.

Predictably, the opinions of the men who were there on September 1, 1862, tend to fall along lines drawn by their respective personal roles in the fight, leaving us little firsthand source material from which to evaluate the battle's impact. Those Union men who fought at Chantilly considered it a great fight, if only because so many of their comrades fell on that rain-soaked field. The analysis of Captain Horatio Belcher, the man Stevens had sent to find reinforcements on September 1, sums up the views of many who were there that day. The victory at Chantilly was, he wrote, "one of the most important of the campaign & war in its results—had we have been defeated again here our army would have been annihilated & Washington taken." Also typical of the battle participants' accounts is that by Captain Walcott of the 21st Massachusetts: "Hard as the fortune of the 21st had been in it, the battle was a decided victory for the Union arms: the rebels had entirely failed in their attempt upon the Union right, and the safety of the troops, artillery, and supplies at Centreville, was assured." Those Union men who instead marched by the battle in the general retreat—most of whom heard the fight but saw nothing of the struggle—saw their rearward move as further proof of Pope's folly. For them, the battle of Chantilly simply meant, as the colonel of the 55th New York recorded, "that the enemy was no longer at our heels." For the Confederate soldiers present at Ox Hill, the battle was simply a skirmish that had little consequence, save the loss of those killed. And after the then-impending battle of Antietam, few would consider the experience at Chantilly, even its human cost, worth mentioning in their letters home or their personal journals.[4]

The battle of Chantilly appears not to have been the key battle that many late-19th-century writers portrayed it to be. Certainly the fight played no role in immediately "saving Washington" from Confederate attack. There is no evidence that Lee would have tried to attack Washington even if he had achieved his strategic objective of capturing or destroying the Union army and, in any case, Lee's battle-weary army was in no position to fight its way through the thousands of fresh troops guarding the Federal capital.

While the battle of Chantilly may not have saved Washington from attack, it was the impetus for Pope's general retreat from the flanked position at Centreville, a decision that ultimately avoided a potentially costly fight and allowed the army to rebuild to fight another day. But it had taken a fight that cost 679 Union casualties to persuade him to take the action that would ultimately preserve the army intact.

The struggle near Chantilly also forced Jackson to stop and fight near Ox Hill and thus ended any further prospect of his command threatening the demoralized and ill-prepared Union army. Although Jackson's drive to seize Jermantown had stopped short of its original goal, Stonewall certainly had other options open to him to continue on General Lee's directed flanking march. He could have sent his force down Ox Road—or any of the other roads running south into the Warrenton Turnpike—to cut off the retreating Union army before potentially turning west to threaten

Centreville. Indeed, that Jackson had stopped at Ox Road, rather than pressing ahead to attack Jermantown in force, leaves open the question of what Stonewall was considering as his next move during the late afternoon of September 1. Was he waiting for General Lee to arrive with Longstreet's Command before taking action or was he considering what avenue of attack to take now that the Jermantown route was closed? In any case, the question of Jackson's next move was resolved for him by the appearance of Stevens's troops on his right flank at 4:00 that afternoon. Whatever Jackson may have been considering before that time, he had to fight there at Ox Hill, forsaking any plans he might have entertained of changing his route of attack.

Another result of the action at Chantilly that certainly had an impact on the outcome of the war were the deaths of Generals Stevens and Kearny. We can only speculate about the personal role these two senior officers might have played had they lived beyond September 1, 1862. But one thing is clear; given the dearth of qualified and competent battle-tested general officers available for higher command, both of these men most certainly would have gone on to more important posts had they lived longer. Isaac Stevens might very well have had a corps-level command by the year's end. We may safely assume this because when General Burnside departed the IX Corps to assume command of the Army of the Potomac on November 5, 1862, he was replaced by Brigadier General Orlando B. Wilcox, the man who replaced Isaac Stevens at the head of the IX Corps' 1st Division.

It may be the death of Philip Kearny, though, that was the single most lasting and dramatic result of the Ox Hill fight. By mid-1862, General Kearny was already being eyed for higher command, having earned a reputation as an aggressive, first-rate general whose antislavery politics simply aided his prospects for promotion. And perhaps more importantly for the time, Philip Kearny had not pitched his "career tent" in the camp of any of the recently departed commanders of the army and so he was well liked, as well as respected, by nearly all his fellow senior officers. Had he lived Kearny certainly would have moved up to a corps-level command by the close of 1862, for on October 30 of that year command of the III Corps was officially given to Brigadier General George Stoneman, the man who replaced Kearny at the helm of that corps' 1st Division. Had Kearny lived and been given the opportunity to apply his aggressive, battle-eager demeanor to an army-level command, the Civil War may well have run a very different course, indeed. While it would have been unlikely that General Kearny would have replaced Ambrose Burnside or Joseph

Hooker in their turn commanding Lincoln's army, he may well have had an edge on George Meade by the middle of 1863. Both Brigadier Generals Kearny and Meade officially assumed brigade-level command in the I Corps during March of 1862, Kearny of the 1st Brigade of the 1st Division and Meade of the 2nd Brigade of the 2nd Division. But Kearny assumed a division-level post in May 1862, nearly five months before Meade took control of his first division command on September 12. And Kearny's extensive combat command experience and reputation as a respected fighting general suggests that he would have been a more logical choice than Meade to replace Hooker in command of the Army of the Potomac after the Union failure at Chancellorsville. While we can only speculate how the course of the war might have changed had Kearny had a chance to lead the army, I suspect that at the very least Robert E. Lee and his army would not have been allowed to retreat south to safety after the battle of Gettysburg if Philip Kearny had been in command instead of George Meade.

In the end, the 1,195 Americans who fell in the shadow of Ox Hill did not die needlessly in a pointless firefight in a thunderstorm. The Union dead, including Generals Stevens and Kearny, did indeed give their lives to preserve the safety of the Union army, even if not in the way that their contemporaries would later portray it. And their Confederate counterparts, too, gave their lives in pursuit of their own goal, even if that effort ultimately failed. Who can say how differently the war—and our subsequent history—might have been if Stonewall Jackson and his men had successfully seized Jermantown or broken Stevens's and Kearny's lines and once again routed the Union army? Considering any of these alternate outcomes is little more than idle speculation. But what is certain is that each man who died at Chantilly did so in pursuit of his own noble goal, regardless if it was to preserve that unique political union known as the United States of America or the experiment in independence known as the Confederate States of America. Clearly, they who fell at Chantilly did not die in vain.

Order of Battle

Forces Engaged at Chantilly and Jermantown

Union
Army of Virginia
Major General John Pope

I Corps
Major General Franz Sigel
    Cavalry Brigade
    Colonel John Beardsley
        1st Connecticut Battalion (two companies)
        1st Maryland – Detached
        4th New York – Detached
        9th New York
        6th Ohio
III Corps
Major General Irvin McDowell
    1st Division
    Brigadier General Rufus King
        3rd Brigade
        Brigadier General Marsena Patrick
            21st New York
            23rd New York
            35th New York
            80th New York (20th Militia)
    2nd Division
    Brigadier General James B. Ricketts
        1st Brigade
        Brigadier General Abram Duryee
            97th New York
            104th New York
            105th New York
            107th New York
        2nd Brigade
        Brigadier General Zealous B. Tower
            26th New York
            94th New York
            88th Pennsylvania
            90th New York
        3rd Brigade
        Colonel Robert Stiles
            12th Massachusetts
            13th Massachusetts
            83rd New York (9th Militia)
            11th Pennsylvania

4th Brigade – On Detached Duty Beginning August 31
Artillery
    Maine Light Artillery, 2nd Battery
    Maine Light Artillery, 5th Battery
    1st Pennsylvania Light Artillery, Battery C
    Pennsylvania Light Artillery, Battery C

Army of the Potomac
(Units placed under the command of Major General John Pope)

II Corps
Major General Edwin V. Sumner
    2nd Division
    Brigadier General John Sedgwick
        1st Brigade
        Brigadier General Willias Gorman
            15th Massachusetts
            1st Minnesota
            34th New York
            82nd New York
        2nd Brigade
        Brigadier General Oliver O. Howard
            69th Pennsylvania
            71st Pennsylvania
            72nd Pennsylvania
            106th Pennsylvania
        3rd Brigade
        Brigadier General N. J. T. Dana
            19th Masssachusetts
            20th Massachusetts
            7th Michigan
            42nd New York
        Artillery
            1st Rhode Island Light Artillery, Battery A
            1st Rhode Island Light Artillery, Battery B
            1st Rhode Island Light Artillery, Battery G
            1st United States Artillery, Battery I
III Corps
Major General Samuel P. Heintzelman
    1st Division
    Major General Philip Kearny
        1st Brigade
        Brigadier General John Robinson
            20th Indiana
            63rd Pennsylvania
            105th Pennsylvania
        2nd Brigade
        Brigadier General David B. Birney
            3rd Maine
            4th Maine

   1st New York
   38th New York
   40th New York
   57th New York
   101st New York
  3rd Brigade
  Colonel Orlando M. Poe
   2nd Michigan
   3rd Michigan
   5th Michigan
   37th New York
   99th Pennsylvania
  Artillery
   1st Rhode Island Light Artillery, Battery E
   1st United States Artillery, Battery K

IV Corps
Brigadier General Erasmus D. Keyes
 1st Division
 Brigadier General Darius N. Couch
  1st Brigade
  Brigadier General Albion P. Howe
   55th New York
   62nd New York
   93rd Pennsylvania
   98th Pennsylvania
   102nd Pennsylvania
  2nd Brigade
  Brigadier General John L. Abercrombie
   65th New York
   67th New York
   23rd Pennsylvania
   31st Pennsylvania
   61st Pennsylvania
  3rd Brigade
  Brigadier General Innis Palmer
   7th Massachusetts
   10th Massachusetts
   2nd Rhode Island
   36th New York
  Artillery
   1st New York, Battery H
   7th New York Light Artillery

VI Corps
Major General William B. Franklin
 1st Division
 Brigadier General Henry W. Slocum
  1st Brigade
  Colonel Alfred T. A. Torbert
   1st New Jersey
   2nd New Jersey

3rd New Jersey

4th New Jersey

IX Corps

Major General Jesse L. Reno (acting)

1st Division

Brigadier General Isaac I. Stevens

1st Brigade

Colonel Benjamin Christ

8th Michigan

50th Pennsylvania

2nd Brigade

Colonel Daniel Leasure

46th New York

100th Pennsylvania

3rd Brigade

Lieutenant Colonel David Morrison

28th Massachusetts

79th New York

Artillery

2nd U.S. Artillery, Battery E

2nd Division

Major General Jesse L. Reno

1st Brigade

Colonel James Nagle

2nd Maryland

6th New Hampshire

48th Pennsylvania

2nd Brigade

Colonel Edward Ferrero

21st Massachusetts

51st New York

51st Pennsylvania

Artillery

Pennsylvania Light Artillery, Battery D

Confederate

Army of Northern Virginia
General Robert E. Lee

Jackson's Command
Major General Thomas J. Jackson

Jackson's Division

Brigadier General William E. Starke

1st (Stonewall) Brigade

Colonel Andrew J. Grigsby

2nd Virginia

4th Virginia
5th Virginia
27th Virginia
33rd Virginia
2nd Brigade
Colonel Bradley T. Johnson
    1st Virginia Battalion
    21st Virginia
    42nd Virginia
    48th Virginia
3rd Brigade
Colonel William Booth Taliaferro
    10th Virginia
    23rd Virginia
    37th Virginia
    47th Alabama
    48th Alabama
4th Brigade
Colonel Leroy A. Stafford
    1st Louisiana
    2nd Louisiana
    9th Louisiana
    10th Louisiana
    15th Louisiana
Coppens's Battalion

Division Artillery
    Brockenbrough's Battery, Baltimore Artillery
    Carpenter's Battery, Allegheny Artillery
    Caskie's Battery, Hampden Artillery
    Cutshaw's Battery, Winchester Battery
    Poague's Battery, Rockbridge Artilley
    Raine's Battery, Lee Artillery
    Rice's Battery
    Wooding's Battery, Danville Artillery
    Light Division
    Major General A. P. Hill
Branch's Brigade
Brigadier General Lawrence O. Branch
    7th North Carolina
    18th North Carolina
    28th North Carolina
    33rd North Carolina
    37th North Carolina
Archer's Brigade
Brigadier General James J. Archer
    5th Alabama Battalion
    19th Georgia
    1st Tennessee
    7th Tennessee

14th Tennessee
Pender's Brigade
Brigadier General William D. Pender
    16th North Carolina
    22nd North Carolina
    34th North Carolina
    38th North Carolina
Field's Brigade
Colonel James M. Brockenbrough
    22nd Virginia
    40th Virginia
    47th Virginia
    55th Virginia
Gregg's Brigade
Brigadier General Maxcy Gregg
    1st South Carolina
    1st South Carolina Rifles
    12th South Carolina
    13th South Carolina
    14th South Carolina
Thomas's Brigade
Colonel Edward L. Thomas
    14th Georgia
    35th Georgia
    45th Georgia
    49th Georgia
Division Artillery
    Braxton's Battery, Fredericksburg Artillery
    Crenshaw's Battery
    Davidson's Battery, Letcher Artillery
    Fleet's Battery, Middlesex Artillery
    Latham's Battery, Branch Artillery
    Pegram's Battery, Purcell Artillery
    McIntosh's Battery, Pee Dee Artillery
Ewell's Division
Brigadier General Alexander R. Lawton
Lawton's Brigade
Colonel Marcellus Douglas
    13th Georgia
    26th Georgia
    31st Georgia
    38th Georgia
    60th Georgia
    61st Georgia
Trimble's Brigade
Captain W. F. Brown
    15th Alabama
    12th Georgia
    21st Georgia
    21st North Carolina

Hay's Brigade
Col. H. B. Strong
    5th Louisiana
    6th Louisiana
    7th Louisiana
    8th Louisiana
    14th Louisiana
Early's Brigade
Brigadier General Jubal A. Early
    13th Virginia
    25th Virginia
    31st Virginia
    44th Virginia
    49th Virginia
    52nd Virginia
    58th Virginia
Divisional Artillery
    Balthis's Battery, Fredericksburg Artillery
    Brown's Battery, Chesapeake Artillery
    D'Aquin's Battery, Louisiana Guard Artillery
    Dement's Battery
    John R. Johnson's Battery
    Latimer's Battery, Courtney Artillery
Cavalry
Major General J. E. B. Stuart
Robertson's Brigade
Brigadier General Beverly H. Robertson
    2nd Virginia Cavalry
    6th Virginia Cavalry
    7th Virginia Cavalry
    12th Virginia Cavalry
    17th Virginia Cavalry
Lee's Brigade
Brigadier General Fitzhugh Lee
    1st Virginia Cavalry
    3rd Virginia Cavalry
    4th Virginia Cavalry
    5th Virginia Cavalry
    9th Virginia Cavalry

Chapter Notes

Chapter 1

1. O.R., Vol. XVI, Pt. 1, p. 5.
2. O.R., Vol. XVI, Pt. 1, p. 20.
3. Donald, David Herbert, ed. *Inside Lincoln's Cabinet: the Civil War Diaries of Salmon P. Chase* (New York: 1954), pp. 96-97.
4. Sears, Stephen, Ed. *The Civil War Letters of George B. McClellan* (New York: DaCapo Press, 1992), p. 367.
5. Ibid., pp. 369-400.
6. Ibid., pp. 388-389; O.R., Vol. XVI, Pt. 1, p. 5.
7. O.R., Vol. XVI, Pt. 1, pp. 20-21.
8. O.R., Vol. XVI, Pt. 1, pp. 551-552; 553
9. O.R., Vol. XVI, Pt. 1, pp. 553-554.
10. O.R., Vol. XII, Pt. 2, p. 653.
11. O.R., Vol. XVI, Pt. 1, p. 14; 36-37.
12. O.R., Vol. XVI, Pt. 1, p. 555.
13. Worsham Letters, Unpublished MS, p. 14.
14. O.R., Vol. XVI, Pt. 1, p. 16; 36-38.
15. O.R., Vol. XVI, Pt. 1, p. 36.
16. O.R., Vol. XVI, Pt. 1, p. 55.
17. O.R., Vol. XVI, Pt. 1, pp. 37-39.
18. Gaff, Alan D. *Brave Men's Tears: The Iron Brigade at Brawner Farm* (Dayton, Ohio, Morningside Publishers, 1996), pp. 58-59.
19. Ibid.
20. O.R., Vol. XVI, Pt. 1, p. 39.
21. O.R., Vol. XVI, Pt. 1, p. 39.
22. O.R., Vol. XVI, Pt. 1, pp. 39-41.
23. O.R., Vol. XVI, Pt. 1, p. 15.
24. O.R., Vol. XVI, Pt. 1, pp. 416-417.
25. O.R., Vol. XVI, Pt. 1, p. 14.
26. O.R., Vol. XVI, Pt. 1, p. 41.
27. O.R., Vol. XVI, Pt. 1, p. 557.
28. Sears, Stephan W., Ed. *The Civil War Papers of George B. McClellan, Selected Correspondence 1860-1865*, (New York: Da Capo Press, 1989), p 404; O.R., Vol. XVI, Pt. 1, p. 5. For an extensive firsthand view of both sides of the Pope-McClellan conflict, see *The Military Memoirs of General John Pope*, pp. 143-170, and *The Civil War Papers of George B. McClellan*, pp. 404-429.
29. Sears, *The Civil War Papers of George B. McClellan*, pp. 407-413.
30. Ibid., p. 416.
31. Ibid., p. 421.

32. O.R., Vol. XII, Pt. 2, p. 537.
33. O.R., Vol. XII, Pt. 2. p. 537.
34. O.R., Vol. XII, Pt. 2, p. 537.
35. O.R., Vol. XII, Pt. 2, p. 537.
36. O.R., Vol. XVI, Pt. 1, p. 557.
37. O.R., Vol. XVI, Pt. 1, p. 76.
38. O.R., Vol. XVI, Pt. 1, pp. 42-43; 558.
39. O.R., Vol. XVI, Pt. 1, p. 43.
40. Wallcott, Charles F. , *History of the Twenty First Regiment Massachusetts Volunteers in the War for the Preservation of the Union, 1861-1865* (Boston: Houghton, Mifflin, and Co., 1882), pp. 158-159.
41. Fletcher, Daniel Cooledge, *Reminiscences of California and the Civil War* (Ayer, Mass.: Press of Huntley S. Turner, 1894), pp. 172-173.
42. O.R., XII, Pt. 2, pp. 746-747; Vautier, John D., *History of the 88th Pennsylvania Volunteers in the War for the Union, 1861-1865* (Philadelphia: J.B. Lippincott Co., 1894), p. 67; Jackman, Lyman, *History of the Sixth New Hampshire Regiment in the War for the Union* (Concord, N.H.: Republican Press Association, 1891), p. 87; Walcott, *History of the Twenty First Regiment Massachusetts Volunteers*, p. 151.
43. Parker, Thomas H., *History of the 51st Regiment of P.V. and V.V* (Philadelphia: King & Baird, 1869), p. 218.
44. *Report of Major General John Pope, Part 2* (Millwood, New York; Kraus Reprint Co., 1977), p. 25; O.R., Vol. XII, Pt. 2, p. 44.
45. Veil, Enos B., *Reminiscences of a Boy in the Civil War,* Unpublished MS, Civil War Misc. Collection, USAMHI, 1915, p. 29.
46. *Report of Pope*, pp. 245-246.
47. O.R., Vol. XII, Pt. 2, p. 557.
48. Richard O'Sullivan, *55th Virginia Infantry* (Lynchburg: H.E. Howard, Inc. 1989), p. 20.

Chapter 2

1. Sears, Stephen W., *To the Gates of Richmond—The Peninsula Campaign* (New York: Tichnor & Fields. 1992), pp. 16-17.
2. O.R. Vol. XVI, Pt. 1, pp. 415-416.
3. Styple, William B., Ed., *Letters From the Peninsula: The Civil War Letters of General Philip Kearny* (Kearny, N.J.: Belle Grove Publishing Co., 1988), pp. 166-167; O.R., Vol. XVI, Pt. 1, pp. 416-418.
4. Styple, *Letters From the Peninsula*, p. 11.
5. Ibid., pp. 11-12.
6. Kearny, Thomas, *General Philip Kearny—Battle Soldier of Five Wars* (New York: G.P. Putman's Sons. 1937), pp. 42-44; Whitehorne, Joseph W. A., "The Battle of Chantilly" (*Blue and Gray Magazine*, April-May, 1987), p. 51.
7. Styple, *Letters From the Peninsula*, p. 12.
8. Kearny, *General Philip Kearny*, pp. 20-21; Whitehome, "The Battle of Chantilly," p. 51.
9. Waugh, John C., "The Proving Ground" (*Civil War Times Illustrated*, April 1996), pp. 36-38.
10. Styple, *Letters From the Peninsula*, p. 13.
11. Ibid., pp. 13-14.
12. Ibid., p. 14
13. Ibid.
14. Ibid.

15. Ibid., pp. 14-17.
16. Kearny, *General Philip Kearny*, p. x.
17. Styple, *Letters From the Peninsula*, p. 17.
18. Ibid.
19. Ibid., p. 19.
20. Kearny, *General Philip Kearny*, p. x.
21. Styple, *Letters From the Peninsula*, pp. 19-20.
22. Ibid., pp. 32-33.
23. Ibid., p. 37.
24. Ibid., p. 45.
25. Ibid., pp. 46-47.
26. Ibid., p. 55.
27. Sears, *To the Gates of Richmond*, p. 78.
28. Styple, *Letters From the Peninsula*, pp. 74-78.
29. Ibid., p. 89.
30. Ibid., pp. 89-92.
31. Sears, *To the Gates of Richmond*, p. 274.
32. Styple, *Letters From the Peninsula*, p. 125.
33. Ibid., p. 137.
34. Ibid., pp. 125-145.
35. Ibid., pp 136-137.
36. Ibid., pp 144-145.
37. Ibid., p. 162.
38. Kearny, *General Philip Kearny*, p. xi; Sears, *To the Gates of Richmond*, p. 303.
39. Carse, Robert, *Department of the South: Hilton Head Island in the Civil War* (Hilton Head, S.C.: Impressions Printing Co., 1987), p. 44; For a thorough and comprehensive biography of Isaac Ingalls Stevens, see *Isaac I. Stevens: Young Man In a Hurry* by Kent D. Richards. This modern biography is a much more balanced and accurate volume than Hazard Stevens's biography of his father (although that volume nonetheless is useful for events and quotes).
40. Carse, *Department of the South*, p. 44-45.
41. Ibid., p. 44; Richards, Kent D., *Isaac I. Stevens: Young Man In a Hurry* (Pullman, Washington: Washington University, 1993), pp. 31-33.
42. Richards, *Isaac I. Stevens*, p. 47.
43. Ibid., p. 53.
44. Ibid., p. 55.
45. Ibid., pp. 54-55.
46. Ibid., p. 57.
47. Ibid., p. 89.
48. Ibid., pp. 93-94.
49. Ibid., p. 137.
50. Ibid., pp. 174-175.
51. Carse, *Department of the South*, p. 46.
52. Mottelay, Paul F. and Campbell-Copeland, T., Eds. *The Soldier in Our American Civil War* (New York: Stanley Bradley Publishing Co. 1890), p. 129.
53. Carse, *Department of the South*, p, 47.
54. Ibid., pp. 3-4.
55. Brennan, Patrick, *Secessionville: Assault on Charleston* (Campbell, California: Savas Publishing Co., 1996), pp. 46-48.
56. Richards, *Isaac I. Stevens*, pp. 372-373.

57. Ibid., pp. 376-377.
58. Carse, *Department of the South*. pp. 60-64.
59. Ibid., pp. 65-67.
60. Marvel, William, *Burnside* (Chapel Hill, N.C.: The University of North Carolina Press, 1991), pp. 100-102.
61. O.R., Vol. XVI, Pt. 1, p. 416.

Chapter 3

1. Todd, William, *The Seventy-Ninth Highlanders New York Volunteers in the War of the Rebellion, 1861-1865* (Albany, N.Y.: Press of Brandow, Barton, & Co., 1886), p. 211.
2. Woodward, Evan Morrison and Zamonski, Stanley W., Eds., *Our Campaigns; the Second Regiment Pennsylvania Reserve Volunteers, 1861-1864* (Shippensburg, PA: Burd Street Press. 1995), p. 144.
3. Ford, Lieutenant H. E., *History of the 101st Regiment* (Syracuse: Times Publishing Co., 1898), p. 38.
4. Pryor, Elizabeth Brown, *Walney* (Fairfax, Virginia: Fairfax County Printing Office, 1984), pp. 83-84.
5. Ibid., p. 84.
6. Bosbyshell, Oliver Christian, *The 48th in the War* (Philadelphia: Avil Printing Co., 1895), p. 69.
7. Todd, *The Seventy-Ninth Highlanders*, p. 211.
8. O.R., Vol. XVI, Pt. 1, pp. 5-6.
9. O.R., Vol. XII, Pt. 2, pp. 537-538.
10. Lewis, George, *The History of Battery E, First Rhode Island Light Artillery* (Providence: Snow & Farnham, Printers, 1892), p. 100; Todd, *The Seventy Ninth Highlanders*, pp. 211-212; *Shoemaker's Battery*, Butternut Press Reprint, pp. 20-21.
11. O.R., Vol XII, Pt. 2, p. 647.
12. O.R., Vol. XII, Pt. 2, p. 743.
13. James Longstreet, *From Manassas to Appomattox* (New York: Smithmark Publishers, Reprint, 1992), pp. 191.
14. Southern Historical Society Papers, Vol. XL, 1915, p. 229; Hennessey, *Return to Bull Run*, pp. 182; 188.
15. Henry Kyd Douglas, *I Rode with Stonewall* (New York: Mockingbird Books, 1989), p. 142.
16. Longstreet, *From Manassas to Appomattox*, p. 192; Taylor, Walter H., *General Lee: His Campaigns in Virginia, 1861-1865* (Lincoln: University of Nebraska Press. 1994), p. 115.
17. Catton, Bruce, *The Army of the Potomac: Mr. Lincoln's Army* (New York; Doubleday & Co., 1951), pp. 43-44.
18. Report of Pope, pp. 246-247; Netherton, Nan and Von Lake Wyckoff, Whitney. *Fairfax Station: All Aboard!*, (Fairfax, Virginia: The Friends of Fairfax Station, 1995), p. 31.
19. *Report of Pope*, p. 247.
20. Ibid., p. 246; O.R., Vol. XII, Pt. 2, p. 79.
21. Hennessey, John, Typescript for *Return to Bull Run*, p. 777.
22. *Report of Pope*, p. 248.

Chapter 4

1. Welch, Spencer Glasgow, *A Confederate Surgeon's Letters to His Wife* (Marietta: The Neale Publishing Co., 1911), p. 27.

2. O.R., Vol. XII, Pt. 3, p. 809.
3. O.R., Vol. XII, Pt. 3. pp. 742; 810.
4. O.R., Vol. XII, Pt. 3, p. 538. It is unclear exactly who sent the dispatch to Col. Torbert. It certainly was not General Pope or probably anyone else in the higher levels of the army's command. It is likely that whomever Torbert placed in temporary command at Jermantown in his absence sent this dispatch bearing the intelligence provided by Lt. Harrison.
5. O.R., Vol. XII, Pt. 3, p. 538; O.R., Vol. XII, Pt. 1, p. 85.
6. Jones, William Ellis, Diary, August 31, 1862; O.R., Vol. XII, Pt. 2, p. 682.
7. Jones, Diary, August 31, 1862; Longstreet, *From Manassas to Appomattox*, pp. 192-193; O.R., Vol. XII, Pt. 2, p. 566.
8. Von Borcke, Heros, *Memoirs of the Confederate War for Independence* (London: William Blackwood and Sons, 1866), p. 167; O.R., Vol. XII, Pt. 2, p. 744.
9. O.R., Vol. XII, Pt. 1, p. 745.
10. Baquet, Camile, *History of the First Brigade, New Jersey Volunteers from 1861 to 1865* (Trenton: n.p.,1910), p. 43
11. Von Borcke. *Memoirs of the Confederate War for Independence*, p. 167.
12. Baquet, *History of the First Brigade*, p. 43; O.R., Vol. XII, Pt. 1, p. 538.
13. Von Borcke. *Memoirs of the Confederate War for Independence*, pp. 167-168; O. R., Vol. XII, Pt. 2, p. 744.
14. Von Borcke. *Memoirs of the Confederate War for Independence*, p. 168-169.
15. O.R., Vol. XII, Pt. 2, p. 647.
16. Freeman, Douglas Southall, *Lee's Lieutenants: A Study in Command, Vol. 2* (New York: Charles Scribner's Sons, n.d.), p. 130; Hotchkiss MS Diary, p. 81.
17. O.R., Vol. VII, Pt. 2, pp. 404-405.
18. O.R., Vol. VII, Pt. 2, pp. 404-405.
19. Ibid.; O.R., Vol. XXIV, p. 749.
20. Lewis, George, *The History of Battery E, First Rhode Island Light Artillery in the War of 1861 and 1865 to Preserve the Union* (Providence: Snow & Farnham, Printers, 1892), p. 100; Woodward, *Our Campaigns*, p. 144.
21. Stevens, Hazard, *The Life of Isaac Ingalls Stevens Vol. II*, (Boston: Houghton, Mifflin and Co. 1900), pp. 477-478.
22. Styple, *Letters From the Peninsula*, p. 169.

Chapter 5

1. Exactly how Pope learned of the fight at Jermantown or the capture of Hight's command is unknown. However, Col. Torbert noted in several different records that he dispatched a staff officer to Centreville to notify Pope; his time of arrival and the events probably noted in his report make it reasonable to assume that this is the note that informed Pope of both developments. In any case, Pope's own comments in his September 2, 1862, and this 1863 reports indicate that he knew of Lee's flanking movement either very late on August 31 or very early on September 1.
2. *Report of Pope*, p. 249; O.R., Vol. XVI, Pt. 1, p. 81.
3. O.R., Vol. XVI, Pt. 1, p. 81.
4. *Report of Pope*, pp. 249-250.
5. Walcott, *History of the 21st Regiment Massachusetts Volunteers*, p. 161; Todd, *The Seventy-Ninth Highlanders*, p. 212; Davis, Charles E., *Three Years in the Army, The Story of the Thirteenth Massachusetts 9. Volunteers from July 16, 1861, to August 1, 1864* (Boston: Estes and Lauriat, 1894), p. 119.

6. O.R., Vol. XII, Pt. 2, p. 538.
7. O.R., Vol. XII, Pt. 2, p. 538.
8. O.R., Vol. XII, Pt. 2, p. 714.
9. Neese, George M., *Three Years in the Confederate Horse Artillery* (Dayton: Morningside Bookshop, 1983), p. 110.
10. O.R., Vol. XII, Part 2, p. 742.
11. Jackson, Mary Anna, *Life and Letters of Gen. Thomas J. Jackson* (New York: Harper & Brothers, 1892), pp. 304-305; Hennessey, *Return to Bull Run MS*, p. 790.
12. Von Borcke, *Memoirs of the Confederate War for Independance*, p. 170.
13. Jackson, *Life and Letters of General Thomas J. Jackson*, pp. 341-342.
14. O.R., Vol. XII, Pt. 2, p. 714.
15. Howard, Oliver Otis, *Autobiography of Oliver Otis Howard, Major General United States Army. Vol. 1* (New York: The Baker & Taylor Co. 1908), p. 268.
16. Ibid., p. 268.
17. Pryor, Elizabeth Brown, *Walney, Two Centuries of a Northern Virginia Plantation* (Fairfax: Fairfax County Office of Comprehensive Planning, 1984), pp. 84-85; Machen Family Correspondence, 1818—1917, Emmeline Machen letter September 2, 1862. Library of Congress.
18. O.R., Vol. XII, Pt. 2. p. 744.
19. *Report of Pope*, pp. 250-251.
20. Ibid., pp. 250-251.
21. Ibid.

Chapter 6

1. Todd, *Seventy-Ninth Highlanders*, p. 215.
2. *Report of Pope*, p. 252.
3. Ibid.
4. Ibid., pp. 252-253; O.R., Vol. XVI, Pt. 1, p. 538.
5. *Report of Pope*, p. 252.
6. O.R., Vol. XII, Pt. 2, p. 414.
7. Todd, *Seventy-Ninth Highlanders*, p. 215.
8. Stevens, *The Life of Isaac Ingalls Stevens*, pp. 478-479.
9. Ibid., p. 479.
10. Ibid., pp. 478-479.
11. Attachment to Porter's letter to Franklin, July 6, 1876.
12. Ibid., July 6, 1876.
13. O.R., Vol. XII, Part 2, p. 414.
14. Mills, J. Harrison, *Chronicles of the Twenty First Regiment New York State Volunteers; Buffalo's First Regiment* (Buffalo: the 21st Regt. Veteran Association of Buffalo, 1887), p. 276; O.R., Vol. XXIV, p. 877.
15. Denison, Rev. Frederic, *Sabres and Spurs: the First Regiment Rhode Island Cavalry in the Civil War, 1861-186.* (The First Rhode Island Cavalry Veteran Association, 1876), p. 148.
16. Ibid.
17. Von Borcke. *Memoirs of the Confederate War for Independence*, pp. 170-171.
18. Hall, Isaac, *History of the Ninety-Seventh Regiment New York Volunteers ("Conkling Rifles") in the War For the Union* (Utica, N.Y.: Press of L. C. Childs & Son, 1890), p. 78.
19. Hall, *History of the Ninety Seventh Regiment*, p. 78.
20. Gates, Theodore B., *The Ulster Guard (20th New York State Militia) and the War of the Rebellion* (New York: Benjamin H. Tyrrel,1879), pp. 282-283.

21. Ibid., p. 283.
22. Ibid., p. 284.
23. Ibid.
24. O.R., Vol. XII, Pt. 2, p. 647.
25. O.R., Vol. XVI, Pt. 1, p. 677.

Chapter 7

1. The identities of these two cavalry guides were not recorded. That there were such guides and that nothing about them, beyond their existence, was recorded is not surprising, however. Serving as a guide for infantry troops was a common role for cavalry troops throughout the war and so such an act would be unremarkable and probably, in the minds of those present, unworthy of recording. It also seems likely that both Hazard Stevens and William Todd, as well as others in the 79th New York on whom Todd drew for his 1886 history of the regiment, would have observed their actions or heard of their role in leading the IX Corps to the field at Chantilly on September 1; Stevens, *The Life of Isaac Ingalls Stevens*, p. 481; Todd, *Seventy-Ninth Highlanders*, p. 215.
2. Parker, George C., George C. Parker Letters, *Civil War Times Illustrated* Collection, U.S. Army Military Historical Institute, Carlisle Army Barracks, PA.
3. Fletcher, *Reminiscences of California and the Civil War*, p. 174.
4. Ibid.
5. Todd, *Seventy-Ninth Highlanders*, p. 215.
6. Ibid.
7. Stevens, *Life of Isaac Ingalls Stevens*, p. 482.
8. Ibid.
9. Ibid.
10. Ibid., p. 484.
11. Ibid., p. 482.
12. Todd, *Seventy-Ninth Highlanders*, p. 216.
13. Ibid., p. 217.
14. Ibid.
15. Ibid.; Stevens, *Life of Isaac Ingalls Stevens*, p. 483.
16. Todd, *Seventy-Ninth Highlanders*, p. 217
17. Ibid., p. 218; Pegram-Johnson-McIntosh Papers, September 4, 1862 letter; O.R., Vol. XII, Pt. 2, pp. 672.
18. Todd, *Seventy-Ninth Highlanders*, p. 218.
19. This regiment unfortunately remains unidentified.
20. Walcott, *History of the 21st Regiment Massachusetts Volunteers*, p. 162.
21. Belcher, Horatio G., Diary. University of Michigan, Bentley Historical Library.
22. Todd, *Seventy-Ninth Highlanders*, p. 218.
23. Stevens, *The Life of Isaac Ingalls Stevens*, p.484.
24. Todd, *Seventy-Ninth Highlanders*, pp. 218-219.
25. Cuffel, Charles A., *History of Durell's Battery in the Civil War* (Philadelphia: Craig, Finnley, & Co., n.d.), p. 68.
26. Walcott, *History of the 21st Regiment Massachusetts Volunteers*, p. 162.
27. Bosbyshell, Oliver, *The 48th in the War* (Philadelphia: Avil Publishing Co., 1893), pp. 69-70.
28. Stevens, *The Life of Isaac Ingalls Stevens*, p. 484.
29. Todd, *Seventy-Ninth Highlanders*, p. 219.

30. Stevens, *The Life of Isaac Ingalls Stevens*, p. 484.

31. Ibid., p. 485.

32. Ibid.

33. Ibid.

34. Todd, *Seventy-Ninth Highlanders*, p. 219.

35. Whitehorne, Joseph, "The Battle of Chantilly," *Blue and Gray Magazine*, April-May 1987, p. 45; Crater, Lewis, *History of the Fiftieth Regiment, Penna. Vet. Vols, 1861-1865* (Reading, PA: Coleman Printing House, 1884), p.29.

36. Gavin, William Gilfillan, *Campaigning With the Roundheads, the History of the Hundredth Pennsylvania Veteran Volunteer Infantry Regiment in the American Civil War 1861-1865* (Dayton: Morningside, 1989), pp. 149-150.

37. Jackman, Lyman, *History of the Sixth New Hampshire Regiment* (Concord, N. H.: Republican Press Association, 1891), pp. 87-88.

38. Ibid, p. 88.

39. Loving, Jerome M. *Civil War Letters of George Washington Whitman* (Durham, NC: Duke University Press), 1975, p. 63.

40. Early, Jubal Anderson, *Lieutenant General Jubal Anderson Early C.S.A.: Autobiographical Sketch and Narrative of the War Between the State* (Wilmington, NC: Broadfoot Publishing Company, 1989), pp. 129-130.

41. Greely, Major General A.W., *Reminiscences of Adventure and Service* (New York: Charles Scrivner's Sons, 1927), pp. 68-69.

42. Todd, *Seventy-Ninth Highlanders*, pp. 219-220.

43. Ibid., p. 220.

44. Stevens, *The Life of Isaac Ingalls Stevens*, pp. 485-486.

45. Early, *Lt. General Early, C.S.A*, p. 130.

46. Ford, Dennis, Letter, 6 September, 1862.
http://mars.acnet.wnec/~dwilliam/history/archive.htm

47. Early, *Lt. General Early, C.S.A*, p. 130.

48. Todd, *Seventy-Ninth Highlanders*, p. 220.

49. Much of Colonel Christ's actions in this battle are conjecture because there are no sources to provide a detailed account of his actions. Though the movements of the regiments under his command were generally recorded in their regimental histories, little to nothing is said in those volumes about Christ's personal role in the fighting.

50. O.R., Vol. XII, Pt. 2, p. 647.

51. Jackman, *History of the Sixth New Hampshire Regiment*, pp. 88-89.

52. Stone, James Madison, *Personal Recollections of the Civil War* (Boston: Published by the Author, 1918), p. 73.

53. Walcott, *History of the 21st Massachusetts Volunteers*, p. 163.

54. Ibid.

55. Stone, *Personal Recollections of the Civil War*, p. 73; Walcott, *History of the 21st Massachusetts Volunteers*, p. 163.

56. Freeman, *Lee's Lieutenants*, pp. 142-143; Walcott, *History of the 21st Regiment Massachusetts Volunteers*, p. 169; Stone, *Personal Recollections of the Civil War*, p. 73; Two contemporary articles detailing the history of the battle of Chantilly have mistakenly recorded that the 21st Massachusetts' Colonel Clark was captured in the woods east of the Ox Road during their clash there. Walcott, who witnessed the regiment's movements in detail that day, recorded Colonel Clark's presence and command of the regiment as it left the woods on pages 163-167 of his *History of the Twenty First Massachusetts Volunteers*.

Chapter 8

1. Martin, James M., et. al. *History of the Fifty-Seventh Regiment, Pennsylvnaia Veteran 2. Volunteer Infantry* (n.p., n.d.), p. 56.
2. Todd, *Seventy-Ninth Highlanders*, p. 221.
3. Lewis, George, *The History of Battery E, First Rhode Island Light Artillery*, (Providence: Snow & Farnham, Printer, 1892), p. 102; O.R., Vol. XII, Pt. 2, p. 419.
4. O.R., Vol. XII, Pt. 2, pp. 647, 654.
5. Freeman, *Lee's Lieutenants*, p. 134; Hale, Laura V., *History of the Forty-Ninth Virginia Infantry C.S.A. "Extra Billy Smith's Boys"* (Lynchburg: Howard Publishers, 1981), p. 48.
6. O.R., Vol. XII, Pt. 2, p. 698; Sorting out the movements of the Confederate brigades engaged at Chantilly is difficult, largely because of the confusing way in which the various brigade commanders wrote their reports (those who bothered to comment on the Ox Hill fight at all). In particular, they tended to run movements together, rarely indicating how much time elapsed between each move. A careful read of all the reports, however, suggests that some significant periods of time passed between these moves.
7. O.R., Vol. XII, Pt. 2, p. 682.
8. Early, *Lieutenant General Jubal Anderson Early, C.S.A.*, p. 129.
9. Fletcher, *Reminiscences of California and the Civil War*, pp. 174-175; Ford, *History of the 101st Regiment*, p. 39.
10. O.R., Vol. XII, Pt. 2, p. 418.
11. Whitehome, "The Battle of Chantilly," p. 48.
12. Floyd, Sergeant Fred C., *History of the Fortieth (Mozart) Regiment* (Boston: F. H. Gilson Company, 1909), p. 178.
13. O.R., Vol. XII, Pt. 2, p. 418.
14. Fletcher, *Reminiscences of California and the Civil War*, p. 174.
15. Whitehome, "The Battle of Chantilly," p. 48.
16. Ford, *History of the 101st Regiment*, p. 39; Whitehome, "The Battle of Chantilly," Blue and Grey, p. 48. Recent archeological excavations in the area behind the center of Jackson's line suggest Birney's line may have advanced far enough to fire on the Little River Turnpike. Available firsthand sources, such as Ford, Fletcher, and Floyd, fail to support this view.
17. Fletcher, *Reminiscences of California and the Civil War*, p. 175.
18. Freeman, *Lee's Lieutenants*, Vol. 2, pp. 134-135. This quote appears in various forms and sometimes mentions Hill, sometimes Branch, or an unnamed officer. If indeed the message was sent to Jackson and he replied in a form similar to the quote attributed to him, then it was probably A. P. Hill who sent the message. It was, after all, Hill's Division that was confronting Birney's brigade and it would have been unusual for Branch to have sent such a message directly to Jackson without going to his immediate superior, A. P. Hill. Perhaps the confusion has arisen from both Branch and Hill sending messages about the impact of wet ammunition on their commands.
19. Styple, *Letters From the Peninsula*, p. 191.
20. Lewis, *History of Battery E, First Rhode Island Light Artillery*, pp. 102-103.
21. Styple, *Letters From the Peninsula*, p. 191.
22. O.R., Vol. XII, Pt. 2, p. 418; Styple, *Letters From the Peninsula*, p. 191.
23. Kearny, *General Philip Kearny*, p. 382.
24. Hennessy, *Second Manassas Battlefield Study*, pp. 461-462.
25. Walcott, *History of the 21st Regiment Massachusetts Volunteers*, p. 164.
26. George C. Parker Letters, *Civil War Times Illustrated collection*, USAMHI.
27. Walcott, *History of the 21st Regiment Massachusetts Volunteers*, pp. 164-165.

28. Ibid., p. 165.

29. Ibid.

30. George C. Parker Letters, *Civil War Times Illustrated* collection, USAMHI.

31. Walcott, History of the 21st Regiment Massachusetts Volunteers, p. 165.

32. O.R., Vol. XII, Pt. 2, p. 703.

33. Walcott, *History of the 21st Regiment Massachusetts Volunteers*, pp. 164.

34. Ibid., p. 165; Stone, *Personal Recollections of the Civil War*, p. 75.

35. Walcott, *History of the 21st Regiment Massachusetts Volunteers*, p. 165; Stone, *Personal Recollections of the Civil War*, p. 73.

36. Whitehome, "The Battle of Chantilly," p, 54.

37. The stories reporting just who had killed General Kearny proliferated after the war to such an extent that it is hard to choose one authoritative version. I believe the 49th Georgia is the regiment responsible for firing the fatal shot based on their position in Thomas's line and their proximity to the 21st Massachusetts just prior to Kearny's death. No less authoritative a source than General Lee, in a letter written to Agnes Kearny in October 1862, reported that Kearny had fallen in front of Thomas's Brigade. I do not accept any of the personal claims of those who argue they fired the fatal shot; nearly all accounts agree it was pitch dark at the time of his death and I believe it little more that wishful thinking for any man to have seen his shot kill the general; Styple, *Letters From the Penninsula*, pp. 175-176.

38. The exact details of this Confederate advance on the 21st Massachusetts remain sketchy. Walcott notes in his regimental history that after Kearny's departure (and death) there was an attack "of rebels against our front and flank." This description suggests the attack was made by a unit larger than a regiment and suggests a Confederate brigade, almost certainly Thomas's Brigade given its proximity to the 21st Massachusetts at that point in the battle. Unfortunately, General Thomas, in his October 1862 report, devoted one short general paragraph to the Ox Hill fight. The description of the movements of Thomas's Brigade in this and the next few paragraphs is my best-educated guess, based on the few available sources, of what actually happened.

39. Walcott, *History of the 21st Massachusetts Regiment Massachusetts Volunteers*, p. 166.

40. George C. Parker Letters, *Civil War Times Illustrated collection*, USAMHI.

41. Ibid.; Walcott, *History of the 21st Regiment Massachusetts Volunteers*, p. 166.

42. Stone, *Personal Recollections of the Civil War*, pp. 74-75.

43. Walcott, *History of the 21st Regiment Massachusetts Volunteers*, pp. 166-167.

44. Ibid., p. 166.

45. O.R., Vol. XII, Pt. 2, p. 418.

46. O.R., Vol. XII, Pt. 2, p. 419.

47. Ibid.

48. Haynes, Martin A., *A History of the Second New Hampshire Volunteer Infantry in the War of the Rebellion* (Lakeport, New Hampshire: n.p., 1896), pp. 139-140.

49. Andrews, W. H., *Footprints of a Regiment, a Recollection of the 1st Georgia Regulars, 1861-1865* (Atlanta: Longstreet Press, 1992), pp. 69-70.

50. Longstreet, *From Manassas to Appomattox*, p. 194.

Chapter 9

1. Ford, *History of the 101st Regiment*, p. 39.

2. Whitehome, "The Battle of Chantilly," p. 55; Walcott, *History of the 21st Regiment Massachusetts Volunteers*, pp. 174-175.

3. Buck, Samuel D., *With the Old Confeds: Actions and Experiences of A Captain in the*

Line (Baltimore: H. E. Hauck & Co., 1925), p. 58. The sun set on September 1, 1862, at 6:30 P.M. local time, although the heavily overcast skies made the battlefield much darker at that point in the day. The half moon—it would reach a full moon on September 7—had begun to rise at 1:30 that afternoon and remained in the night sky until setting at 11:00 P.M.

4. Kearny, *General Philip Kearny*, pp. 388-389.
5. Walcott, *History of the 21st Regiment Massachusetts Volunteers*, p. 174.
6. Stone, *Personal Recollections of the Civil War*, pp. 75-77.8
7. Whitehome, "The Battle of Chantilly," p. 55.
8. George Parker Letters, *Civil War Times Illustrated Collection*, USAMHI.
9. Donald, David Herbert. *Gone for a Soldier, the Civil War Memoirs of Private Alfred Bellard* (Boston: Little, Brown, and Co., 1975), pp. 145-146.
10. Fletcher, *Reminiscences of California and the Civil War*, pp. 175-176.
11. Ibid., p. 176.
12. Ibid., p. 177.
13. Welch, *A Confederate Surgeon's Letters to His Wife*, pp. 28-29.
14. George Parker Letters, *Civil War Times Illustrated* collection, USAMHI; Walcott, *History of the 21st Regiment Massachusetts Volunteers*, pp. 167-169.
15. Dunaway, *Reminiscences of a Rebel*, pp. 45-47.
16. Early, *Lieutenant General Jubal Anderson Early, C.S.A.*, p. 131.
17. O.R., Vol. XVI, Pt. 1, p. 15.
18. Howard, *The Autobiography of Gen. O. O. Howard*, p. 269; Greely, *Reminiscences of Adventure and Service*, p. 69.
19. Catton, *Mr. Lincoln's Army*, p. 46.
20. Edward Schweitzer Diary and Letters, USAMHI, p. 12; Sears, Stephen, ed., *For County, Cause, and Leader, the Civil War Journal of Charles B. Haydon* (New York: Ticknor & Fields, 1993), p. 282.
21. Priest, John Michael, *Captain James Wren's Civil War Diary from New Bern to Fredericksburg* (New York: Berkley Books, 1991), p. 75.
22. Catton, *Mr. Lincoln's Army*, p. 46.
23. Parker, Thomas, *51st Regiment of P.V and V.V.* (Philadelphia: King & Baird, Printers, 1869), p. 221.
24. Todd, *Seventy-Ninth Highlanders*, p. 224; O.R., Vol XII, Pt. 2, p. 805.
25. Fletcher, *Reminiscences of California and Civil War Service*, p. 175.
26. Walcott, *History of the Twenty First Regiment Massachusetts Volunteers*, p. 167; Gavin, *Campaigning With the Roundheads*, p. 150.
27. Fletcher, *Reminiscences of California and Civil War Service*, pp. 177-179.

Chapter 10

1. Todd, *Seventy-Ninth Highlanders*, p. 224.
2. Stevens, *The Life of Isaac I. Stevens*, pp. 498-499.
3. George Parker Letters, *Civil War Times Illustrated* collection, USAMHI.
4. Ibid.
5. Andrews, *Footprints of a Regt.*, p. 70; Kearny, *Philip Kearny: Battle Soldier of Five Wars*, p. 388; Richmond Examiner, Sept. 8, 1862.
6. Styple, *Letters from the Peninsula*, pp. 194-195.
7. Ibid.
8. Taylor, *General Lee*, p. 116.
9. Martin, James M., et.al. *History of the Fifty-Seventh Regiment Pennsylvania Veteran*

Volunteer Infantry. (n.p., n.d.), p. 57.

10. Kearny, *General Philip Kearny,* pp. 390-392.
11. Styple, *Letters From the Peninsula,* p. 181. Apparently rumors circulated in the press and the army claiming that no wound could be found on Kearny's body. To put these tales to rest an autopsy was performed in Alexandria, which proved that the general was killed by a minie ball during battle.
12. Styple, *Letters From the Peninsula,* pp. 224-225.

Chapter 11

1. O.R. , XII, Pt. 3, p. 797.
2. *Report of Pope,* p. 254.
3. Ibid., pp. 254-255.
4. O.R., Vol. XII, Pt. 2, p. 647.
5. McCrea, Henry Vaughn, *Red Dirt and Isinglass* (n.p., 1992), p. 104; Welch, *A Confederate Surgeon's Letters to His Wife,* pp. 30-31.
6. Jed Hotchkiss Diary, Entry for 2 Sept.
7. Kegel, James A., *North with Lee and Jackson* (Mechanicsburg, Pa.: Stackpole Books, 1996), pp. 99-114.
8. Allan, *Jackson, Lee, and the ANV,* p. 319; O.R., Series 1, Vol. XII, Pt. II, p. 558.
9. O.R., Series 1, Vol. XII, Pt. II, pp. 744-745.
10. Greely, *Reminiscence of Service,* p. 69.
11. History Committee, *History of the Nineteenth Regiment Massachusetts Volunteer Infantry, 1861-1865* (Salem, Mass: The Salem Press Co., 1906), pp. 122-123.
12. Greely, *Reminiscences of Adventure and Service.* pp. 70-71.
13. *Report of Pope,* p. 171.
14. Sears, *Civil War Letters of George B. McClellan,* p. 428.
15. Welles Diary, Vol. I, p. 105.
16. Sears, *Civil War Letters of George B. McClellan,* pp. 428-429.
17. Ibid., p. 429; O.R., Series I, Vol. XIX, Pt. 1, p. 38.
18. Sears, Stephen. *George McClellan, the Young Napoleon* (New York: Ticknor & Fields, 1988), pp. 261-263.
19. Sears, *George McClellan, the Young Napolean,* pp. 261-263; Weld, War Diary, Entry for Sept. 4, 1862, p. 136.
20. For a full description of Lee's thinking on this, and subsequent days prior to the battle of Antietam, see *Antietam: The Soldier's Battle* by John Michael Priest or *Confederate Tide Rising: Robert E. Lee and the Making of Southern Strategy, 1861-1862* and *Taken at the Flood: Robert E. Lee and Confederate Strategy in the Maryland Campaign of 1862,* both by Dr. Joseph Harsh.
21. Ford, Dennis, Letter of 6 September, 1862.

Chapter 12

1. Walcott, *History of the Twenty First Regiment Massachusetts Volunteers,* pp. 166-167; Dennis Ford, Letter of 6 September, 1862; Tondee, Robert P. Letter.
2. O.R., Vol. XII, Pt. 2, p. 558.
3. Allan, William, "Conversations with R.E. Lee" February 16, 1868. The Southern Historical Collection, No. 2764, University of North Carolina, Chapel Hill.
4. Walcott, *History of the 21st Regiment Massachusetts Volunteers,* pp. 166-167; Caton, *Mr. Lincoln's Army* pp. 46-47; Horatio Belcher Diary.

Bibliography

Published Works

Allan, William. "Conversations with R.E. Lee." February 16, 1868. The Southern Historical Collection, No. 2764, University of North Carolina, Chapel Hill.

Andrews, W. H. *Footprints of a Regiment, a Recollection of the 1st Georgia Regulars, 1861-1865.* Atlanta: Longstreet Press, 1992.

Barnes, Charles H. *History of the Philadelphia Brigade.* Philadelphia: J.B. Lippencott & Co., 1876.

Bates, Samuel P. *History of the Pennsylvania Volunteers, 1861-1865.* Wilmington, North Carolina: n.p., 1899.

Beale, R.L.T. *History of the Ninth Virginia Cavalry in the War Between the States.* Richmond: B.F. Johnson Publishing Co., 1879.

Blackford, W.W. *War Years with Jeb Stuart.* New York: Charles Scribner's Sons, 1945.

Bosbyshell, Oliver Christian. *The 48th in the War.* Philadelphia: Avil Printing Co., 1895.

Brennan, Patrick. *Secessionville: Assault on Charleston.* Campbell, California: Savas Publishing Co., 1996.

Brown, Henri Le Ferre. *History of the Third Regiment Excelsior Brigade 72d New York Volunteer Infantry 1861-1865.* n.p., n.d.

Buck, Samuel D. *With the Old Confeds: Actions and Experiences of A Captain in the Line.* Baltimore: H. E. Hauck & Co., 1925.

Caldwell, J.F.J. *History of the Brigade of South Carolinians Known First As Gregg's, Then as McGowan's.* Marietta, Georgia: Continental Book Co., 1866.

Carse, Robert. *Department of the South: Hilton Head Island in the Civil War.* Hilton Head, S.C.: Impressions Printing Co., 1987.

Catton, Bruce. *The Army of the Potomac: Mr. Lincoln's Army.* New York: Doubleday & Co, 1951.

Cheney, Newel. *History of the Ninth Regiment, New York Volunteer Cavalry, War of 1861-1865.* Poland Center, New York: Martin Merz & Co., 1901.

Cozzens, Peter. *General John Pope: A Life for the Nation.* Urbana: University Press of Illinois, 2000.

Cozzens, Peter and Robert I. Girardi. *The Military Memoirs of General John Pope.* Chapel Hill: University of North Carolina Press, 1998.

Crater, Lewis. *History of the Fiftieth Regiment, Penna. Vet. Vols, 1861-1865.* Reading, PA: Coleman Printing House, 1884.

Cuffell, Charles A. *History of Durrell's Battery in the Civil War* (Independant Battery D, Pennsylvania Volunteer Artillery). Philadelphia: Craig Finley & Co., 1904.

Curtis, Newton Martin. *From Bull Run to Chancellorsville: The Story of the Sixteenth New York Infantry Together With Personal Reminiscences.* New York: G.P. Putnam's Sons, 1906.

Davis, Charles E. *Three Years in the Army, The Story of the Thirteenth Massachusetts Volunteers from July 16, 1861, to August 1, 1864.* Boston: Estes and Lauriat, 1894.

Denison, Rev. Frederic. *Sabres and Spurs: the First Regiment Rhode Island Cavalry in the Civil War, 1861-1865.* The First Rhode Island Cavalry Veteran Association, 1876.

Denney, Robert. *Civil War Medicine: Care and Comfort of the Wounded.* New York: Sterling Publishing Co. Inc., 1995.

DePeyster, John Watts. *Personal and Military Biography of Philip Kearny, Major General United States Volunteers.* New York: Rice and George, Publishers, 1869.

Donald, David Herbert. *Gone for a Soldier, the Civil War Memoirs of Private Alfred Bellard.* Boston: Little, Brown, and Co., 1975.

Dowdey, Clifford, Ed. *The Wartime Papers of R. E. Lee.* New York: DaCapo Press, 1987.

Douglas, Henry Kyd. *I Rode with Stonewall.* New York: Mockingbird Books, 1989.

Dunaway, Rev. Wayland Fuller. *Reminiscences of a Rebel.* New York: The Neale Publishing Co., 1913.

Early, Jubal Anderson. *Lieutenant General Jubal Anderson Early C.S.A.: Autobiographical Sketch and Narrative of the War Between the States.* Wilmington, N.C: Broadfoot Publishing Company, 1989.

Ford, Lieutenant H.E. *History of the 101st Regiment.* Syracuse: Times Publishing Co., 1898.

Fletcher, Daniel Cooledge. *Reminiscences of California and the Civil War.* Ayer, Mass.: Press of Huntley S. Turner, 1894.

Floyd, Sergeant Fred C. *History of the Fortieth (Mozart) Regiment.* Boston: F. H. Gilson Company, 1909.

Freeman, Douglas Southall. *Lee's Lieutenants: A Study in Command,* Vol. 2. New York; Charles Scribner's Sons, n.d.

Gaff, Alan D. *Brave Men's Tears: The Iron Brigade at Brawner Farm.* Dayton, Ohio: Morningside Publishers, 1996.

Gates, Theodore B. *The Ulster Guard (20th New York State Militia) and the War of the Rebellion.* New York: Benjamin H. Tyrrel, 1879.

Gavin, William Gilfillan. *Campaigning With the Roundheads, the History of the Hundredth Pennsylvania Veteran Volunteer Infantry Regiment in the American Civil War 1861-1865.* Dayton: Morningside, 1989.

Greely, Major General A.W. *Reminiscences of Adventure and Service.* New York: Charles Scribner's Sons, 1927.

Hale, Laura V. *History of the Forty-Ninth Virginia Infantry C.S.A.* "Extra Billy Smith's Boys." Lynchburg: Howard Publishers, 1981.

Hall, Isaac. *History of the Ninety-Seventh Regiment New York Volunteers ("Conkling Rifles") in the War For the Union.* Utica, N.Y.: Press of L. C. Childs & Son, 1890.

Harsh, Joseph L. *Confederate Tide Rising: Robert E. Lee and the Making of Southern Strategy, 1861-1862.* Kent, Ohio: Kent State University Press, 1998.

Harsh, Joseph L. *Taken at the Flood: Robert E. Lee and Confederate Strategy in the Maryland Campaign of 1862.* Kent, Ohio: Kent State University Press, 2000.

Haynes, Martin A. *A History of the Second New Hampshire Volunteer Infantry in the War of the Rebellion.* Lakeport, New Hampshire: n.p., 1896.

Hays, Gilbert Adams. *Under the Red Patch: Story of the Sixty Third Regiment Pennsylvania Volunteers 1861-1864.* Pittsburgh: n.p. 1908.

Hennessy, John. *Return to Bull Run, The Campaign and Battle of Second Manassas.* New York: Simon and Schuster, 1993.

Hennessey, John. *Second Manassas Battlefield Map Study.* Lynchburg: Howard Publishing Co., n.d.

History Committee. *History of the Nineteenth Regiment Massachusetts Volunteer Infantry, 1861-1865.* Salem, Mass: The Salem Press Co., 1906.

Hough, Franklin B. *History of Duryee's Brigade.* Albany: J. Munsell, 1864.

Howard, Oliver Otis. *Autobiography of Oliver Otis Howard, Major General United States Army.* Vol. 1. New York: The Baker & Taylor Co. 1908.

Howe, Mark De Wolfe, ed. *Touched With Fire: Civil War Letters and Diary of Oliver Wendell Holmes, Jr.* 1861-1864. Cambridge: Harvard University Press, 1946.

Hutchinson, Gustavus B. *A Narrative of the Formation and Services of the Eleventh Massachusetts Volunteers, From April 15, 1861 to July 14, 1965.* Boston: Alfred Mudge & Sons, Printers, 1893.

Jackson, Mary Anna. *Life and Letters of Gen. Thomas J. Jackson.* New York: Harper & Brothers, 1892.

Jones, Terry L. *Lee's Tiger's: The Louisiana Infantry in the Army of Northern Virginia.* Baton Rouge: Louisiana University Press, 1987.

Jones, Archer and Herman Hattaway. *How the North Won.* Urbana: University of Illinois Press, 1983.

Kearny, Thomas. *General Philip Kearny—Battle Soldier of Five Wars.* New York; G.P. Putman's Sons., 1937.

Kegel, James A. *North with Lee and Jackson.* Mechanicksburg, Pa.: Stackpole Books, 1996.

Krick, Robert. *The Fredericksburg Artillery.* Lynchburg: Howard Publishing Co., 1986.

Krick, Robert. *40th Virginia Infantry.* Lynchburg: Howard Publishing Co., 1989.

Lewis, George. *The History of Battery E, First Rhode Island Light Artillery.* Providence: Snow & Farnham, Printers, 1892.

Longacre, Edward G. *Jersey Cavaliers: A History of the First New Jersey Volunteer Cavalry, 1861-1865.* Hightstown, N.J.: Longstreet House, 1992.

Longstreet, James. *From Manassas to Appomattox.* New York: Smithmark Publishers, reprint, 1992.

Loving, Jerome M., Ed. *Civil War Letters of George Washington Whitman.* Durham, N.C.: Duke University Press, 1975.

Lusk, William Thompson. *War Letters of William Thompson Lusk.* New York: privately printed, 1911.

Martin, James M., et. al. *History of the Fifty-Seventh Regiment, Pennsylvania Veteran Volunteer Infantry.* n.c.: n.p., n.d.

Marvel, William. *Burnside.* Chapel Hill, N.C.: The University of North Carolina Press, 1991.

McCrea, Henry Vaughn. *Red Dirt and Isinglass.* n.c.: n.p., 1992.

Mills, J. Harrison. *Chronicles of the Twenty First Regiment New York State Volunteers; Buffalo's First Regiment.* Buffalo: The 21st Regt. Veteran Association of Buffalo, 1887.

Moorell, Robert H. *The Danville, Eight Star, New Market, and Dixie Artillery.* Lynchburg: Howard Publishing Co., 1989.

Mottelay, Paul F., and T. Campbell-Copeland, Eds. *The Soldier in Our American Civil War.* New York: Stanley Bradley Publishing Co., 1890.

Neese, George M. *Three Years in the Confederate Horse Artillery.* Dayton: Morningside Bookshop, 1983.

Netherton, Nan and Whitney Von Lake Wyckoff. *Fairfax Station: All Aboard!.* Fairfax, Virginia: The Friends of Fairfax Station, 1995.

O'Sullivan, Richard. *55th Virginia Infantry.* Lynchburg: Howard Publishing Co, 1989.

Oldaker, Glenn C. *Centennial Tales: Memiors of Colonel "Chester" S. Bassett French, Extra Aide-de-Camp to Generals Lee and Jackson, Army of Northern Virginia, 1861-1865.* New York: Carlton Press, 1992.

Osborne, Seward R. ed. *The Civil War Diaries of Col. Theodore B. Gates, 20th New York State Militia.* Hightstown, N.J.: Longstreet House, 1991.

Parker, Thomas H. *History of the 51st Regiment of P.V. and V.V.* Philadelphia: King & Baird, 1869.

Priest, John Michael. *Captain James Wren's Civil War Diary from New Bern to Fredericksburg.*

New York: Berkley Books, 1991.

Pryor, Elizabeth Brown. *Walney*. Fairfax, Virginia: Fairfax County Printing Office, 1984.

Pyne, Henry R. Ride to War: The History of the First New Jersey Cavalry. New Brunswick: Rutgers University Press, 1961.

Report of Major General John Pope, Parts 1 & 2. Millwood, New York: Kraus Reprint Co., 1977.

Richards, Kent D. *Isaac I. Stevens: Young Man In a Hurry*. Pullman, Washington: Washington University, 1993.

Robertson, James J. *General A.P. Hill: The Story of a Confederate Warrior*. New York: Random House, n.d.

Scott, Kate M. *History of the One Hundred and Fifth Regiment Pennsylvania Volunteers*. Philadelphia: New World Publishing Co., 1877.

Sears, Stephen W., ed. *For County, Cause, and Leader, the Civil War Journal of Charles B. Haydon*. New York: Ticknor & Fields, 1993.

Sears, Stephen W., ed. *The Civil War Papers of George B. McClellan, Selected Correspondence 1860-1865*. New York: Da Capo Press, 1989.

Sears, Stephen W., *To the Gates of Richmond - The Peninsula Campaign*. New York: Tichnor & Fields, 1992.

Shoemaker's Battery. n.c: Butternut Press Reprint, n.d.

Stevens, Hazard. *The Life of Isaac Ingalls Stevens*, Vol. II. Boston: Houghton, Mifflin and Co., 1900.

Stone, James Madison. *Personal Recollections of the Civil War*. Boston: Published by the author, 1918.

Styple, William B., ed. *Letters From the Peninsula: The Civil War Letters of General Philip Kearny*. Kearny, NJ: Belle Grove Publishing Co., 1988.

Taylor, Walter H. *General Lee: His Campaigns in Virginia, 1861-1865*. Lincoln: University of Nebraska Press, 1994.

Todd, William. *History of the Ninth New York N.Y.S.M. – N.G.S.N.Y. (Eighty Third N.Y. Volunteers) 1845-1888*. New York: n.p., 1889.

Todd, William. *The Seventy-Ninth Highlanders New York Volunteers in the War of the Rebellion, 1861-1865*. Albany, N.Y.: Press of Brandow, Barton, & Co., 1886.

United States War Department. *War of the Rebellion. A Compilation of the Official Records of the Union and Confederate Armies*. 128 Vols. Washington, D.C.: 1881-1902.

Von Borcke, Heros. *Memoirs of the Confederate War for Independence*. London: William Blackwood and Sons, 1866.

Vautier, John D. *History of the 88th Pennsylvania Volunteers in the War for the Union, 1861-1865*. Philadelphia: J.B. Lippincott Co., 1894.

Wallcott, Charles F. *History of the Twenty First Regiment Massachusetts Volunteers in the War for the Preservation of the Union, 1861-1865*. Boston: Houghton, Mifflin, and Co., 1882.

Welch, Spencer Glasgow. *A Confederate Surgeon's Letters to His Wife*. Marietta: The Neale Publishing Co., 1911.

Whitehorne, Joseph W. A. "The Battle of Chantilly." *Blue and Gray Magazine*, April-May, 1987.

Woodward, Evan Morrison and Stanley W. Zamonski, eds. *Our Campaigns; the Second Regiment Pennsylvania Reserve Volunteers, 1861-1864*. Shippensburg, PA: Burd Street Press. 1995.

Unpublished Works

Belcher, Horatio G. Diary. University of Michigan, Bentley Historical Library.

Buck, Samuel D. Diary. William R. Perkins Library, Duke University.

Elliott, Thomas J. Letters. William R. Perkins Library, Duke University.

Ford, Dennis. Letter. 6 September, 1862.
http://mars.acnet.wnec/~dwilliam/history/archive.htm

Hennessey, John. Typescript for Return to Bull Run. Manassas National Battlefield Library.

Hotchkiss MS Diary. United States Army Military History Institute.

Jones, William Ellis. Diary. United States Army Military History Institute.

Machen Family Corresponsence, 1818 – 1917. Library of Congress.

Parker, George C. Letters. *Civil War Times Illustrated* Collection. United States Army Military History Institute.

Pegram-Johnson-McIntosh Papers. United States Army Military History Institute.

Porter, Fitz John. Attachment to Letter to William B. Franklin. Library of Congress.

Schweitzer, Edward. Diary and Letters. United States Army Military History Institute.

Southern Historical Society Papers. Vol. XL. Fairfax County Public Library.

Stevens, Isaac I. Isaac Ingalls Stevens's Papers, 1831-1862. University of Washington Libraries.

Tondee, Robert P. Letters. William R. Perkins Library, Duke University.

Veil, Enos B. "Reminiscences of a Boy in the Civil War." United States Army Military History Institute.

Weld. Diary. United States Army Military History Institute.

Welles, Gideon. War Diary. Library of Congress.

Wolcott, Charles. Letters. Massachusetts Historical Society.

Index

Anderson, Richard, 28, 34, 193
Anderson's Division, 28, 34, 193
Andrews, First Sgt W. (1st GA), 193
Andrews, Gov. (MA), 209
Archer, James J., 27
Archer's Brigade, 27, 147, 193
Army Corps, Union
  Army of the Potomac
    I, 216
    II, 54, 83, 85-86, 92, 110, 125, 135,
      216, 220-221
    III, 25, 41, 52, 54, 83, 124, 125, 129-
      130, 138, 141, 169, 192, 205-206,
      214, 216, 246
    IV, 135
    V, 25, 26, 27, 28, 29, 30, 33, 55, 83,
      110, 216, 220
    VI, 30-31, 83, 85, 86, 92, 216
  Army of Virginia
    I, 20, 25, 83, 216, 220
    II, 20, 83, 216
    III, 20, 23, 25, 83, 111, 216
    Reserve, 20, 216, 220
  Independent Corps
    IX, 29, 60, 77, 83-84, 106, 126-127,
      129, 137-167, 205-206, 216, 232-
      234, 246

Baker, Capt. (1st NJ), 32, 85
Ball, Rev. George (21st MA), 207
Ballard, John, 13
Banks, Nathaniel P., 15, 16, 20, 83
Barrington, John (28th MA), 199
Baylor, Colonel, 115
Beauregard, P. G. T., 58, 63, 66
Beckwith, Lt. (21st MA), 198
Belcher, Horatio G. (21st MA), 149, 169,
  234, 244-245
Bellard, Alfred (5th NJ), 199
Bellegrove, 46

Benham, Henry, 75-77
Benjamin, Lt., 126-127
Benjamin's battery, 127, 148-149, 151, 153
Berry's brigade, 56, 170. *See also* Poe's
  brigade
Birney, David, 169-170, 173, 175-181, 191,
  195, 206, 213, 230, 234
Birney's brigade, 55, 169-170, 173, 175,
  176-181, 182, 191
Bosbyshell, Oliver (48th PA), 84, 151
Branch, Lawrence O'Brian, 27, 163-164,
  171-172, 178
Branch's Brigade, 136, 147, 163-164, 171-
  172, 177, 178, 193, 202
Brawner's Farm, battle of, 25, 89
Breckinridge, John C., 70
Brockenbrough, James, 136
Brown, William F., 147, 166
Browne, Rev. Robert Audley (100th PA),
  208
Bull Run, Second Battle of, 25-36
Burks, R. H. (12th VA Cavalry), 105
Burnside, Ambrose, 78, 84, 246
Butterfield, Daniel, 33
Butterfield's division, 33

Cameron, James, 71
Cameron, Simon, 70-71
Centreville, VA, 9, 24, 31, 35, 37-39, 41,
  50-51, 78-79, 81-82, 85-87, 91-92, 97-98,
  103, 105, 109, 112, 121, 123, 126-127,
  138, 203-204, 237-238, 240
Chantilly, VA, 15, 103, 105, 117, 125, 202-
  203
Chase, Salmon P., 18, 223
Christ, Benjamin, 146, 163-164
Clark, William S. (21st MA), 181, 183-185
Connecticut Cavalry Regiments
  1st, 135
Cornwell, George (40th VA), 202

Couch, Darius, 135
Couch's division, 135, 223
Cox, Jacob D., 224
Cross Key's, battle of, 16
Cuffel, Charles (Durrell's Bty.), 198

Dana's brigade, 110, 221
Davis, Charles (13th MA), 111
Davis, Jefferson, 67, 218, 238
de Peyster, John Watts, 43
Doubleday, Abner, 28
Dunaway, Wayland (40th VA), 202
Durrell's Independent Battery D (PA
    Light Artillery), 149-150, 175, 198
Duryee's brigade, 131-133

Early, Jubal, 158, 162
Early, Lt., 162
Early's Brigade, 147, 158, 162, 171
Edwards, Col. (13th SC), 201
Eggleston, Capt. (97th NY), 133
Elliott, Samuel, 72
Ewell, Richard S., 21, 45, 89
Ewell's Division, 21-22, 89, 112, 147

Fairfax Court House, VA, 31-32, 41, 51,
    85, 98-99, 104, 106, 110-111, 120, 123-
    125, 127, 129, 203, 205-206, 212, 215,
    219- 220, 222, 224
Fair Oaks, battle of, 54-55
Ferrero's brigade, 127, 137, 149-150, 156
Field's Brigade, 136, 147, 171-172
1st U. S. Artillery, 170
1st U. S. Dragoons, 43
Fitzpatrick, Marion (45th GA), 217
Fletcher, Daniel (40th NY), 35, 138, 173,
    176, 177-178, 199-201, 207, 208
Flynn, Cpl. (40th NY), 208
Fogerty, Dennis (21st MA), 197
Ford, Dennis (28th MA), 162, 226
Ford, Lt. (101st NY), 82, 172-173, 195
Franklin, William, 30-31, 50, 83, 85, 92,
    93
Frayser's Farm, battle of, 55-56
Frazer, John (21st MA), 166
Fremont, John C., 15-16
Fruitwood. See Reid house

Gardner, Sgt. (49th GA), 183
Garnett, James (Stonewall Brigade), 89
Gates, Theodore (80th NY), 133-135
Georgia Infantry Regiments
    1st, 193
    45th, 217
    49th, 183-187, 210
Germantown, VA. See Jermantown
Gibbon, John, 25, 42, 91
Gibbon's brigade, 25, 42, 91
Glendale, battle of, 55-56
Gould, Lt. (40th NY), 173
Graham's Battery (1st U. S. Artillery),
    170
Graves, Col. (40th NY), 175
Greely, Andrew (19th MA), 158, 220
Gregg's Brigade, 12, 26-27, 147, 155, 164,
    171-172, 177
Grigsby, Andrew, 157
Grover, Cuvier, 26, 138, 179, 192
Grover's brigade, 26, 138, 179
Groveton, VA, 28, 33, 149

Halleck, Henry W., 18-19, 21, 29-30, 38,
    39, 91-94, 120-121, 123-124, 127, 215,
    222, 223-224
Hampton's Cavalry Brigade, 98, 216-
    217, 219
Hancock, Winfield S., 53
Harrison, Lt. (2nd U. S. Cavalry), 97, 98,
    109
Hastings, Dr. Joseph (21st MA), 207
Hatch, John, 28, 224-225
Hatch's division, 25, 28, 29, 33
Haydon, Charles (2nd MI), 205
Hayes, John L., 209
Haynes, Martin (2nd NH), 192
Hays's Brigade, 12, 147, 154, 158, 159,
    161, 162, 203
Heath family, 145
Heintzelman, Samuel P., 25, 29, 58, 83,
    92, 125, 128-129, 138
Hight, Thomas (2nd U. S. Cavalry), 97,
    109
Hill, Ambrose P., 21, 55, 89, 99, 136, 148,
    178, 211, 230, 239
Hill's (Gen. A. P.) Light Division, 21-22,
    27, 95, 112, 147, 178

Hill's (Gen. D. H.) Division, 101
Hinks, Edward W., 110, 112, 125, 129
Hinks's brigade, 112
Hood, John Bell, 28, 34
Hood's Division, 28
Hooker, Joseph, 23, 52-53, 125, 129-130, 131, 133, 192, 214, 247
Hooker's brigade. *See* Grover's brigade
Hooker's 2nd Division, 179
Hopkins, Charles (1st NJ), 48-49
Hotchkiss, Jed (Stonewall Brigade), 104
Howard, Oliver O., 118, 204, 220-221
Howard's brigade, 112, 117, 220-221
Hunter, David, 75-77

Ives, Robert (79th NY), 143, 145

Jackman, Lyman (6th NH), 37
Jackson, Mary Anna, 115
Jackson, Thomas J. "Stonewall," 12, 15-17, 21-28, 35, 58-59, 87-90, 99, 103-104, 112-117, 119, 130, 135-136, 147, 167, 170-171, 172, 178, 192-193, 202-203, 211, 216, 217, 218, 229, 230-231, 232, 233, 235-237, 239, 241, 242, 245-246
Jackson's Command, 21-28, 35, 87-90, 95, 99, 101, 104, 112-117, 119, 120, 130, 135-136, 141, 147-148, 153, 154-156, 157-158, 161-166, 170-172, 195, 202, 211, 225, 229-230, 235, 239, 241
Jackson's Division. *See* Starke's Division
James Island, battle of, 75-77
Jastram, Lt. (Randolph's Battery), 179
Jay, Peter Augustus, 43
Jermantown, VA, 32, 85, 87, 97-98, 101, 106, 110, 112-113, 123-136, 138, 147, 231, 325, 242-243, 245
Johnson, Bradley T., 117, 119
Johnston, Joseph, 54

Kearny, Agnes Maxwell, 42, 45-47, 49, 50, 51, 52, 53, 55, 58, 59, 106, 212
Kearny, Archibald K., 47, 49
Kearny, Diana Bullitt, 44, 46-47
Kearny, John Watts, 47
Kearny, Philip
    battle of Chantilly, 169-170, 173, 174, 175, 178-186, 230, 232, 234-235

burial, 210-214
childhood, 43
commands New Jersey Brigade, 48-52
death, 12, 14, 185-187
during Peninsula campaign, 51-59
early army career, 43-45
French army service, 44, 47, 48
marriage problems, 44, 45-46
Mexican War service, 44-45
misc., 27, 35, 41, 60, 78-79, 106-107, 138, 191, 192, 226, 246-247
promotion to major general, 59
receives division command, 52
Kearny, Stephen Watts, 43
Kearny, Susan Watts (daughter), 47
Kearny, Susan Watts (mother), 43
Kearny's division, 4, 52-59, 138, 169, 207, 230
Kelton, Ira (21st MA), 187, 198-199, 201
Kemper, James, 28
Kemper's Brigade, 28
Kenedy, Dr., 201
Kilgore, Dr., 201
King, Rufus, 25, 50
King's division, 25. *See also* Hatch's division

Lane, Joseph, 70
Lawton, Alexander R., 89, 158
Lawton's Brigade, 147, 193
Leasure, Daniel, 27, 146
Leasure's brigade, 27, 146, 156
Lee, Fitzhugh, 86, 95, 97-98, 114, 130, 131, 134, 135, 219, 235
Lee, Lt. (Kearny's division), 191
Lee, Robert E., 20-23, 24-29, 33-35, 39-40, 44-45, 55, 56, 58, 63, 85-90, 98, 112, 123-124, 136, 167, 192, 204, 211-212, 214, 216-219, 225-226, 230, 237-241, 245-247
Lee, Stephen D., 33
Lee's (Fitzhugh) Cavalry Brigade, 95, 97-98, 114, 219, 221
Lewis, George (1st RI Light Artillery), 85, 106
Lincoln, Abraham, 16, 30, 70, 208, 223-224, 244
Linden Lee, 211

Little Sorrell, 192
Longstreet, James, 22, 26, 28, 34, 52, 55, 58, 87, 101, 104, 113, 130, 193, 239
Longstreet's Command, 22, 24, 26-28, 34, 87, 99-101, 104, 119, 130, 136, 192-193, 203, 211, 216, 239, 246
Lusk, William T. (79th NY), 143, 145, 153-154, 155, 158

Machen, Arthur, 82, 118-119
Machen, Caroline, 82-83
Machen, Emma, 118-119
Magruder, John, 48
Maine Cavalry Regiments
  1st, 118
Maine Infantry Regiments
  3rd, 176
  4th, 173, 176-177
Major, Nelson (48th PA), 205
Manassas, Second Battle of. See Bull Run, Second Battle of
Manassas Junction, VA, 23, 86, 220
Maryland Infantry Regiments
  2nd, 156
Mason, James, 62, 63
Massachusetts Artillery Batteries
  8th Light, 127
Massachusetts Infantry Regiments
  11th, 57
  13th, 111
  19th, 112, 204, 220-221
  20th, 112
  21st, 34-35, 37, 111, 127, 138, 151, 156, 163, 164-166, 181-185, 187-190, 195, 197-199, 200, 207, 211, 234, 245
  28th, 14, 146, 153-156, 162-163, 180, 196, 199, 226, 227
Maxwell, Agnes. See Kearny, Agnes Maxwell
McClellan, George B., 15-20, 23, 29-30, 31, 38-39, 50, 51-52, 53-54, 56-57, 58, 66, 68, 71, 75, 77, 86, 92, 121, 122, 215, 222, 223-224, 225-226
McClellan, Mary Ellen, 18-19, 29, 223
McDowell, Irvin, 16, 20, 29, 83, 124, 130, 203, 224, 225
McGeorge, T. J. (55th VA), 40
McGowan, Gen., 12

McLean's brigade, 34
Meade, George G., 247
Michigan Infantry Regiments
  2nd, 191, 205
  3rd, 191
  7th, 112
  8th, 77, 146, 156
Millan, Sgt. (Randolph's Battery), 179
Millan house, 10, 13, 200-201, 206, 208
Minnesota Infantry Regiments
  1st, 220-221
Monford, Capt., 213
Morrison, David, 111, 146, 209
Morrison's brigade, 27, 146, 153-156, 159-163, 180, 233
Morrow, Billy (21st MA), 197
Mozart Regiment. See New York Infantry Regiments, 40th
Munford, T. T. (2nd VA Cavalry), 219

Nagle, James, 27
Nagle's brigade, 27, 151, 156-157
Neale, Julia, 95
New Hampshire Infantry Regiments
  2nd, 192
  6th, 37, 156-157, 158, 163
New Jersey Artillery Batteries
  1st Light: Battery A, 32
New Jersey Brigade, 13, 23, 32, 48-52, 56
New Jersey Cavalry Regiments
  1st, 118
New Jersey Infantry Regiments
  1st, 32, 48-49, 99
  2nd, 32, 48-49, 85, 102
  3rd, 32, 48-49, 99
  4th, 32, 48-49, 98, 112
  5th, 199
New York Cavalry Regiments
  9th, 135
  10th, 104-105
New York Highlanders. See New York Infantry Regiments, 79th
New York Infantry Regiments
  1st, 176
  9th, 135
  21st, 99, 106, 111, 129, 135
  23rd, 99, 106, 111, 129
  38th, 176

40th, 35, 138, 173, 175, 176, 177-178, 199-200, 208
42nd, 112
46th, 146, 156
51st, 10, 127, 150, 156, 157, 164-165
55th, 204, 245
79th, 14, 71-73, 77, 81, 111, 139, 143-146, 148-149, 153-155, 158-164, 180, 196, 209-210, 233
80th (20th Militia), 133-135, 147
97th, 133
101st, 82, 172, 176-177, 195
New York Zouaves, 34
North Carolina Infantry Regiments
16th, 172
18th, 164
22nd, 172
34th, 172
38th, 172

Ohio Cavalry Regiments
6th, 135
30th, 205
Ox Hill, VA, 9-10, 101, 120, 130, 136, 172, 202, 212, 216-217, 220, 225-227, 239, 245, 247

Parker, Cortlandt, 58-59
Parker, George (21st MA), 138, 181, 183, 187-188, 198-199, 201, 210-211
Parker, Thomas (51st PA), 37, 206
Pate, Major (49th GA), 186
Patrick, Marsena, 99, 110-111, 129, 133
Patrick's brigade, 111, 129-130
Pelham's Battery, 85, 131, 219, 224
Pender's Brigade, 147, 148, 172, 177, 193, 202
Pennsylvania Infantry Regiments
2nd Reserves, 81, 106
48th, 84, 151, 156, 205
50th, 146, 155-158, 163
51st, 37, 127, 150, 206
57th, 176, 213
88th, 37
100th, 146, 156, 179, 208
105th, 191
Pennsylvania Light Artillery, Battery D, 149-150, 175, 198

Philadelphia Brigade. See Howard's brigade
Phillips, Lt. (Kearny's division), 191
Pierce, Franklin, 67
Plunkett, Sgt. (21st MA), 196
Poe, Orlando, 170, 175, 191
Poe's brigade, 170, 175, 178, 179-180, 181, 191, 195
Pope, John, 16, 17-23, 24, 25, 26, 27, 28-29, 31, 33-35, 37-40, 41-42, 59, 67, 77, 83, 84-87, 90-94, 98-99, 103, 107, 109-112, 120-122, 123-126, 127-130, 135-136, 167, 170, 192, 202, 203-204, 208, 212, 215-216, 218, 221-225, 229, 230, 231, 237, 240, 241, 242-244, 245
Porter, Fitz John, 25, 27, 28, 33-34, 58, 83, 92, 93, 110, 112, 117, 118, 128
Pratt, Capt. (10th NY Cavalry), 104-105
Preston, Willie, 115
Pryor, Roger, 101

Randolph's Battery (1st Rhode Island Artillery, Battery E), 85, 106, 170, 175, 179
Reid house, 13, 145, 151, 157, 176, 191, 205-206, 208, 227
Reno, Jesse, 12, 26-27, 78, 83, 84, 126-127, 149-151, 156-157, 167, 173, 179, 203, 206, 209, 230, 232, 233-234
Reno's division, 83-84, 127, 142, 207
Reynolds, John, 26-27, 34, 92, 106
Rhode Island Artillery Batteries
1st, Battery A. See Tompkin's Battery
1st, Battery E. See Randolph's Battery
Rhode Island Cavalry Regiments
1st, 129-131
Rice, Henry, 75
Rice's Battery, 117, 118
Richardson, Israel, 54
Richardson's division, 54
Robertson, Beverly, 119-120
Robertson's Cavalry Brigade, 98, 105, 114, 119-120
Robinson, John, 170
Robinson's brigade, 55, 170, 178, 181, 191, 195
Rock Hill, 117
Rosser, Thomas (5th VA Cavalry), 86, 131

Saxton, Rufus, 77
Schweitzer, Edward (30th OH), 205
Scott, Winfield, 44-45, 48, 62-65, 66, 70
2nd U. S. Artillery, 127
2nd U. S. Cavalry Regiment, 97, 98
Sedgwick's division, 135
Seven Days' Campaign, 17, 55-57
Seven Pines, battle of, 54-55
Sherman, Thomas, 73-75
Shoemaker, J. (Pelham's Battery), 85
Showell, Pvt. (6th NH), 157
Sickles, Daniel, 214
Sigel, Franz, 20, 24-26, 83
Slocum, Henry W., 31-32
Smith, John L., 63
Smith, William "Extra Billy," 171
South Carolina Artillery Batteries
    1st, 76
South Carolina Infantry Regiments
    13th, 95, 172, 201
    14th, 172
Sowell, Pvt. (6th NH), 157
Sprague, Gov. (RI), 209
Stafford, Leroy, 147
Stanton, Edwin, 15, 16, 223
Starke, William E., 89, 157-158, 162, 165
Starke's Brigade, 117, 119, 147, 172
Starke's Division, 89, 112, 147, 157, 162, 172
Stevens, Catherine, 68
Stevens, Gertrude, 66
Stevens, Hannah, 60
Stevens, Hazard (79th NY), 62, 68, 126, 143-146, 148, 151-155
Stevens, Isaac I. Jr.,
    battle of Chantilly, 137-143, 146, 148-151, 153-161, 163, 167, 169-170, 175, 230-232
    battle of James Island, 75
    brigade command, Dept. of the South, 73-78
    burial, 209-210
    death, 12-13, 161
    campaign manager of Breckinridge-Lane ticket, 73
    childhood, 60
    Colonel of 79th New York, 71-73

    early army career, 61-62, 65-66
    governor of Washington Territory, 67-70
    marriage, 61
    Mexican War service, 62-65
    misc., 10, 27, 42, 78-79, 83, 84, 106, 126-127, 129, 192, 244, 246, 247
    Port Royal skirmish, 73-74
    published works, 66-67, 75
Stevens, Isaac I. Sr., 60
Stevens, Jonathan, 60
Stevens, Margaret Hazard, 61-63, 68, 74
Stevens, Susan, 66
Stevens, Virginia, 61-62
Stevens's division, 84, 126-127, 137-167, 173, 179, 180, 196, 207, 209, 230, 232, 233-234
Stone, James (21st MA), 164, 165, 166, 188-189, 197-198
Stoneman, George, 246
Stonewall Brigade, 89, 130, 133, 147, 157, 172
Strong, Col. (Hays's Brigade), 12, 158, 161-162
Stuart, J. E. B., 86-87, 98-99, 101-103, 113-114, 119-120, 131, 202, 219, 230, 241-242
Stuart's Horse Artillery, 131, 219. See also Pelham's Battery
Sturgis, Samuel D., 20
Sullivan, Timothy, 28
Sullivan's brigade, 28
Sumner, Edwin V., 83, 85, 92, 93, 97, 110, 111, 112, 117, 125
Sykes's division, 34

Taliaferro, William B., 21, 89
Taliaferro's Brigade, 147, 172
Taliaferro's Division, 21, 24. See also Starke's Division
Taylor, George, 23
Taylor, Henry, 212-213
Taylor, Walter H., 90, 212-213
Thomas, Edward L., 26, 186-190
Thomas's Brigade, 26, 147, 148, 161, 170, 172, 177, 183-184, 186-190, 198, 210, 235

Todd, William (79th NY), 81, 139, 144, 146, 150, 209
Tompkin's Battery (1st Rhode Island Artillery, Battery A), 200-221
Toombs's Brigade, 193
Torbert, Alfred T. A., 32, 85, 98-101, 102, 106, 109, 125, 129
Torbert's brigade, 32, 98-101, 106, 112, 130, 135
Tower, Zealous, 42, 62-63
Tower's brigade, 34, 37
Trimble's Brigade, 22, 27, 147, 165-166, 172
Twiggs, Gen., 64-65

U.S. Regular Army Regiments
2nd U.S. Artillery, Battery E, 127
2nd U.S. Cavalry, 97-99, 109

Vautier, John (88th PA), 37
Virginia Cavalry Regiments
2nd, 219
5th, 130-131
12th, 105
Virginia Infantry Regiments
1st Battalion, 117
4th, 89
13th, 162
21st, 23, 117-118
25th, 162

31st, 162
40th, 202
42nd, 117
48th, 117
49th, 171
55th, 40
Von Borcke, Heros, 101, 102, 103, 131

Walcott, Charles (21st MA), 37, 165, 182, 183, 185, 188, 189, 245
Warren, Gouverneur, 34
Warren's brigade, 34
Washington Artillery, 101
Watts, John, 43, 213
Welch, Dr. Spencer (13th SC), 95, 201, 217
Weld, Stephen, 225
Welles, Gideon, 223
Wheat, Robardeau, 48, 59
White, High, 115
Whitman, George (51st NY), 157
Wilcox, Cadmus, 28
Wilcox, Orlando B., 246
Wilcox's brigade, 28
Williamsburg, battle of, 52-53
Witcher, William (21st VA), 117, 118
Woodward, Evan (2nd PA Reserves), 81, 106
Wren, James (48th PA), 205
Wright's brigade, 76